EXTRACTION

ALSO BY THEA RIOFRANCOS

Resource Radicals:
From Petro-Nationalism to Post-Extractivism in Ecuador

A Planet to Win:
Why We Need a Green New Deal
(coauthored with Kate Aronoff,
Alyssa Battistoni, and Daniel Aldana Cohen,
with a foreword by Naomi Klein)

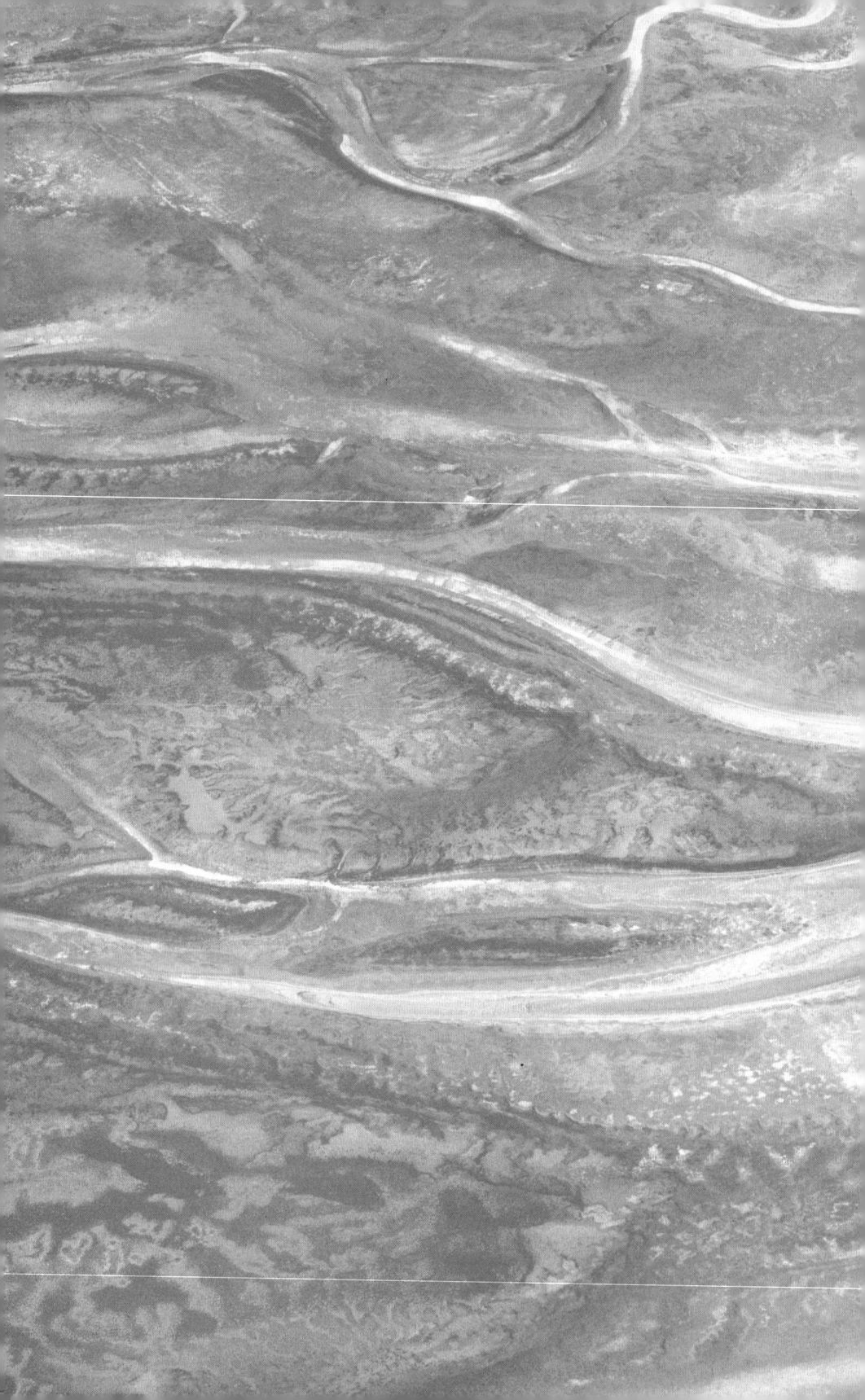

EXTRACTION

THE FRONTIERS OF GREEN CAPITALISM

THEA RIOFRANCOS

W. W. Norton & Company
Independent Publishers Since 1923

Copyright © 2025 by Thea Riofrancos

All rights reserved
Printed in the United States of America
First Edition

For information about permission to reproduce selections from this book, write to
Permissions, W. W. Norton & Company, Inc., 500 Fifth Avenue, New York, NY 10110

For information about special discounts for bulk purchases, please contact
W. W. Norton Special Sales at specialsales@wwnorton.com or 800-233-4830

Manufacturing by Lakeside Book Company
Book design by Daniel Lagin
Production manager: Julia Druskin

ISBN: 978-1-324-03676-0

Frontispiece: Photograph from Lithium Series II, by Tom Hegen

W. W. Norton & Company, Inc.
500 Fifth Avenue, New York, NY 10110
www.wwnorton.com

W. W. Norton & Company Ltd.
15 Carlisle Street, London W1D 3BS

10 9 8 7 6 5 4 3 2 1

CONTENTS

PART I
EXTRACTION

PROLOGUE: Mining Water in a Desert   3

1. Earthly Entanglements   15

PART II
FRONTIERS

2. Peripheries and Power   33
3. Lithium Frontiers   47
4. Lithium for Chile   73
5. The Return of Resource Nationalism   101

PART III
GREEN CAPITALISM

6. Green Dominance   125
7. Green Mining   147

PART IV
BEYOND GREEN CAPITALISM

8. Resisting Green Extractivism — 173

9. Green Futures — 205

ACKNOWLEDGMENTS — 215

NOTES — 223

INDEX — 265

PART I

EXTRACTION

Los Flamencos National Reserve, Atacama Salt Flat, Chile

PROLOGUE

Mining Water in a Desert

A high-altitude desert plateau traverses Argentina, Bolivia, and Chile. I am on the Chilean side, in the passenger seat of a Jeep, along with two other researchers. The afternoon air is thin and brisk, but the sun is piercing—a combination I am familiar with from years of living and traveling in South America's Andean range. The landscape is a study in contrasts and contours: broad basins suddenly cut off by sweeping curves, flat expanses sliced by near vertical ascents. The Licancabur Volcano looms large above us. Vegetation and humidity levels change rapidly with the rising altitude, bringing cooler temperatures, wetter air, and denser plant life. We are driving from San Pedro, once a small town but now a metastasizing tourist hub, to the Salar de Atacama, the vast salt flats that contain the largest lithium reserves in the world.[1]

The space and time of our journey are occasionally marked by passing through one or another of the eighteen Indigenous (Atacameño, or Lickanantay) communities that ring the salt flat, each organized around one of the spring-fed streams that run down the deep ravines sliced into the slopes of the surrounding mountains. Each community has a relationship to its deified and named mountain, which a range of practices aim to appease in return for water and harvests. Local irrigation infrastructures channel this water to homes and small farms. The resulting "Mediterranean" microclimate creates fertile conditions for figs, pomegranates, quince, grapes, and maize.

We detour into the high mountains bordering Bolivia before careening back down toward the alluvial basin and the salar. En route, we pass an Atacameño family in the midst of an outdoor celebration. I buy a kilogram of fresh goat cheese, and then we take off for the salt flat.

A sandstorm, improbably though quite palpably interspersed with a rainstorm, engulfs us for most of the remainder of our drive. I'm not sure if I've ever felt so buffeted by so many elements at once: the whipping wind, the sky alternately grainy with sand and sparkling with raindrops, intense sunlight barely veiled by enormous gray clouds. And then, abruptly, the environment rearranges itself. The sand and sandstorm disappear, replaced by gradations of white and gray that stretch all the way to the mountains that still form the horizon.

This is the Salar de Atacama—the Atacama Salt Flat—the largest of several dozen salt flats in northern Chile and the third largest in the world, about two-thirds the size of my home state of Rhode Island. The brilliant white flat lies in a high basin 7,500 feet above sea level, enclosed by the even higher Andean Mountains to the east and the Domeyko Mountains to the west. We park and enter Los Flamencos National Reserve, 285 square miles of protected ecosystem, by foot. It is extremely dry and the solar radiation extremely high (the day we visited the UV levels were literally off the charts). To our left stretches unending salt crust. To our right, the crust is interspersed with lagoons. But the landscape is not all gray and white. Upon closer inspection, elegant Andean flamingos with pastel pink feathers are backed by the muted red water of the lagoons, an effect produced by the interaction of algae, sun, and wind.

This striking landscape—the salt flat, the flamingos, and the neighboring Indigenous communities—is under threat from a counterintuitive source: our efforts to save the planet from catastrophic climate change. Just beneath my feet are nearly one-third of the world's lithium reserves, suspended in water saltier than the ocean.[2] Lithium is essential to addressing the climate crisis. It is a key ingredient in the rechargeable batteries that play a starring role in eliminating carbon emissions from transportation and energy—the two highest emitting sectors. But extracting this lithium will come at escalating social and environmental costs. It is this dilemma that has brought me to the salt flat.

THE ATACAMA IS THE WORLD'S OLDEST DESERT. THE HIGH-ALTITUDE, bone-dry landscape, with its dazzling days and spectacularly starry nights, formed twenty million years ago. And despite forbidding conditions, humans began living in the Atacama at least eleven or twelve thousand years ago.[3] Nor were they isolated. The Andean plateau long enabled north-south movement, and by at least fifteen hundred years ago, the settlements of the plateau had become intensively linked by networks of trade and travel across the Domeyko Mountains' passes with those of the more hospitable Pacific coastal plain.

But those more interested in the region's minerals than its people or ecology have repeatedly declared it to be empty and lifeless. The narrative penned by Spanish historian Jerónimo de Vivar, who accompanied the conquistador Pedro de Valdivia in the 1540s, painted an enduring portrait of the landscape as "barren" and "unpopulated," except for the valleys. In all of this expanse, he wrote, "it does not rain."[4] The winds were frigid, the risk of death by thirst palpable. Accordingly, Vivar called the vast space "*el gran despoblado.*" In Spanish, the word *despoblado* is ambiguous. It can mean simply unpopulated, or it can mean depopulated, implying a change over time.[5] A deserted desert, in other words.

To the Spanish, this imagined emptiness justified their colonial domination. After independence in 1818, Chilean authorities appointed experts to explore and map the region and to assess the desert's "economic potential"—specifically, its "mineable wealth."[6] They reproduced the tropes of colonial conquest, emphasizing the same extreme aridity, hostility to life, and emptiness.[7] They urged the state to provide support for private firms to exploit the riches of this ostensible terra nullius—and it did.

Government policies encouraged resource extraction, which then incentivized more government support, in an accelerating cycle. In 1858, because of the discovery of copper nearby, the government declared the fishing village of Taltal a state harbor.[8] Railroads would later link it to new inland nitrate mines, confirming it as the coastal logistical hub of multiplying extractive spokes. The state built an elaborate system of wells and pipelines to provide crucial water access for mining operations. The legal infrastructure of Chile's Mining Code of 1874 further facilitated the private appropriation of subsoil wealth. By the late nineteenth century, silver, gold, copper, and nitrate production was booming. Over a century later, the state still depends on the revenues generated by mining and is looking toward its next resource boom.

Today the Atacama Desert is best known as an extractive frontier, rich in two minerals key to the energy transition: lithium and copper. Abundant in resources—but supposedly devoid of life. Wealth, free for the taking, with purportedly no one and nothing harmed in exchange. State and capital, scientists and maps, minerals and water, laws and property rights, pipes and ports... and narratives that erase thousands of years of human habitation and flatten a complex ecosystem into a lifeless blank slate. This is how extractive frontiers are made.

WHEN IT DOES RAIN IN THE ATACAMA, IT'S HARD TO OVERSTATE the intensity of the floods. I once found myself caught in what is called *invierno boliviano*, or Bolivian winter, a paradoxical name for a weather phenomenon that occurs during the Southern Hemisphere's summer months. These rainy fronts originate in the Amazon and travel up the steep slopes of the Andean Mountains, where Bolivia's high-altitude winds then drive them up and over the ridges, until their torrents drench the Chilean high plateau.

Rainbows were the first sign that precipitation was making its way toward us. I was on a guided trek with a group of tourists, walking on the path along a narrow ridge in *el Valle de la Luna* (the Valley of the Moon), trying to keep from falling over the steep cliffs on either side while gazing up at the deep red, undulating mountains and impossibly smooth sand dunes. Suddenly, multicolored banners appeared in the sky, one after the other, tracing myriad arcs from peak to peak. There were so many rainbows, I lost track trying to count them. The enchantment was dizzying. But by the time we had driven back to San Pedro de Atacama, the landscape was shrouded in rain. Our preparations for the dry heat, our sunglasses and water bottles, suddenly seemed absurd. The town itself was submerged in darkness—the rain and winds had cut the power supply. We ate by candlelight, still shivering in our damp clothes.

The morning's light revealed the damage. All roads south of Toconao, an Atacameño village 20 miles from San Pedro, were closed. The desert grasses of the alluvial plain to the left of the road, like the jaunty tufts of gold-green paja brava, were completely submerged. The water, made dark by the sediment it carried, was still rushing past, even though it was no longer raining.

My plans to visit a lithium mining operation foiled by the flooding, I entered Toconao instead. The river running through the town was the main attraction. Here, high up on the Andean plateau, rivers form the centerpieces to ancestral irrigation systems. They are literal oases: You can spot a village from miles away by the cluster of green trees standing out against the otherwise muted tones of the surrounding landscape. On that day, the river ran so high, swirling with white rapids, that the residents had closed all the town's locks to protect farm plots from flooding.

The scientific term for closed basins like the Atacama is "endorheic" (etymologically, "inside" and "flow") for water can flow down into the Atacama basin, but it cannot leave—except by evaporation. And this is the key to Atacama's extraordinary lithium brine.

After deluges like the one I experienced, water pours down the surrounding mountains; during the long dry spells between storms, it trickles down ravines from the precious mountain springs. As it flows, the water leeches lithium from the volcanic rock, picks up wind-scoured lithium dust, and carries it down to the nucleus, or center, of the salar.[9] This pooled surface water can only escape through evaporation, and with every drop of water that evaporates, the concentration of lithium in the remaining brine increases. Without the parched and sun-blasted Atacama's extraordinarily high evaporation rate, lithium concentrations would not reach the "economical" levels prized by mining companies.

Yet further lithium enrichment takes place out of sight. Remaining water gradually seeps into the ground, creating underground wells of lithium-rich brine. These wells are linked into complex hydrothermal systems. Then the heat of magma, especially near the Andes' active fault lines, drives circulations of subsurface brine through fissures and porous geological strata, dissolving even more lithium out of the subsurface rock.[10]

The resulting brine deposits anywhere from 4 to 200 feet below the Atacama's salty crust represent a potential bonanza to corporations. The Atacama's singular coincidence of climactic, geological, geothermal, and hydrological conditions makes it one of the least expensive places on earth to mine lithium.[11] And at each step, the process of "mining water" is intimately related to the very environmental conditions that formed the valuable deposits in the first place: Miners pump the underground brine to vast evaporation ponds on the surface, where natural evaporation concentrates the brine yet again, increasing its lithium levels fortyfold from approximately 0.15 percent to a whopping 6 percent. One cycle of the process can take ten to twenty-four months, depending on brine quality and weather conditions.[12]

Two of the world's largest lithium miners, SQM and Albemarle, tout this extraction method as "environmentally friendly" and "sustainable." Official corporate statements celebrate that compared with hard rock mines, such as Western Australia's spodumene deposits, "brine production is a very eco-friendly way to produce lithium," with a "very low CO_2 footprint" and using "very few [sic] freshwater."[13] But this relatively low-cost, low-tech, and supposedly low-impact extractive process nonetheless imperils the species and communities that call the Atacama Desert home. And it is a microcosm of a planetary phenomenon: the expanding extractive frontiers of green capitalism. Everywhere that mines are dug up to provide raw materials for the energy transition, global climate action comes into conflict with local environmental protection.

Mining always transforms, in many ways irrevocably, the landscapes in which it occurs.[14] In remaking the earth in the image of extractive capital, physically and chemically separating what is deemed valuable from often toxic waste, mining evokes the image of terraforming so central to science fiction. But if terraforming is supposed to make a lifeless planet as verdant as Earth, mining, to the contrary, often leaves parts of the Earth itself uninhabitable. While the environmental impacts of mining brine are less obvious to the naked eye than, say, mountaintop removal, extracting the lithium-rich liquid does in fact threaten a fragile, desert water system, along with the ecosystems and people that depend on it.

The anthropogenic reshaping of nature is complex when the deposit in question is fluid. Unlike traditional hard rock mining, mining water rearranges both the brine deposits at the center of the salt flat and the freshwater aquifers at its perimeter.[15] Pumping brine on an industrial scale creates a cone-shaped subsidence around each extraction well. As a result, freshwater at the salar's perimeter flows toward its center, away from the aquifers between the foothills of the towering mountain ranges and the edge of the vast salar.[16] Meanwhile, precipitation replenishes those vital freshwater sources very slowly. A recent study found that nearly all the freshwater stored in aquifers is at least sixty-five years old.[17]

There is active scientific debate about precisely how much lithium mining reduces freshwater availability in the Atacama. But even those researchers who are most sanguine about the impacts of the lithium industry admit that current legal freshwater allotments to mining and agricultural companies have little basis in hydrological reality.[18] Even though copper mining and agriculture consume much more freshwater than the lithium sector, side-by-side comparisons of the consequences of each use of water obscures the simple fact that all three are happening simultaneously in the Atacama, constituting a direct threat to water access in the driest desert on earth—with severe consequences for the eighteen Atacameño communities that ring the salt flat.

THE WORLD'S OLDEST, DRIEST DESERT MAY APPEAR BEREFT OF LIFE. Ecologists call it a "polyextreme" environment, given its altitude and high direct solar radiation, its intense aridity, its huge diurnal temperature swings, and its densely saline lakes. Those who study such polyextreme environments alternately describe them as low-diversity, with relatively "simple" webs of life,[19] or "astonishing" in their biodiversity.[20] It all depends on perspective. Plants and animals have evolved to make do with less and saltier water and, above all, the abundant energy of relentless sun. Extremity stimulates nature's creativity.

Artemia, or brine shrimp, thrive in hypersaline lakes that would be intolerable to most species.[21] These tiny creatures are a key node in the plateau's food chain. The brine shrimp eat bacteria and phytoplankton (microscopic plants) and are, in turn, food for Chilean flamingos. The flamingos, too, have adapted to the saline lagoons, evolving a filter in their bills akin to the lamellar membranes of oysters or whales to strain the microscopic plants and animals from the brine.[22] The relationship isn't just one of predator and prey. The tiny crustaceans cling to the flamingos, hitching a ride as the birds migrate and thus dispersing themselves across the myriad salty lakes of the Andean plateau.

The flamingos are a barometer of wetland health. As the birds travel the salt flats in search of food and mates (attracted through a courtship ritual of synchronized dancing), they link together the saline lakes into a web of habitats.[23] And as these habitats suffer, so do flamingo populations: All three of the Atacama Salt Flat's endemic flamingo species are in decline.[24] The distinct drivers of this population loss reveal the compounding harms afflicting this fragile environment. Warmer average temperatures due to climate change evaporate surface water faster, reducing the blue-green algae essential to flamingo and *Artemia* diets. And the noise and traffic associated with mining operations appear to directly disrupt the flamingo's breeding.

Though less charismatic than the improbably pastel pink birds, unique endemic plants have achieved impressive feats of resourcefulness and endurance. Indeed, scientists have called the region an "unparalleled natural laboratory" to understand how plants adapt to "extreme environmental conditions."[25] Species like *Solanum chilense*, a wild desert tomato, or the flowering *Azorella atacamensis*, with its anti-virulent properties, cope with high solar radiation and frigid nights and can likewise survive prolonged droughts punctuated by intense rains. Given the desert soil's limited absorptive capacity, much of the rain runs off in flash floods, offering the plants only a short and unpredictable window to quench their thirst.

These plants of the Atacama, whether wild or domesticated, tell stories. One story is of human knowledge accumulated across millennia, enabling communities to cultivate sustaining harvests in a hostile environment. Another is of the origins of organic life on earth—and its possibility on other planets. And another is how aspects of our future may be prefigured in the desert's past. The very conditions that these plants have evolved to withstand are more and more common the world over. As humanity faces a warmer and drier future, researchers are exploring whether relatives of the staple crops able to thrive in Atacama, like legumes and potatoes, might help feed future generations in a hotter and more arid world. For plant biologists concerned about global food security, the Atacama is a "genetic goldmine."[26]

The Atacama offers access to other realms of knowledge as well. Its vast and austere geometries, its mountains and basins, valleys and ridge lines, its craggy textures, and its palette of gray and white and red and brown conjure up the landscapes of the moon or Mars. But its link to other worlds is not just a poetic analogy. Atop a ridge 5,000 feet above sea level, far from any light pollution, through the moistureless air, the world's largest astronomical project, the ALMA (Atacama Large Millimeter/submillimeter Array), has an unparalleled view of the galaxy.[27]

And, out of view, there is yet another real alien world in the hypersaline lakes and subsurface brine deposits of the Andean plateau. These are liquid habitats for the captivating microorganisms classified as "extremophiles"—literally, lovers of the extreme, because of their ability to withstand salty water, parched air, and relentless sun.[28] The very existence of these bacteria upend prior scientific assumptions about microbial habitats and deepen our understanding of biological evolution on earth—and of the possibility of life on other planets. Such organisms were at the origin of the earth's evolutionary history, and they in turn propagated yet more life, enabling oxygenation and helping cause what evolutionary biologists call a "biodiversity explosion" 2.5 billion years ago. In this sense, the salt flats and their salty lakes are at once a living record and an ongoing recapitulation of billions of years of planetary history.[29]

In the lithium-rich brine deposits far below the desert surface, one of the saltiest environments on earth,[30] single-celled archaea predominate. Without access to the sun, they generate energy from inorganic chemicals in a process known as chemosynthesis, rather than the more familiar photosynthesis. Amazingly, this life can still be found in the dense, super salty water even once the brine is pumped to the surface. But the pumping and evaporation of brine fundamentally alters its microbial profile, allowing bacteria to overgrow the archaea. Some scientists have therefore called for a "framework of conservation" to protect the bacteria and archaea that are lithium's neighbors.[31]

Researchers are struggling to predict the overall direction of the multiple compounding and confounding processes changing the Atacama. Global warming leads to faster rates of evaporation of water in the surfacing lagoons, making their salinity more than species had originally evolved to withstand, at the same time that lithium mining's rapid pumping up of brine draws freshwater from aquifers into the subsurface brine, reducing its salinity.[32] Science can only play catch-up, documenting the impacts long after the harm has occurred. Lithium extraction's threat to the liquid supporting its ecosystem is a slow-motion disaster with planetary causes and consequences.

Mining companies typically portray brine as lacking any environmental value. Yet scientific research has revealed that the brine is not only an essential constituent of the plateau's broader ecology, but an entire ecosystem unto itself. This fact raises existential questions for the planet's zero-carbon future.

In the Atacama, global supply chains intersect with local food chains, webs of economic production undermine webs of life, and colonization and postcolonial state-building erase ancient histories of continuous Indigenous settlement. And these unexpected entanglements are just the beginning of the story. In more ways than I could have imagined when I first stepped foot on the Atacama Salt Flat on that blustery day, this extractive frontier is a portal into our planetary future.

CHAPTER 1

Earthly Entanglements

Lithium is the third element in the periodic table. It is the lightest, least dense metal—although it is never encountered as such in nature, as it's too reactive to exist without being bonded in a compound. Lithium ions and minerals appear in an impressive range of environments: hard rocks, liquid brines, soft clays, and even oceans (albeit at very low concentrations). It has an equally impressive number of uses, from oven-safe cookware to psychotropic pharmacology to the role it is now playing on history's grand stage: as an essential ingredient in rechargeable batteries.

The renewable energy transition depends on electrification—and electrification depends on rechargeable batteries. If we are to have any chance whatsoever of avoiding the most catastrophic climate scenarios, we have no choice but to slash carbon emissions, especially in transportation. The transportation sector is the single largest contributor to the US carbon footprint and the second largest source of global carbon emissions. And the batteries that make it possible for cars to run on wind and sun instead of fossil fuels depend, in turn, on refined, high-purity lithium compounds. Lithium batteries are also emerging as essential for the energy sector. As our energy systems incorporate more electricity from intermittent sources like sun and wind, storage is crucial—otherwise the energy would only be available when the sun is shining or the wind is blowing. Large, "utility-scale" batteries are thus vital to balance the energy grid.

Lithium has become a "critical" element in the energy transition. The International Energy Agency (IEA), an intergovernmental organization, predicts that demand for lithium will skyrocket under a scenario of rapid green transition. The organization estimates that the demand in 2050 will be ten times that of demand in 2023—the single largest growth forecast of any of the "critical minerals" the agency surveyed.[1] And lithium is not the only energy transition material that is forecasted for increased demand. The manufacturing of solar panels, wind turbines, and electric vehicles, to name just three essential technologies of our renewable era, requires a veritable periodic table of inputs wrested from the earth's crust: lithium, graphite, copper, iron, rare earth elements, nickel, cobalt, bauxite, silicon, manganese, and many more. The copper sector, which already serves an enormous global market, will need to grow by 150 percent by 2050.[2] We will need twice the amount of aluminum in 2050, refined from mined bauxite, than what we produce today.[3]

Skyrocketing demand means more mines. Benchmark Mineral Intelligence estimates that meeting global lithium demand in 2035 will require between 59 and 74 new and fully operational lithium mines (the exact number depends on recycling capacity).[4] Looking at a range of minerals required for battery production, the analytics firm predicts between 336 and 384 entirely new mines will need to be built and in production by 2035 to satisfy global demand for lithium, graphite, cobalt, and nickel. This would be in addition to 54 plants pumping out synthetic graphite (which, by the way, is made from coal).

And this is just for batteries. If we add figures from the World Bank for other renewable energy supply chains, solar panel production could require over 200 million tons of cumulative mineral demand by 2050, primarily aluminum (and secondarily copper).[5] Wind turbines would need as much as 350 million tons more iron—their single largest raw material input—in addition to 125 million combined tons of zinc, copper, aluminum, chromium, manganese, and rare earth elements.

The numbers are staggering. Every single supply chain of green technologies and infrastructures involves mining—and every kind of mining since the dawn of capitalism has brought with it boom-and-bust cycles, social conflicts, and environmental harm.

Extraction is the material foundation of a zero-carbon world. And that is a key reason that "green capitalism" can read like an oxymoron. How can capitalism ever be green if even the technologies and infrastructures needed to harness renewable energy require digging several hundred new large-scale mines in the span of a decade?

Green capitalism does not mean that capitalism is becoming ecologically sustainable. Instead, it refers to the emergence of new economic sectors and supply chains labeled as "green" because of their role—proven or unproven—in addressing the climate crisis, whether by decarbonization or adaptation. It likewise refers to a worldview. Promoters of green capitalism see profit-maximizing firms and business-friendly governments as the main protagonists in the drama of the energy transition—and assert that market-driven innovation can save the planet, without major changes in how our economy works.

Extractive frontiers are not just unfortunate blemishes on otherwise "clean" energy, nor are they tragic but inevitable flaws in an otherwise virtuous economic system. Instead, extractive frontiers provide a fresh, if bracing, perspective on green capitalism from the vantage point of the earthly origins and entanglements of everything around us. This perspective cautions us against the temptations of technical fixes, escape-from-nature fantasies, or a purely post-extractive society. It links the brutal past of colonialism to the stark injustices of the green future—and the geopolitical battles pitting the Great Powers against emerging powers, with governments around the world trying to find their foothold in the supply chains of the twenty-first century.

WILL THERE BE ENOUGH LITHIUM TO POWER THE TENS OF MILLIONS of new electric vehicles slated for production by the end of this decade? In theory, the answer is yes. Lithium is not scarce. Deposits have been discovered on all seven continents, including Antarctica, and it is the thirty-third most common element in the earth's crust and waters.[6] And although almost all the world's lithium currently emanates from a handful of countries (Australia, Chile, China, and Argentina), the list is expanding, with lithium mining ramping up in Zimbabwe, Brazil, Canada, and elsewhere.

Notwithstanding these developments, the IEA expects that lithium demand will outstrip market supply after 2030, based on existing and announced lithium mine projects.[7] Wood Mackenzie predicts this inflection point will happen a few years later, in 2033.[8] In contrast, Benchmark Mineral Intelligence predicts this will happen sooner, in 2028.[9] Copper, too, will "fall significantly short" of global needs by 2040.[10] This is part of what it means to call these raw materials "critical minerals": Experts have deemed these minerals essential to energy systems, national security, or the broader economy, yet supplies are either insufficient or vulnerable. Bringing new mineral supplies into the global market is rarely a rapid or smooth process. Depending on the country, it can take ten to thirty years for the discovery of a new deposit to become a productive mine.[11] Those lengthy time frames reflect the surprising number of things that, from a corporate perspective, can go wrong: permitting challenges, financing woes, community protest, labor strikes—not to mention increasingly unpredictable weather and ever-scarcer water, which can disrupt operations. This by no means implies that minerals are always in shortfall. The underlying unpredictability entails that supply can just as easily overshoot demand. That's because the same factors that make mining so time-intensive also mean that when supply does ramp up, demand may have softened for other reasons.

But it gets even more complex. The economics of critical minerals is not a simple matter of supply and demand. Today, market dynamics take place in a world increasingly defined by "geoeconomics": the fusion of national security and economic policy that is a hallmark of our era.[12] States compete against each other in a global contest to achieve national dominance over the supply chains for electric vehicles, solar panels, and semiconductors. To this end, governments cajole multinational corporations to invest within their borders—or send them packing if they're too closely allied with an adversarial state.[13] And amid these contests of economic and political power, marginalized communities and precarious workers are demanding a say in the future of mining. The only certainty, in other words, is volatility.

To understand the high stakes, let's imagine two very different futures.[14]

First picture a world in the grip of recurrent shortages of the metals needed to build solar panels or electric vehicles. Especially in today's geopolitical climate, interstate competition for dwindling reserves could get fierce. Governments might increasingly resort to trade protectionism—including outright bans on exports—or, worse, the use of force to secure access to raw materials. Now factor in the profound inequalities separating the globe's richest countries from its poorest. If affluent countries hoard resources, how will the majority of the earth's inhabitants access renewable energy technologies? An undersupply of lithium, copper, or graphite would mean a slower and more uneven energy transition, with global consequences for our ability to mitigate the climate crisis.

In stark contrast, imagine an alternate future of mineral abundance, in which electric vehicles are more affordable to working- and middle-class people around the world. With the problem of scarcity removed, low- and middle-income countries also have access to the minerals so critical for renewable energy. With fewer tensions around supply chains, nations are willing and able to cooperate on emissions targets and ensure access to climate finance. In such a world of plenty, massive deployment of green technologies generates economies of scale that further drive down cost, buttressing not only the economic feasibility but also the political popularity of the energy transition, all while spreading its benefits more broadly.

These radically different futures map onto two schools of thought on energy transition minerals. One set of experts contends that there are enough minerals; the other predicts chronic gaps between available supplies vis-a-vis growing demand. These are simplifications, of course. For example, the optimists acknowledge the possibility of temporary shortfalls. But as self-identified "ecomodernists," they have faith in the combination of market forces and technological progress to drive new mining and innovative substitutions.[15] They point, for example, to the growing popularity of cheaper cathode chemistries, such as lithium iron phosphate, or to replacements for lithium altogether, such as sodium batteries, which are growing closer to commercial viability.

The doomsday view, for its part, offers a few off-ramps from apocalypse. While the pessimists tend to present supply as a hard constraint, some among them see demand as more malleable, embracing a philosophy known as "degrowth." From this perspective, the best solution to mineral scarcity is to reduce consumption, particularly the elite lifestyles that produce the largest carbon footprints: bans on private jets, caps on energy use, and a massive shift from individual cars to mass transit.[16] Degrowth, the thinking goes, would alleviate pressure not only on market supplies but also on the ecosystems, watersheds, and communities that bear the brunt of extractive harm.

Both the optimists and the pessimists have valuable insights. At the same time, both schools of thought miss key dynamics of the political economy of extraction. "Is there enough?" is the wrong question to ask. As the pages of this book will make clear, extraction is never just about what's underground. And, besides, our understanding of "what's underground" changes over time. Improvements in geological knowledge, innovations in mining techniques, and shifts in global markets create new extractive frontiers. In the mid-1950s, American geologist M. King Hubbert predicted that US oil production would "peak" in 1970—one of many moments of recurrent concern that oil supplies, whether in the United States or globally, were near exhaustion.[17] Decades later, the shale revolution, more commonly known as fracking, opened entirely new territories for oil and gas. These days, the United States is the world's top oil and gas producer, with production of both exceeding the predicted 1970 apex.[18] It is increasingly likely—and of course from a climate perspective, eminently desirable—that demand for fossil fuels will dwindle before supplies do.

WHILE RESEARCHING THIS PROJECT, I HAVE WALKED SOMEWHAT unsteadily across the uneven ground of the Atacama Salt Flat, scrambled up to a ridge in Nevada's Silver Peak Range, and sat by the banks of the Covas River in northern Portugal, where I enjoyed a cool breeze for the first time all day.

These locales are singular, striking, incommensurable. At the same time, each of these places occupies only one of so many nodes in a vast economic web. Flows of money, goods, people, and knowledge link peripheral zones to the centers of economic and political decision-making in financial districts and capital cities. Seemingly defying the laws of physics, each of these locales is in fact "two places at once," in the words of environmental historian Jason W. Moore.[19]

On the one hand, mineral deposits are necessarily rooted in place, artifacts of the deep time of geological history, with their accessibility to humans conditioned by topography and climate. For globetrotting capitalists, these territorial specifics are at once a blessing and a curse. Just as their offerings—copper or oil, lithium or gold—appear as "free gifts of nature" ripe for the picking, so, too, does their fixity in space pose problems.[20] Capital craves movement. Mobility optimizes profitability by allowing corporations to scan the world for where they can obtain the highest returns on investment and the least exposure to risk. Mobility also offers a degree of protection from taxes or regulations—and strikes or protests. In contrast, place-based investments come with sunk costs that tether companies in place, potentially boosting the leverage of local governments, communities, and workers. The costs start with the very first stake in the ground, and they accumulate over time.

On the other hand, as fixed in place as such frontiers are, they are also as intimately bound to the volatilities of global capitalism as Wall Street or the City of London, and to geopolitics as Washington DC, Brussels, or Beijing. At first glance, extraction would appear to be the very moment at which a supply chain starts. But the minerals being mined are as much outcomes as inputs, their utility and value shaped by the goods and services they play a role in creating. Likewise, a frontier's political importance, or the policy decision to designate its natural resources as "critical" or strategic, is not a given, but wholly contingent on the shifting calculi of state officials and the evolving needs of global production.

I first started connecting these dots in Chile. In Santiago, the country's capital, I frequented the elegant government buildings of the historical downtown, speaking with water regulators who bemoaned their limited powers to calibrate the delicate balance of freshwater and expanding extractive sectors in the Atacama Desert. I also confronted a wall of security guarding an opaque corporate bureaucracy in the toniest part of the city, the headquarters of lithium giant SQM. In the graffiti-strewn headquarters of a national labor federation, a longtime organizer who had spent time in prison under the infamous Pinochet dictatorship captivated me with his dream to nationalize lithium and use it for the public interest. From there I traveled to the tiny offices of a regional anti-mining network where a stoic leader I had first met years ago, on the frontlines of a fight over a gold mine in highland Ecuador, recounted the transnational struggles brewing over lithium across the Andean plateau.

On my trips to the country's north, competing imaginaries of the lithium frontier took shape before my eyes. After my first breathtaking encounter with the Atacama Salt Flat, I witnessed a heated public debate as the local Indigenous council's position on the sector evolved. The group had recently radicalized its stance on mining, vowing to oppose all new projects. That same week, an unusually intense—but now more frequent due to climate change—rainstorm temporarily flooded the desert, submerging the hardy paja brava grasses and rendering impassable all roads south of the beautiful village of Toconao. The rains prevented me from visiting mining installations and reminded me that an increasingly unruly nature can impede not only fieldwork but also extractive operations. These experiences were bookended by dusty hour-long rides between Calama's airport and San Pedro. Those journeys took me past wind turbines that brought to life the dream of "green mining": the notion that lithium and copper extraction could occur with minimal environmental impact and be fully powered by renewable energy before making their way into supply chains that stretched to Europe, China, and the United States.

It was in Chile, then, where I first saw Indigenous communities and environmentalists, labor unions and left-wing parties, globally connected elites and multinational corporations, scientists, lawyers, and regulators conjure different green futures. It was in Chile where lithium's "strategic" status was first encoded into law and where politicians and corporations have branded the sector as the vanguard of "sustainable" extraction. And it was in Chile where I first encountered the dilemmas at the heart of this book: conflicts between renewable energy and Indigenous rights; between climate action and biodiversity preservation; between green sacrifice zones and green profiteering.

If Chile inspired this book, though, it was a serendipitous trip to the headquarters of the European Union that gave me my first inkling of the world-historic dimensions of battles over the strategic minerals of the twenty-first-century green economy. What I learned during that visit upended assumptions I had formed over more than a decade of research on mining and oil in Latin America. I went into this project assuming that the extractive frontiers of green capitalism would recapitulate the sordid history of global inequality and injustice: five centuries of Great Powers pillaging copper, silver, gold, tin, oil, timber, rubber, cotton, sugar, tobacco, opium, and much more from the places they dominated.[21] It is still very much the case that capital extracts the most from nature and workers in former colonies in the Global South and that natural resources continue to flow from south to north. However, as I would soon discover, the world's dominant powers had begun to revise their cold calculus.

Mining proceeds apace in the vast extractive zones of the planet's peripheries, but the governments of the most powerful countries now also seek the comforting security of raw materials sourced closer to home. In Brussels, I was startled to learn that policymakers aspired to European "self-sufficiency" in "critical minerals"—a bold, and perhaps unachievable, goal for a continent almost entirely dependent on metals imported from abroad. This was late 2019, mere months before COVID-19 was detected in Italy, triggering a series of events that only further reinforced EU officials' new interest in supply chain security.

On the other side of the Atlantic, similar ideas were taking hold in Washington, DC. It was Trump's first term, and he had campaigned on economic nationalism: nostalgia for a bygone era of American manufacturing combined with xenophobia toward China, immigrants, or anyone who could be scapegoated for hollowing out domestic industry. Biden likewise embraced the domestic production of green technologies from mine to factory, with top officials openly criticizing the prior paradigm of free trade and globalization.[22] This push has only gained momentum. On the same day that he was inaugurated for a second term as president, Trump signed an executive order aiming to "restore" America's "mineral dominance."[23] In both the European Union and

United States, policymakers have particularly emphasized the strategic importance of onshoring "critical minerals"—with electric vehicles, their batteries, and their essential input of lithium taking center stage.

If the very affluent countries that had long benefited from faraway resource frontiers actually began bringing extraction home, I wondered, would the stark economic and ecological inequalities of the world order be reversed? In other words, would onshoring be a step toward a more even distribution of the harms and benefits of extraction? But as I learned in my journeys to Nevada and Portugal—two places slated for more lithium mining as a result of US and EU policies—extraction is not just distributed unequally between world regions, or between poor and rich countries. It is also experienced differentially *within* regions and countries. Expanding lithium mining in the southwestern United States, with its intertwined legacies of Indigenous dispossession, toxic mining, and nuclear testing, does not repair harm in Chile, nor does it advance the cause of global justice.

As important as it is to govern extraction better and to distribute its costs and benefits more equally, I have come to believe that it is also vital to reduce extraction overall. I'm agnostic about whether or not we should call such a change "degrowth." But one thing is clear: The race for new frontiers is fed by the relentless demand for raw materials to feed the factories of global capitalism that furnish consumer lifestyles, especially for the affluent.

DISCUSSIONS OF GREEN CAPITALISM INCREASINGLY FOCUS ON SUPply chains. But what, precisely, is a supply chain? The term calls to mind a linear process that starts when raw materials are extracted or harvested and ends with a consumer purchasing a finished product (or, more accurately, discarding or recycling it). As we will see throughout this book, however, although mining chronologically precedes manufacturing, it is manufacturing's voracious appetite for raw materials that compels the extraction of resources in the first place. To drive this point home, some scholars call the zones where large-scale mining and agriculture take place "commodity frontiers," emphasizing the intimate connection between extraction and commodity production.[24]

Rubber is a great example of this dynamic.[25] For centuries, Indigenous peoples in the Brazilian Amazon had foraged wild rubber. They did so at a small scale, intermittently, and without recognition of property rights. It was not until the mid-nineteenth century that the growth in British, American, and European tire production (initially for bicycles, later and more massively for the automobile) drove a boom in Brazilian rubber. By the early twentieth century, Brazil's rubber exports came second only to coffee. The relentless demand from those downstream industries transformed the rubber extraction process. Corporations enslaved and otherwise coerced Brazilian laborers to tap rubber from trees in massive plantations. The production of tires at the "end" of the supply chain drove extraction and exploitation at the "beginning."

Over the past five hundred years, the world's commodity frontiers have been remade many times over. From the late fifteenth through mid-twentieth centuries, colonial and imperial powers often procured raw materials directly from the territories they conquered. Brazil, for example, lost its status as top rubber producer when the British Empire began to source domesticated rubber from its colonies in Sri Lanka and Malaysia.

With the takeoff of industrial capitalism, large corporations emerged as key players in the global hunt for resources. During the era of Fordism (ca. 1913–1973), titans of industry attempted to establish their own mini-empires.[26] With the goal of vertical integration, large corporations internalized various stages of production—including raw materials and energy. Ford's River Rouge plant, completed in 1927, not only integrated the manufacturing of the car's components, but also produced the necessary steel on-site using iron ore and coal from Ford's own mines. A year after bringing River Rouge into operation, Ford attempted to integrate rubber into his operations, too, establishing a plantation in northern Brazil. That effort, unlike the coal mines, ultimately failed.[27]

The economic crisis of the 1970s brought Fordism to an end, prompting the reorganization of global supply chains. Innovations in finance, container shipping, and logistics allowed corporations to *dis*-integrate, offshoring and outsourcing their operations not just across different firms, but around the world.[28] The result was the complex, spatially dispersed, "sliced and diced" supply chains we know today.[29] These corporate strategies aligned with, and were enabled by, government policies that encouraged capital, raw materials, and finished goods to move across borders with minimal regulations. This logic of economic efficiency extended to extractive frontiers: Mining would happen wherever it was easiest and cheapest, in low-income countries with abundant deposits and pliable governments.

Today, it almost seems like history is running in reverse. Neither policymakers nor downstream firms trust those bywords of globalization, "free trade" and "open markets," to ensure reliable access to lithium battery supply chains. Instead, world powers like China, the United States, and the European Union are actively encouraging lithium mining to take place within their borders. "Onshoring" is being complemented by "friend-shoring," in which countries sign agreements with allied nations to secure mineral supplies. And after decades of offshoring and outsourcing, automakers are directly investing in vertically integrated lithium mines, refineries, and battery factories. Just as combustion engines defined the history of an earlier era, lithium batteries reveal the fundamental transformations of today's global economy as it passes through the triple crucible of climate change, energy transition, and geopolitical conflict.

FROM A DISTANCE, RHYOLITE RIDGE APPEARED AS A CHALKY WHITE hill, its soft curves set against a cobalt blue sky. As I approached, shape and color fragmented into a jumble of irregular polygons whose hues spanned the spectrum of grayness. And the motley crew of rocks had company. A cluster of teardrop-shaped green leaves, each covered in tiny pale hairs, nestled among the jagged edges. Three hardy stems, crowned by a globe of delicate cream petals, sprung from their center.

The desert wildflower was here for the same thing I was, the same thing that had brought an Australian mining company and their drilling equipment to the Silver Peak Range in southwestern Nevada. Tiehm's buckwheat (*Eriogonum tiehmii*), like the other species in its genus, has evolved to thrive in harsh conditions, including intense heat and aridity. The exceedingly rare plant lives only in soil abundant in both lithium and boron—and so, it grows only on Rhyolite Ridge, one of two such combined deposits in the world.[30] These rocky 10 acres of public land are the only home Tiehm's buckwheat has ever known.[31]

Rhyolite Ridge, the only habitat for this endangered species, is also the site for a planned open-pit mine. Between these two possibilities stand contradictory regulatory decisions, hundreds of millions of dollars in outside investment and US government loans, state and federal permits, and a tenacious campaign to save Tiehm's buckwheat from extinction. The fate of this flower and the future of the energy transition are bound together.

The day before I visited Rhyolite Ridge, I drove west on US-95 from Las Vegas, where I had spent the week at a corporate lithium convention, to the ghost town of Goldfield. As the name implies, Goldfield was once a booming hub for gold mining. The parallels of past and present were impossible to ignore and imbued the looming lithium rush with a spectral quality. In 1906, Goldfield's population was twenty thousand. Just four years later, three-quarters of the town was gone. In the interim, the state government had colluded with mine owners to brutally repress militant labor organizing, even convincing President Theodore Roosevelt to send hundreds of federal troops.[32] In the years that followed, mining companies abandoned the town. Sources attribute the capital flight to the cost of extracting gold in Goldfield, where subsurface brine was liable to fill mining pits and had to be pumped out.[33] The violent class conflict may also have played a role. Either way, a series of catastrophic fires ultimately sealed the town's fate.[34]

Looking at what was left of Goldfield, I couldn't help wondering whether the patterns of boom-and-bust cycles and state-sponsored violence would repeat in the extractive frontiers of the energy transition. History can weigh heavily on the present and the future. It can evoke nightmares. But it can also take the form of unfulfilled dreams: dreams of justice, of self-determination, of global cooperation; dreams of living well on our one and only planet.

But something else hit home during my drive to Goldfield. A radio announcement warned me of dangerous air quality, with toxic gases, pollutants, and particulate matter blowing in from across the border in California. The smoke came from the tail end of the Caldor Fire, which burned over 200,000 acres of forest in the Sierra Nevada in late 2021. Global warming scorched the western United States, setting more than ten thousand fires ablaze across the region that year alone. The fires themselves released an estimated 37 billion metric tons of carbon dioxide into the atmosphere, promising a future of relentless fires and floods. Looking out the window, a thick haze cloaked the Amargosa Range that runs along the eastern perimeter of Death Valley. The smoke tinged the mountains with subdued shades of light blue and gray, ombré tones that faded smoothly into the blue-gray sky. It suddenly struck me: *Everything will happen at once.*

The climate crisis, lithium mining, the energy transition, and, hopefully, something like climate safety: These aren't sequential steps in a linear trajectory but intersecting processes unfolding at increasing speed, bumping up against one another in time and space. We are currently in what energy systems analyst Emily Grubert calls the "mid-transition."[35] Renewables are being deployed, but fossil fuels remain dominant. Some corners of the economy are being decarbonized, while others continue to spew emissions and warm the atmosphere. This likewise implies multiplying extractive frontiers. Fossil capitalism is painfully undead; the mines to supply green capitalism are still being built.

There is no one simple trick to escape our earthly entanglement with nature's bounty—nor to dismantle power relations that have sedimented into their own force of nature, transforming the planet in the image of extractive capitalism. The implications are quite material. The impacts of lithium mining will be intensified by the very climate crisis that its extraction is intended to allay. The political and economic insecurity exacerbated by extreme temperatures will destabilize supply chains, including those for lithium batteries. And the confluence of these processes will reshape conflicts over extraction, ratcheting up their stakes and intensity.

PART II

FRONTIERS

Los Flamencos National Reserve, Atacama Salt Flat, Chile

CHAPTER 2

Peripheries and Power

Extractive frontiers offer a portal to the very origins of capitalist modernity. The model of extraction as we know it today—large-scale, export oriented, and socially and environmentally reckless—originated in the European conquest of the Americas. Famously, Christopher Columbus learned of Hispaniola's abundant gold deposits soon after making landfall on the island in 1492. Infamously, his forces decimated the native Taíno people and forced the survivors to labor in the growing mining industry—a workforce that would soon be supplemented by African slaves—all in the name of transferring the island's mineral wealth to the coffers of the Spanish crown.

Whether during the initial era of European conquest of the Americas; the height of European and American imperialism throughout Africa, Asia, and the Middle East; or the more contemporary "neocolonial" era, Western governments and firms have sought the Global South's oil, minerals, and fertile lands to supply their factories and markets. A classic example is the sprawling scale and scope of England's Industrial Revolution: a small island gaining the ability to "live beyond its means" by obtaining natural resources, agricultural products, and labor from a combination of colonial domination and trade.[1]

This history of colonialism casts a long shadow over the planet's extractive frontiers. Low-income countries, many of which were former colonies of European countries or the United States, provide much more energy, land, labor, and raw materials to the global economy than they consume.[2] Compared with their lower-income counterparts, high-income countries consume six times as much biomass, fossil fuels, metals, and nonmetallic minerals.[3] These raw materials are in turn inputs for downstream manufacturing that primarily takes place in wealthier countries, most of which are former colonizers, and, increasingly, in rapidly industrializing middle-income countries.[4] China is the partial exception that proves the rule. It both exploits and is exploited: an industrial powerhouse that extracts raw materials from Latin America and Africa—yet also provides embodied materials, energy, and labor to the global economy.[5]

The consequences of this highly asymmetric transfer of resources are profound. The same countries that provide more energy, land, labor, and raw materials than they consume also earn less from trade and suffer worse environmental impacts.[6] Wealthier countries, meanwhile, don't just appropriate resources; they also capture the net monetary benefits of trade. Countries with sectors like high-tech manufacturing earn more for their exports—exports that are made possible by extraction and harvesting beyond their borders—while externalizing their socio-environmental costs.

Mining exemplifies this pattern. A recent study of iron, aluminum, copper, zinc, lead, and nickel—six industrial metals absolutely essential for manufacturing infrastructures and technologies, including those linked to the renewable energy transition—found glaring but familiar patterns in where they come from and where they go. North American, Western European, and wealthier Asian countries consume three to four times as much of these metals as the world average.[7] Measured in terms of final consumption, 20 percent of the global population gobbles up 60 to 75 percent of the six metals, while the bottom 20 percent accounts for only about 1 percent.

Supply chains are much more than the geographic routes of material flows. They are vectors of inequality. And with inequality comes conflict. Colonial patterns are entrenched, not uncontested. The grand struggle over who controls the earth's bounty is far from over.

><

EXTRACTIVE FRONTIERS COME INTO BEING AND FADE INTO OBSCUrity at the whims of far-flung corporations, governments, and consumers. This reality helps explain some of the most persistent features of resource sectors and their landscapes: the boom-and-bust price cycles; the sharp swings from underinvestment to overcapacity; the sudden transformation of bustling mining hubs into eerie ghost towns; a given raw material's change in status from essential to expendable, seemingly overnight; the spatial coincidence of so much natural wealth and such high piles of waste.

Resource deposits take up enormous amounts of geological, political, and economic space. Their sheer physicality has long tempted commentators to see them as the root cause of corruption or poverty. Entire academic fields of inquiry have been devoted to studying how resource abundance affects the development of political regimes or a region's economy. Oil, in particular, is said to lead to authoritarianism and prevent industrialization, to breed violent conflict and weaken civil society.[8] How can a country escape this so-called resource curse if the resources are fixed in place? Over and over again, officials and executives from Santiago to Carson City told me, "The resources just are where they are."

Geology, however, is not destiny.[9] In the memorable phrasing of resource economist Erich Zimmermann, "Resources are not; they become."[10] The processes that concentrate and distribute minerals to their locations in the earth's crust—volcanic activity, erosion, precipitation—operate independently of human will. But these minerals only become useful and valued resources as a result of human action.

Geography is not destiny, either. Many factors shape whether a given deposit ultimately becomes a developed mine. Profitability is a sine qua non.[11] However, perhaps more so than in other realms of the economy, the success of an extractive enterprise depends on government decisions.[12] At a fundamental level, states "mediate" capital's access to nature.[13] State agencies grant environmental and social permits, concessions for exploration and exploitation, and subsidies for extractive activity (including the requisite energy, water, and transportation infrastructure). If the state is the owner of the resource in question, state-owned companies may operate with no involvement of the private sector—or may enter into joint ventures with multinational corporations. In such settings, even if private firms acquire concessions to mine a deposit on their own, they must negotiate contracts with state agencies that establish the parameters of their operations: spatial footprint, temporal duration, and, most critically, distribution of revenues between corporations and governments. With environmental regulations, states constrain firms' behavior and thus mitigate capitalism's tendency to deplete and contaminate the natural systems on which all economic production depends. Just as importantly, when states remediate environmental harm and compensate communities for land and livelihoods lost to mining, they help companies acquire and maintain the "social license" to operate.[14]

Resource extraction everywhere and always takes place against a background of public policies. Whether governments act independently of oil and mining companies is another question altogether, but in no other sector of the economy is the state so central. It is for this reason that extractive firms so often attempt to control the government agencies established to govern them in the first place, a phenomenon known as regulatory capture.

The world's states do not govern extraction on an equal footing. The colonial forces that relegated some places to serve as the mines and plantations for global capitalism also hollowed out the heartwood of political capacity. Today, many of these same states are home to large-scale extractive operations and are tasked with regulating multinational corporations—yet the line between public authority and private influence is blurry at best. Changing this reality entails confronting some of the most entrenched power relations on the planet. Latin America was the first formerly colonized world region to try.

IN 1922, ARGENTINA ESTABLISHED YACIMIENTOS PETROLÍFEROS Fiscales (YPF), the first state-owned oil and gas company outside of the Soviet Union.[15] In 1937, Bolivia nationalized Standard Oil's gas assets. Fifteen years later, a revolutionary government kicked out the "tin barons" and founded a state-owned mining company.[16] In 1938, Mexico wrested control of its oil supplies away from foreign companies.[17] These are just four of the many examples of the wave of resource nationalism that surged across Latin America in the middle of the twentieth century.

It makes sense that Latin America was the first region in which political leaders and ordinary citizens alike demanded a response to the yawning gap between nominal political sovereignty and the reality of economic subservience. This is because the vast majority of Latin American countries achieved independence well before much of Africa, the Middle East, and Asia were even fully colonized by European powers. By the mid-nineteenth century, almost all Latin American states were politically independent—but had little control over their economies.[18] US multinational corporations, especially those invested in mining, oil, and plantation-style agriculture, rapidly expanded their operations in the region. These behemoths (including the likes of Standard Oil, Anaconda Copper, and the United Fruit Company) operated with the backing of the US government and against the wishes of many Latin Americans. This set of circumstances provoked nationalist sentiment.

Popular discontent concentrated on extractive sectors—the most enduring links between Latin America and the world system into which it was so violently incorporated. Across twentieth-century

Latin America, there were sixteen nationalizations in the oil and gas sector alone[19] and many more in mining, steel, telecommunications, electricity, and railroads, in some cases without any compensation to the original owner. Some resource nationalizations were later reversed (and then reversed again). But once broached, the idea that the people, and by proxy the state, should own and control extraction within their national borders took hold. The possibility of harnessing natural resources for the public's benefit, rather than using them to line the pockets of foreign investors, formed a potent yearning that has been periodically sidelined but rarely extinguished.

Resource nationalism was much more than a set of policy experiments. It constituted a worldview that achieved political hegemony between the 1930s and 1970s and would return, in force, in the 2000s with the "pink tide," when leftist administrations governed the majority of the region's inhabitants.[20] The practical question of how a state might actually nationalize its resources fell to reform-minded politicians and bureaucrats, who worked out the nitty-gritty of compensation, management, and expertise. But the vision itself emerged from left-wing parties, labor unions (especially in the oil, gas, and mining sectors), and the working class more broadly. The stirring language of national sovereignty and *patrimonio*—a hard-to-translate word that denotes both cultural heritage and economic asset—filled the air.

Latin America, in other words, didn't just export raw materials to global markets. The region also exported a whole vocabulary for describing the economic pains of being former colonies—a set of concepts that later diffused to the several dozen newly independent states in what was formerly called the "Third World." In the 1950s and 1960s, Latin American academics and politicians in United Nations agencies developed and circulated a set of ideas that became known as dependency theory. The Economic Commission for Latin America and the Caribbean (known as CEPAL), established by the UN in 1948, and the organization's Conference on Trade and Development (UNC-

TAD), founded in 1964, spearheaded this movement as it spread first across the region and then globally.[21]

The two main features of what Brazilian sociologist (and later president) Fernando Henrique Cardoso called "the situation of dependency" were unequal exchange and enclave economies.[22] The concept of unequal exchange highlights the inequalities generated by the distinctive patterns of global markets: Exporters of manufactured goods benefit more from trade than do exporters of raw materials. The second concept, enclave economies, observes that mines, oil fields, and agricultural plantations contribute little to national economic development. The result is underdevelopment.

Dependency theory gave Latin American economists a powerful way to understand how a land so rich in natural resources could suffer such poverty. The framework suggested that underdevelopment—economic instability, persistent poverty, and inadequate healthcare and education—was not driven by cultural backwardness but was instead the predictable outcome of colonization. The striking title of Guyanese activist Walter Rodney's 1972 book, *How Europe Underdeveloped Africa*, pithily captures a sentiment shared across the Third World. A corollary to dependency theory held that development could only be achieved by "completing decolonization": by breaking free of the yoke of Western corporations.[23]

By 1960, this Latin American understanding of the roots of global inequality had begun influencing political leaders across the decolonizing world. That year, a set of Third World leaders came together to leverage their possession of a resource that wealthier nations couldn't live without: oil. Oil exemplified the situation of dependency. In the postwar era, a handful of Western companies, known as the "Seven Sisters," controlled 99 percent of Middle Eastern oil and 80 percent of crude in Venezuela and the Dutch Indies.[24] In other words, the literal fuel of capitalist modernity was extracted under profoundly neocolonial conditions. That is what the Organization of Petroleum Exporting Countries (OPEC) sought to transform. Established in 1960 by oil-producing states in the Middle East and Latin America, OPEC soon grew to include countries in Southeast Asia and North Africa. Venezuelan state officials played a particularly vital role in creating the organization and sharpening its core argument. Colonialism had divided the world to conquer it. Now, OPEC proposed that resource exporters band together to force multinational corporations to the negotiating table. The logic was undeniably compelling.

In 1971, Algeria nationalized its oil. By the end of that decade, every OPEC member nation, from Venezuela to Iraq, had done the same.[25] As anti-colonial uprisings accelerated in Africa and the Caribbean, Third World leaders around the world confidently asserted not only that their states should control how, when, and where their domestic natural resources were extracted, but also that they should ally with one another in transnational producer cartels to manage how those resources would be sold. Organizations like OPEC would set production levels and establish prices—and in so doing would exert leverage over the wealthier nations they exported to. OPEC became a model for transnational partnerships for other primary commodity sectors, whether copper or sugar.[26]

By the mid-1970s, the new understanding that formerly colonized countries should control the wealth generated within their borders had become a powerful force in international politics. The sheer number of newly independent countries generated its own political momentum. In 1974, the so-called Group of 77 (G77) led the UN in passing a declaration calling for a "New International Economic Order" that emphasized national sovereignty and self-determination, particularly when it came to natural resources.[27]

Almost five hundred years after the twin forces of mining and massacre had thrust the Western Hemisphere into a properly global capitalism, extraction was finally experiencing its first properly global reckoning. The West had learned that the system it had created and dominated for so long could in fact escape its grasp; the rest of the world had discovered that if they united, a different global order was possible.

But as the decade wore on, budding Third World solidarity faced challenges. By the late 1970s, the category encompassed almost a hundred countries, featuring a dizzying range of languages, cultures, religions, and geographies. Another name for this group, the Non-Aligned Movement (NAM), references an ideological debate over whether the situation of dependency should be addressed via reform or revolution. These divergent approaches mapped onto geopolitical divides. During the Cold War, Third World governments aligned with either the United States or the Soviet Union—or attempted a third option of non-alignment. Despite the connotation of neutrality, many non-aligned states adopted ambitious policies—including resource nationalization. Such attempts at economic sovereignty were met with swift retaliation. Thus, perhaps the most important challenge to Third World ascendancy came from the obdurate power of Western states and multinational corporations. Third World coordination challenged this dominance, but the backlash from powerful governments, particularly that of the United States, was fierce.

Nowhere are these sharp reversals in resource sovereignty more evident than in Chile. Starting in the mid-1960s, the government "Chileanized" copper mines previously owned by US companies, giving the Chilean state substantial equity stakes in the mines. In 1971, a democratically elected socialist administration finished the job, achieving full nationalization. Not coincidentally, CEPAL, the home of dependency theory, is headquartered in Chile. Soon enough, however, a violent US-backed reaction came in the form of a coup that rejected socialism. While state-owned mines were retained to fund the military, the dictatorship avidly courted private investment in copper and all other sectors of the economy.

The year that General Augusto Pinochet seized control of Chile was the same year that OPEC played its hand, precipitating a global oil crisis. In retrospect, 1973 was both the high-water mark for resource nationalism and Third World solidarity and the beginning of the West's search for new approaches to resource security and control.

><

DEPENDENCY IS DANGEROUS.

For centuries, high-wealth nations had preferred to obtain their natural resources from elsewhere, capturing the economic benefits of trade and externalizing the costs onto those they first colonized and later dominated. But the emergence of OPEC and calls for a New International Economic Order challenged this model. As OPEC member states nationalized their oil sectors, they gained more leverage over foreign multinationals. At the same time, they faced pressure from their own societies to address poverty, inequality, and underdevelopment. Given that the oil sales generated the bulk of these states' revenues, the only way to meet their citizens' demands was to squeeze more rent from oil. Demand from the industrialized West, meanwhile, was skyrocketing on the heels of the postwar boom and labor victories that boosted working- and middle-class consumption.[28]

OPEC leaders saw the situation clearly—and acted accordingly. For the first time in history, raw materials exporters took coordinated, unilateral action to transform the terms of trade. In October 1973, OPEC member states doubled oil's "posted price," or the price used to calculate the revenues petrostates receive. They did so without negotiating with oil companies. In January 1974, they did so again. European and US companies, and by extension their governments, suddenly lost control over the most vital commodity in the global economy, the lifeblood of all production and consumption.[29]

This turned out to be the high point of OPEC's power, but the "oil revolution"—or from the perspective of the West, the oil "shock" or "crisis"—fundamentally changed the course of history.[30] OPEC's demands upended the power relations embedded in the resource extraction economy and revealed the limits of Western dominance.

Among importing countries, the price shock drove governments to encourage their residents and manufacturers to use less oil and adopt alternative energy sources and technologies. Wealthy nations also instituted policies designed to increase domestic fossil fuel production. Within a decade, new oil frontiers had appeared in Alaska, the Gulf of Mexico, and the North Sea.[31] Having experienced a rare moment of vulnerability, Western policymakers were now intent on reducing "dependency" on imports of this critical resource.[32]

The same word—dependency—took on radically different meanings in the Global South and Global North. In the former, it meant economic subordination to the West; in the latter, it meant reliance on imported raw materials, including energy resources, from poor countries that, for more than five centuries, had been expected to follow orders rather than make demands. Both interpretations responded to the fundamental fact of global interdependency. But interdependency doesn't entail equality, or even reciprocity. The two meanings of dependency betrayed the intimate, and enduring, links between the colonizers and the colonized.

THE OPPOSITE OF DEPENDENCE IS INDEPENDENCE.

It is only fitting, then, that in late 1973, US president Richard Nixon launched "Project Independence" to recover "the strength of self-sufficiency." No longer would the United States expose itself to the vulnerability of "relying on any foreign nation" for crucial resources like oil.[33] After Nixon's resignation in August of the following year, President Gerald Ford signed the Energy Policy and Conservation Act into law, thereby establishing the Strategic Petroleum Reserve.[34] Later in the decade, President Jimmy Carter gave a speech in which he bemoaned the "intolerable dependence on foreign oil" and defined such dependency as a direct threat to national security. Famously known as the "malaise speech," the oration foreshadowed Carter's defeat at the polls the following year. To add some color to his address, he quoted the words of participants in an energy crisis summit he had convened at the presidential retreat in Camp David, Maryland. Among the concerns shared by leaders in business and politics was a statement the president characterized as particularly "vivid": "Our neck is stretched over a fence and OPEC has a knife."[35]

In establishing a link between resources and security, Nixon, Ford, and Carter were drawing on prior moments of American history. The United States first began mineral stockpiling in the years between the First and Second World Wars.[36] In the years leading up to World War II, Congress directed the executive branch to catalog and store "strategic and critical minerals."[37] During World War II, the War Production Board controlled the production of raw materials for military applications—including lithium. The surrender of the Axis forces in 1945 was almost immediately followed by the first phase of the Cold War, and along with it came a new regime of controlling access to "atomic materials"—again, including lithium.

But in the years immediately following World War II, even as the US government closely monitored supplies of critical minerals, it pivoted to imports to satisfy the demand for raw materials. In 1951, the Paley Commission, which President Truman had asked to examine the country's long-term resource needs, recommended that, aside from minerals needed in a "military emergency," the nation should rely on "lower-cost foreign sources for economic purposes."[38]

The commission's report marked a key inflection point. Over the next two decades, the share of minerals mined in the United States would decline precipitously.[39] During this period, the US government treated extractive resources as something that should be obtained as cheaply as possible, ideally from abroad—with the crucial exception of situations of "military emergency." The embrace of imports was a sign of American prowess. Emerging out of World War II as a global superpower, successive US administrations were confident they could access raw materials. When dollars or diplomacy didn't work, political meddling and military coups did.

But the rise of OPEC and the new assertiveness of Third World mining and oil exporters in the early 1970s forced policymakers in the United States to rethink their assumptions about easy access to other countries' resources. These political challenges arrived concurrently with a "logistics revolution" that eased global trade and thereby fed demand for raw materials. Computerized inventories and container ships enabled the movement of goods across oceans and continents at unprecedented speed and scale. All of this economic activity entailed an enormous material footprint, devouring unprecedented levels of fossil fuels, minerals, water, and land itself. This "Great Acceleration," as environmental historian John McNeill called it, ran roughshod over local ecosystems and the earth's climate system.[40]

Accelerated resource use sparked environmental activism, as witnessed by the millions of Americans who participated in the first Earth Day on April 22, 1970. But it also gave rise to fears of resource scarcity. That same year, US oil production peaked and commenced a slow but steady decline, fueling panic that oil would simply run out (the fears later proved baseless; domestic oil extraction now surpasses 1970 levels).[41] Increasingly, investors worried that scarcity might act as a brake on profits. *The Limits to Growth*, a best-selling report published in 1972, was issued not by radical environmentalists but by the Club of Rome, a global roundtable of leaders from the private and public sector.

In this context, Global South governments, frequently acting in response to social demands, attempted to strengthen their sovereignty over their resources and economies. Global North governments saw these actions as a direct threat. They deployed a potent mix of hard interventions and soft diplomacy to protect multinational corporations and their investors. And some of them, particularly those whose own territories included extensive mineral and fossil fuel deposits, also promoted domestic extraction.

Geopolitics has changed considerably since the 1970s. Yet that moment, dominated as it was by decolonizing demands, Great Power tensions, and energy shocks, also feels uncannily familiar today. The continued salience of resource nationalism in the Global South and the appeal of resource security in the Global North is a testament to the staying power of the languages and logics birthed in that tumultuous period. From contemporary proposals for a "Lithium OPEC" to moves to onshore lithium mining in the United States and the European Union, we are living in a world forged by prior decades of fierce contests over the extractive frontiers of global capitalism.

It is no mere coincidence, then, that the lithium battery, too, traces its origins to the turbulence of the 1970s.

CHAPTER 3

Lithium Frontiers

The idea that lithium batteries could be used to replace oil has an unlikely source: Exxon. At the height of the oil shock in the early 1970s, the fossil fuel company dedicated millions of dollars to researching alternatives to its main product. Working under the assumption that oil production would peak in the next few decades, company scientists sought the energy technologies of the future—with the goal of ensuring that the end of oil would not spell the end of Exxon's profits.[1]

Although it might at first seem counterintuitive for a fossil fuel company to plan for a post-carbon world, it made sense given the long lines at the gas pump and fears of the material limits to growth. As environmental historian James Morton Turner recounts, this moment of corporate farsightedness was fleeting. As soon as oil prices settled, Exxon abandoned its interest in new energy technologies. But the company's Advanced Battery Project formed a crucial node in the transnational story of the lithium battery. That story unfolds across the 1970s and 1980s, coursing through the "hellish industrial sprawl of refineries and storage tanks" of Exxon's facilities in Clinton, New Jersey, to Oxford University's Inorganic Chemistry Laboratory, to

Kanagawa, Japan, the site of a major manufacturing plant operated by petrochemicals giant Asahi Kasei.[2]

Lithium's star role in rechargeable batteries and thus in electric mobility owes much to chemist Stanley Whittingham's key innovation: *intercalation*.[3] This wonky term refers to the ability of solid materials with latticelike structures to play host to itinerant molecules or ions. Whittingham did not himself discover intercalation, which had been known since the mid-nineteenth century. His contribution, developed at Exxon's labs, was in applying the process to batteries. Positively charged lithium ions can nestle into the anode and cathode materials, flowing from anode to cathode when the battery is powering a device, and back in the opposite direction when the device is plugged in and charging.[4] At the same time, the now-liberated electrons move along the external circuit. This movement is the electric current.

Every type of battery—from the lead-acid variety that kickstarts a traditional car's engine to the alkaline type that powers flashlights and portable radios to the lithium-ion version that fuels smartphones and EVs—is a source of electrical power. This basic function is so ubiquitous that it is easy to take for granted. But batteries perform an impressive feat: By storing energy, they decouple the generation of energy from its eventual use, enabling the two processes to occur at distinct moments in time and distinct locations in space.[5] Beyond this essential shared feature, batteries differ in whether or not they can be recharged, in their voltage, and in their energy and power density. In other words, batteries vary in their electric potential, their capacity to store energy per unit volume, and how quickly and reliably they can deliver power.

Lithium excels on all these fronts. Lithium atoms are uniquely lightweight, with just three protons, four neutrons, and three electrons—hence the element's third place in the periodic table. Relative to its mass, lithium can store a lot of energy. In the case of an electric vehicle, thousands of battery cells are integrated into packs, in effect multiplying their power and energy density to a degree thus far unrivaled by any competing battery technology.

Lithium doesn't act alone. The specific materials that compose the cathode and anode have implications for the density, safety, and cost of battery cells. It was Oxford chemist John Goodenough's discovery of three distinct cathode recipes that provided the basis for the battery industry we know today.[6] From his perch as the head of the Inorganic Chemistry Lab, Goodenough built directly on Whittingham's innovations. Instead of drawing lithium from a fire-prone lithium metal anode, Goodenough supplied the batteries' lithium from a variety of compounds in the cathode: lithium cobalt oxide; lithium manganese oxide; and lithium iron phosphate. But what would replace the unstable lithium anode? Here, Goodenough in effect passed the baton of scientific progress to chemist Akira Yoshino. Working at the labs of Asahi Kasei, Yoshino experimented with various carbon-based materials for the anode, ultimately deciding on petroleum coke, or synthetic graphite.[7]

Through this distributed, collaborative, and transnational process of research and development, the lithium-ion battery had come into being by the summer of 1986. Its invention represented a quantum leap in energy storage, density, and performance. In recognition for their combined efforts, Goodenough, Whittingham, and Yoshino were awarded the 2019 Nobel Prize in Chemistry.

Scientific innovation is one thing, commercialization quite another. As a petrochemicals company, Yoshino's employer, Asahi Kasei, lacked battery-making knowhow or facilities. The Japanese firm also wanted to keep its competitors, like Sony and Panasonic, from catching wind of their groundbreaking, energy-dense rechargeable battery. Instead of pursuing the project in their own labs, the company sent a delegation to Boston with three jars of chemical slurry, containing the cathode, the anode, and the electrolyte, with the goal of piloting the new battery design. Their destination was Battery Engineering, Inc., a firm based in a converted garage in

Hyde Park, a neighborhood in the far south of the city. The small company specialized in unusual batteries, ranging in applications from medical (pacemakers) to military (fighter jets).[8] Although they had received no advance notice of the visit, Battery Engineering complied with Asahi Kasei's request, producing a batch of two hundred cylindrical battery cells based on Yoshino's prototype. By the following year, Asahi Kasei had decided that the benefits of collaboration outweighed the dangers of competition. Asahi Kasei executives met with Sony, and the two corporations established a "joint work team."[9]

In 1991, Sony debuted its 8mm camcorder, the first retail electronic device to be powered by a lithium battery based directly on Yoshino's prototype. It was China, however, that revolutionized the mass production of lithium batteries—and did so for their now most important use: electrifying the world's transportation fleet.

IN 2024, OVER 17 MILLION ELECTRIC VEHICLES WERE SOLD— almost one out of every five cars.[10] (This number includes 5.2 million hybrids.) This represents 7 times the 2019 EV sales and over 130 times the 2012 sales.[11] This figure demonstrates the industry's "robust" growth, which is all the more remarkable when we consider that auto sales overall are contracting.[12] The vast majority of these purchases—93 percent—take place in three major EV markets: China, the European Union, and the United States.[13] Of these, China emerges as the clear leader. In 2024, the country accounted for almost 64 percent of global sales.

China's EV market is the direct result of industrial policies that have encouraged mass production and consumption. Market fundamentals—supply and demand—were effectively artifacts of government planning.

The meteoric rise of the China's electric mobility sector has multiple origin points. One was development of mass-produced bicycles—

first powered by humans, then by batteries. After the revolution, the Chinese Communist Party's (CCP) first five-year plan (1953–1957) included ambitious targets for bicycle production; reminiscent of today's EV race, government policies ensured manufacturers' access to scarce inputs.[14] A year after that plan concluded, the country was producing a million bicycles a year. Chairman Mao himself owned a bicycle made by national champion Flying Pigeon. In the early 1960s, the CCP established a commission to study bikes powered by lead-acid batteries. The initial efforts failed. But decades later, the switch to lithium technology expanded e-bike sales, which topped 50 million in 2022 and provided a revenue stream for companies that would later expand into electric cars.[15]

Another origin point was the astronomical rise in car ownership in the 1980s, stoked, in part, by the consumerism of the CCP elite. As car spending reached $3 billion in 1985, leaders fretted about the yawning trade deficit. The worry birthed joint ventures between Chinese (often initially state-owned) and foreign firms as a conduit for technology transfers ("forced" or "fair," depending on your perspective). These partnerships were paired with import restrictions and "Made in China" requirements, a model later replicated across the country's economy. These policies ultimately created a powerful Chinese auto sector—one that, by the end of 2024, was the world's largest car exporter, having surpassed Japan, Mexico, Germany, and South Korea.[16]

Eliminating emissions was the next step. By the 2000s, rampant air pollution in Chinese cities was sparking political unrest. CCP leaders saw electrifying the still nascent domestic auto manufacturing sector as a solution. It helped that electric mobility was a relatively open economic niche, with Western car companies staunchly committed to the fossil capital coalition, clinging to carbon-spewing vehicles and financially contributing to climate denial. In China, meanwhile, the state had been prioritizing the development of "advanced energy technologies" since 1986, when a group of Chinese physicists with a background in applied science had advocated for the approach in a joint letter to Chairman Deng Xiaoping—revolutionary leader turned proponent of market reforms.[17]

In 2001, EVs were for the first time explicitly included in China's five-year plan, a decision that opened the floodgates of state loans and subsidies.[18] The state also encouraged creative experiments, such as the 2009 "Ten Cities, Ten Thousand Vehicles" contest that pitted major cities against one another in a race to deployment.[19]

But success also revealed vulnerabilities. In sourcing batteries—the most sophisticated and essential component of electric mobility—Chinese EV manufacturers remained dependent on imports from Japan, where battery cells were produced via highly capital-intensive automated production lines. Chemist Wang Chuanfo saw the gap as an opportunity. In 1995 he created the company BYD ("Build Your Dreams") by reverse engineering Japanese cell phone batteries and replacing expensive automation with cheaper human workers.[20] As recently as 2000, 90 percent of the world's lithium-ion batteries were produced in Japan.[21] Today, BYD is one of the world's biggest manufacturers of both EVs and their batteries. Six of the top ten battery manufacturers by market share are headquartered in China; the country boasts 85 percent of global battery production capacity.[22]

Entrepreneurial grit and labor exploitation are one side of the story; government policies are another. It is no coincidence that BYD was founded in Shenzhen, the first of four "special economic zones" created by Deng and launched in 1980. In the words of historian Quinn Slobodian, this zone, like other such jurisdictions around the world, is an "enclave carved out of a nation and freed from ordinary forms of regulation" in which "investors effectively dictate their own rules,"[23] a paradise for corporations guarded by barbed-wire fences and government checkpoints.[24] Low taxes and low-wage labor made Shenzhen an ideal location for BYD. To pivot from cell phones to cars, Wang acquired a state-owned auto enterprise in 2003. And to make those cars affordable to a mass market, BYD benefited from state subsidies at the local and national level.

STATECRAFT WAS SUPREMELY RELEVANT TO THE DEVELOPMENT OF another node in China's EV supply chain: raw materials. China's first lithium mine, Koktokay, was located in Xinjiang, as was its first lithium chemical factory. Xinjiang means "new frontier" in Mandarin.[25] Bordering Russia (as well as Central Asia, India, and Pakistan), the province's position between the twentieth century's two red powers made it an ideal site for an extractive frontier. The mine, which also produced beryllium and tungsten, furnished the Soviet Union with resources for industrial and military applications for decades.[26] Even during the Sino-Soviet split of the early 1960s, Koktokay's output helped China repay Soviet loans.[27] In recent years, Xinjiang has only grown in importance as an extractive frontier, with a vast complex of mines and smelters for producing lithium, nickel, manganese, beryllium, copper, and gold.[28] All this extraction comes at a serious cost, with reports of grave human rights violations, including detention camps, forced labor, and sterilization targeting the Uighur population.[29]

When the Koktokay mine was first developed in the 1940s, the lithium was primarily used to produce ceramics and glass.[30] It may also have supplied lithium for Soviet nuclear bombs (an isotope of the element is a crucial ingredient in nuclear weaponry).[31] The mine's significance increased in the early 1960s once China fully committed to a nuclear weapons program.[32]

By this point, the world's first race for lithium was on. The United States was then the top global producer of lithium, with mines located in North Carolina and South Dakota.[33] American lithium mining had expanded during World War II, when it was considered an essential resource with military applications, including inflating naval balloons. In the first months of the Korean War, the US government, under the auspices of the Atomic Energy Commission, the agency responsible for nuclear research for military and civilian applications, invested billions of dollars in the lithium supply chain. The program funded processing plants in Ohio, South Carolina, and Kentucky. The American press, egged on by domestic mining companies, stoked fears of a looming lithium shortage that bear an uncanny resemblance to today's headlines.[34]

But despite this moment in the limelight, it wasn't until 2016 that China declared lithium a "strategic" mineral meriting special attention from the state[35]—still a few years before the United States, the European Union, or the United Kingdom accorded lithium "critical" status. The new "strategic" designation touched off a major push to explore for new deposits within China's borders, with downstream battery makers such as BYD, CATL, and Gotion providing crucial financing.[36] The efforts have paid off. In 2024, the country accounted for 17 percent of the global share of lithium mining (up from 6 percent in 2016).[37] But lithium sourced from China's internal hinterlands—the salt flats of Qinghai and Tibet and the hard rock deposits of Sichuan Province and Jiangxi—remains insufficient in quantity and quality for the country's voracious battery market.

Domestic mining is thus only part of how China came to dominate lithium battery and EV markets. China is the top global importer, refiner, and consumer of lithium.[38] To satisfy China's enormous demand, Chinese supply chains now extend to extractive frontiers around the world. Chinese firms own a majority of the lithium mines in Zimbabwe's growing sector and a third of lithium mines in production or planned in Argentina, to give just two examples.[39]

Even before the EV takeoff, two Chinese companies that would become among the world's lithium powerhouses began eyeing overseas resources.[40] Ganfeng, one of the world's five largest lithium companies and a major supplier for Tesla, now has stakes in projects in Australia, Argentina, Mexico, and, most recently, Mali. Tianqi, meanwhile, holds a quarter of Greenbrushes, Australia's largest lithium mine, making it a partner with US-based Albemarle. Tianqi had previously been the project's majority owner, but it was forced to shed assets to relieve a heavy debt load incurred when the Chinese firm bought 23.77 percent of Chilean mining and chemicals giant SQM. This means that Tianqi is financially intertwined with both of the companies that dominate lithium extraction in Chile's Atacama Desert: SQM and Albemarle. Tianqi is also part owner of Australia's first battery-grade lithium refinery, a venture ironically being billed as a means of weaning the country from its "dependence" on China.[41] But for now, that dependency remains stark: As of 2024, the vast majority (98 percent) of Australia's spodumene (a type of hard rock ore) is processed into lithium hydroxide in China.[42]

Ganfeng, Tianqi, SQM, and Albemarle are four of the "lithium majors."[43] This term refers to the world's largest lithium companies, whether defined in financial terms (by the value of their shares) or, more materially, by the size and productive capacity of their mines. Their presence is a testament to the oligopolistic character of the lithium market, a sector dominated by a handful of corporations with interlocking ownership that make competitors in one country collaborators in another.

As I write, however, lithium capitalism is entering a new phase. Commodity heavyweights like Rio Tinto, the second largest mining company in the world, are making big plays in the lithium market. In the fall of 2024, the megafirm acquired Arcadium Lithium[44]—itself the product of a merger between US-based Livent and Australia's Allkem, which took place earlier the same year.[45] Meanwhile, fossil capital, including coal giants like Glencore, is also pivoting to "green" mining. And, coming full circle to its role in the invention of lithium batteries, oil giant Exxon has purchased mining rights to a lithium deposit in Arkansas.[46]

Through these developments, we witness new varieties of extractive capital—and new extractive frontiers—in the process of being born.

CAN MARKET FORCES SAVE US FROM THE CLIMATE CRISIS?

Proponents of market-driven innovation often point to the

trajectory of lithium batteries as evidence that the answer is yes. Transportation is the second-largest contributor to global carbon emissions and the number one contributor in the United States. Electrifying transportation is thus essential to meeting climate targets. Batteries are the most important and expensive component of EVs. Making them cheaper is therefore a crucial step toward consumer adoption. Over the past few decades, the explosive growth of battery manufacturing has dramatically lowered their price tag, making EVs more attractive to the all-important individual consumer.

Battery cost is calculated in dollars per kilowatt-hour (kWh), a standard unit measuring an hour's worth of energy consumption.[47] (A typical US EV has a 70 kWh battery.[48]) Battery cost reductions over the past few decades have been staggering, dropping 97 percent since the Sony camcorder first came on the market in 1991.[49] Zooming in on a narrower time frame, prices for lithium battery packs plunged from $1,391/kWh in 2013 to $139/kWh in 2023.[50]

How did batteries get so cheap? At first glance, the answer is a felicitous story of manufacturers relentlessly innovating, leading to batteries with greater levels of energy density: the amount of energy stored per unit volume. The gains are, in fact, impressive: Today, a battery the same size as the one in Sony's original camcorder would store 3.4 times as much energy.[51] Concretely, that means more energy bang for materials buck, reducing overall cost.[52]

But innovation isn't only the result of capitalist ingenuity. (Recall that Exxon shelved its plans to commercially develop lithium batteries when the oil shock subsided.) Instead, technological progress is downstream of larger political and economic forces. Government support for research and development (R&D) played a crucial role.[53] This is an example of what Mariana Mazzucato calls "the entrepreneurial state" that guides publicly funded innovation.[54] Increasing economies of scale have also reduced battery cost.[55] Simply put, the more widgets a factory produces, the cheaper it is to produce each widget; the cheaper the widgets, the more people can afford them—a virtuous cycle of production and consumption. But this, too, is shaped by public policies, especially those that create the markets for EVs and their batteries in the first place. These policies include subsidies for EV manufacturers, rebates for EV consumers, and emissions rules discouraging traditional cars. On all these fronts, China has stood out.[56]

On closer examination, however, innovations in manufacturing are only part of the story. The trend of ever-more affordable lithium batteries owes at least as much to the availability of mined materials.[57] For the two decades during which battery prices experienced their most precipitous decline, lithium prices were consistently low. It wasn't until late 2015 that lithium experienced its first major price spike, owing to EV takeoff in China.[58] Since then, the cost of battery cells has continued to fall, but cathode materials—including lithium—have comprised an ever-greater portion of the cost structure—51 percent in 2022, up from around 33 percent in the 1990s and 2000s.[59] Battery prices, in other words, are increasingly vulnerable to commodity shocks.

Just such a shock happened in the late summer of 2022. Demand for lithium was skyrocketing, in part because the United States had adopted major legislation that stimulated the production and consumption of electric vehicles, powered by lithium batteries.[60] Meanwhile, EV sales were up in European markets due to new emissions standards and consumer rebates, and China's EV uptake continued at a rapid clip.[61] But lithium battery supply chains could not respond nimbly to the sudden influx of demand. Pandemic-related disruptions were part of the reason. The lengthy time to open new mines was another. Climate chaos was also complicating lithium extraction. Sichuan, China—a key node of global battery production—was scorched by a seventy-day heat wave.[62] Sichuan provides almost a third of the country's lithium and is home to the lithium powerhouse Tianqi. The fallout transformed the province from bustling battery hub to yet another clogged chokepoint of global supply chains as power cuts forced major producers to slow or even halt operations. As

Sichuan sweltered, the gap between supply and demand widened further, pushing up the price of batteries and vehicles around the world.

The year 2022 marked the first time ever that lithium batteries were more expensive than the year before, primarily due to increasing prices of raw materials—especially lithium, which rose at a faster rate than other cathode inputs.[63]

Although the causes of this lithium price shock were specific, the implications are more general. Extreme weather makes raw materials more expensive. For example, agricultural crops from wheat to potatoes to coffee become harder to grow in drought conditions, resulting in smaller harvests and higher prices. The energy transition, a means of mitigating the climate crisis, can itself spur inflation. At a very basic level, this is because increased demand for wind turbines or e-bikes cannot always be met with immediate new supply, thereby putting upward pressure on prices.[64] But this Economics 101 explanation misses the fact that supply chains are always power relations. The larger the portion of the market a corporation commands, the greater that corporation's ability to protect its profit margins by passing on any cost increases to consumers (or by reducing their workers' wages).[65]

Now, this certainly did not mark the beginning of a new pattern of ever-costlier batteries. Most battery metals saw lower prices again in 2023, with lithium nosediving. Battery prices in turn resumed their downward trajectory, hitting $115/kWh in 2024, with further declines forecast in the years to come.[66] Cheaper batteries meant that some American EV models finally achieved "price parity" with traditional cars that same year.[67] But the episode does serve as a reminder that green capitalism is tethered to boom-and-bust extractive sectors and that "the energy transition"—or even just zero-emissions transportation, which is just one slice of it—is not one smooth process but rather several simultaneous, interacting, and unpredictable operations. Success on one front can result in bottlenecks on another.

BATTERY PRODUCTION HINGES ON THE READY AVAILABILITY OF mined materials like lithium. But mineral supply—what's underground—is a surprisingly complex phenomenon.

In one sense, this supply is static. It is certainly true that minerals are nonrenewable, at least in human time frames. The geological processes that form minerals take thousands to millions of years, many orders of magnitude longer than the time it takes to deplete a given mine (thirty to fifty years).[68] Despite this fact, known supplies increase over time as new discoveries are made.

As the energy transition gains momentum, the fundamental categories that the mining sector uses to describe minerals—deposit, resource, and reserve—have increasingly entered mass media. I frequently read headlines proclaiming discovery of the "world's largest lithium reserve" or that "half of the world's lithium" has been found somewhere or another. Unfortunately, media outlets and even policy experts play fast and loose with these terms. According to the United States Geological Survey (USGS), a *deposit* is "a mineral occurrence of sufficient size and grade that it might, under the most favorable of circumstances, be considered to have economic potential."[69] *Resources* are a smaller subset, indicating deposits where "economic"—that is, profitable—extraction of a commodity is feasible.[70] Lastly, *reserves* are that portion of a resource that can be "economically and legally extracted at the time of determination."[71]

All of these categories involve an interplay of geology, technology, and profitability. A reserve is only a reserve if the deposit has been identified, by surveying and prospecting; if the technical means of extracting it exist; and if expected revenues exceed costs. And these elements interact: A new method of extraction might render a deposit "economic" to exploit—just as high prices for a mineral may make it more attractive for a company to invest in physical infrastructure, equipment, and workers. These categories also involve speculation.

Qualifiers such as "indicated," "inferred," "probable," and "proven" denote varying levels of confidence in a mineral reserve, but even "proven" is a matter of degree (specifically, 90 percent technical and commercial viability).[72] Full certainty may come only decades later, after the mine is fully permitted, constructed, and operational and the income from sales exceeds expenditures on capital and labor. In this sense, in the words of geographer Brett Christophers, reserve estimates are "narrations of [the] future."[73]

Sometimes that future never arrives. I am reminded of a thirty-year battle to protect a cloud forest—a global biodiversity hot spot in the Intag Valley of northern Ecuador, a lush zone of dozens of headwaters of rivers and streams and endangered species like the long-nose harlequin frog—from a copper project that four different mining companies have pursued.[74] The various companies and the national government tried everything to mitigate the opposition of the residents of this highland community, from information sessions to physical assaults meted out by both private and state security forces. But these efforts did not ultimately pay off for those hoping to profit from the mine. After decades of protest and legal battles, a court found that the latest project owners, a joint venture of Ecuadorian and Chilean state-owned mining companies, had violated the community's right to prior consultation and the rights of nature—both of which are recognized in the country's 2008 constitution. For now, at least, the mine will not be built.

A sanguine observer might emphasize that humanity's knowledge of subsoil resources and reserves increases over time in a steady march of scientific progress. The latest research, however, challenges this optimistic view.[75] The "risks" associated with environmental, social, and governance (ESG) factors—including situations like the one I just described—are becoming ever more important in determining whether a discovery becomes a developed deposit. In other words, a mining company must manage such risks to profitably exploit its reserves.

Socio-environmental conflicts like the one in Intag Valley are more and more common. Militant resistance to extraction has proliferated along the ever-expanding frontiers of global capitalism, especially as affected communities have grown more environmentally conscious of the threats that mining poses to their land and water and less tolerant of the social dislocation and violent repression that so often accompanies extraction. For corporations, these conflicts, whatever their causes, directly translate into costs.[76] Interviews with corporate personnel reveal that delays, whether due to legal actions or protest tactics like occupations or blockades, can generate tens of thousands of dollars of losses a day, as operations are on "standby" while the company continues to pay wages and maintain the physical plant.[77]

Of course, what looks like an expensive delay from the point of view of investors is, from another perspective, at least a provisional victory. In these situations, capitalists must decide whether to absorb the costs of opposition in the hope of future profits or to cut their losses and strand their assets. The place-based nature of extractive sectors exposes them to sunk costs: investments that cannot easily be recovered. Context-specific sunk costs can increase the leverage of frontline communities or host governments in negotiations with firms.

ESG factors are not limited to local community protest or regulations protecting the environment over corporate profits. The "G," for governance, can also take the form of industrial policies that increasingly link access to energy transition minerals to larger goals of national security or economic prosperity. To wit, a recent report by the Organisation for Economic Co-operation and Development (OECD) found a fivefold increase in export restrictions on critical raw materials between 2009 and 2020.[78] The International Monetary Fund (IMF) likewise noted a major global increase in industrial policies, including trade barriers, from 2010 through 2023—and observed that "low-carbon technologies" as well as their "critical mineral" components were among the top targets of government interventions.[79] Such restrictions on "upstream" mineral supplies—which can range from taxes to outright bans on exports—make it more cost-effective to keep a commodity within the country where it is extracted and are often intended to stimulate the development of "downstream" domestic industries.

Export bans are a crucial tool for development, especially in the Global South. That's because economies that depend heavily on extracting and exporting raw materials present limited opportunities for sectoral diversification, job creation, or technological upgrading. Extractive economies are also subject to the whims of global markets, with commodity prices particularly prone to dramatic boom-and-bust cycles. At the same time, export bans can reduce the global availability and increase the price of energy transition minerals.[80] And export restrictions tend to beget more restrictions. Once one country limits the outflow of raw materials, others are incentivized to do the same.[81] These government interventions in mineral-producing countries are being complemented by a new assertiveness in importing countries. In the United States and the European Union, policymakers have pursued a combination of onshoring in a bid to expand domestic supplies, while also embracing friend-shoring, which favors imports from allies rather than, as the security state language goes, "foreign entities of concern." In the early months of Trump's second term, a third option emerged, which we could simply call "shoring." With threats to invade Greenland and annex Canada, both abundant in critical minerals, Trump proposed expanding the borders of the US to encompass resource deposits across the Western Hemisphere.[82]

Mineral supply, in other words, is shaped as much by grassroots resistance and tense geoeconomics as by geological processes. A third factor is arguably equally or more consequential: finance. From roughly 2000 to 2014, raw materials from copper to oil to beef experienced a period of historically high prices—a "commodities super cycle"—fueled in large part by rapid industrialization in China, which stimulated demand for a wide range of inputs.

When this commodity boom went bust, the world's multinational mining companies significantly reduced exploration for new deposits.[83] Between the peak in 2012 and the trough of 2016, mining firms reduced expenditures on exploration by almost two-thirds. Budgets recovered slightly over the next few years, but they remained well below half of their prior high.

The hesitation to break new ground is evidence of "capital discipline": pressure from shareholders to maximize returns in the form of dividends or stock buybacks, rather than allocating capital to risky investments that take much longer to yield a profit. An increasing share of mining deposits are being identified by junior mining companies—upstart firms that focus on early-stage exploration—but they lack the financial heft to develop mines beyond the exploration stage.[84] Instead, they need to convince outside investors to fund the project or a larger company to buy it from them. Thus, while people in the industry tend to blame government red tape or community protests for making it difficult to open new mines, the fact that exploration budgets shriveled during the crucial decade leading up to the energy transition takeoff suggests a more complex story that implicates capitalists themselves.

The combined forces of protest, regulation, geoeconomics, and financing all lead to the same result: The percentage of mining discoveries that become active mines is declining over time. Take the example of copper. In the 1950s, just over two-thirds (68 percent) of the moderate-to-large deposit discoveries were converted to productive mines. For discoveries made in the 1990s, the "conversion rate" dropped to just under a third (29 percent). In the 2000s, fewer than one in ten mining deposits were converted into mines (with the caveat that this number may tick up, as some of these more recent discoveries are now being developed).[85] Simultaneously, the lag between discovery and an operational mine is getting longer, now averaging 12.4 years across a wide range of mining sectors.[86]

For all these reasons, timely, affordable, and accessible mineral supplies are far from guaranteed. Minerals are never simply an input, patiently awaiting their turn to enter economic production: They are themselves the outcome of varied processes—and an increasingly unpredictable one, at that.

———

UNDERSTANDING EXTRACTION IS OFTEN AN EXERCISE IN HOLDING two—or more!—contradictory thoughts simultaneously.

On the one hand, it is true that digging up the earth's crust takes longer than it used to. Whether or not that is a good or bad thing depends on your normative perspective, as well as your social position. Shareholders, corporate executives, and often government officials prefer faster time frames, while marginalized communities, along with ecosystems, plants, and animals, certainly benefit from any regulation that requires more careful study of impacts. Movements in opposition to a given project explicitly aim to stall or stop the mine in question, whether to allow for additional participatory or regulatory processes or to prevent it from being built altogether.

On the other hand, the elongated time frames for more recent projects does not mean that the total output from mines around the world has decreased over time. Far from it. Over the past several decades, mining companies have more than tripled the volume of metals they remove from the ground, from 2.7 billion tons in 1970 to 9.6 billion tons in 2020.[87] High-resolution satellite imagery reveals the gargantuan spatial footprint of planetary extraction: over twelve thousand mines covering 65,000 square kilometers.[88] This figure includes a subset of fossil fuels, specifically coal and tar sands. But copper, essential to the energy transition, has the third-largest footprint of all (1,722.6 kilometers).

These numbers do not include the broader reach of mining's impacts. Sludgy mine waste and toxic chemicals can travel far from the point of extraction; likewise, the energy and transportation infrastructure needed to support operations extend well beyond the mine site. Researchers make different assumptions about the size of this "buffer zone." In tropical regions at least, there is evidence that mining can directly and indirectly contribute to deforestation more than 50 kilometers away.[89] If you incorporate the 50-kilometer buffer zone, mining has a global footprint of 24.5 million square kilometers.[90] The sheer spatial scale of extraction and its socio-environmental impacts has never been greater.

On yet a third hand, these facts on the ground are all subject to change. That's because extraction is shaped by a turbulent tangle of political and economic power, climate crisis, and energy transition.

The early 2020s provide a clear illustration of the manifold forces influencing mineral supply. The post-commodity boom phenomenon of constrained exploration budgets began to shift in 2021, as pandemic recovery policies, combined with the build-out of renewable energy supply chains, stoked demand for transition minerals,[91] encouraging more aggressive exploration efforts. Latin America was once again a top destination for extractive capital. The upswing, however, was short-lived. By the end of 2022, many mining investors had retreated to focusing on the profits from their existing assets, rather than developing new mines.

Lithium was initially immune from the downturn, with its record-breaking prices causing some industry analysts to label it "recession-proof."[92] Exploration budgets for lithium mines were the highest on record. But eventually supply caught up with, and then outpaced, demand, which had softened as economic growth slowed.[93] Lithium prices began their decline in late 2022, crashed by the spring of 2023, and stayed low through the end of 2024. Where once battery and EV manufacturers worried about the skyrocketing cost of lithium, lithium miners have now become worried that their sector will be less attractive to investors—and have asked governments for more support.[94]

Most analysts predict future supply crunches. Investor reluctance amid low prices, and thus low profits, is one issue. Another is overall uncertainty regarding the percentage of lithium discoveries that will become operational mines.[95] Some projects in the pipeline involve extractive techniques that have been tested in a pilot setting but have no commercial precedent.[96] The prevailing view is that lithium shortfalls will return after 2030 and onward, as phaseouts of traditional vehicles come into effect around the world.[97]

In the words of one expert, achieving equilibrium between lithium supply and demand hinges on "flawless" execution.[98] That means no major delays in the permits required to open a new mine, no days that are too hot for mines to safely operate, no protesters blocking the mine's entrance, no geopolitical conflagrations that result in barriers to trade, and a smooth pipeline of policy incentives and investor financing. The alternative is market imbalance: a mismatch between demand and supply.

Mismatches are not, of course, permanent. The gap can be narrowed in any number of ways, and governments play a big role. On the supply side, governments can loosen the regulatory requirements for new mines or dangle attractive tax breaks for extractive firms. Policymakers can also take more radical actions targeting profits or consumer lifestyles. These could include controlling prices for commodities deemed "essential" or moderating demand by encouraging less resource-intensive consumption.[99]

Among these various options to correct market imbalances, establishment policymakers and corporations across the lithium battery supply chain prefer expanding supply. For mainstream politicians and green capitalists, this makes perfect sense. Elected officials are understandably concerned with what is politically feasible. From their perspective, it is easier to dramatically ramp up mining in the United States and abroad, thereby increasing the supply of materials like lithium, than it is to discipline corporations by controlling prices or change deeply embedded consumption patterns, such as car ownership. Meanwhile, powerful industries—auto, mining, finance—benefit from incentives to mine and manufacture and would oppose efforts to reduce demand for their products.

Geopolitics also shapes supply and demand. These days, every new lithium mine or battery plant is strategic matériel in the global battle for green dominance. National security has become another reason to support mining projects, whether at home or in friendly states abroad. But geopolitics also constrains supply. Escalating efforts to decouple the West from China could result in an increasingly bifurcated global market, with flows of lithium and other "critical minerals" routed by grand strategy rather than economic efficiency.

⸺

SUPPLY CHAINS ARE VECTORS OF ECONOMIC PROFIT AND POLITICAL power, artifacts of decisions made by firms and states, sites of grassroots protest, and links between far-flung locales connected by the sinews of container ships and corporate contracts.[100] They are also, just as importantly, a set of ecological relations. Embodied in all final products are water, energy, land, and raw materials. A lithium battery and the car it powers carries within not only refined metals, but also the physical waste, water consumption, energy generation, and emissions entailed in their extraction and processing.

In other words, just how *green* is electric mobility?

This is a less straightforward question than it seems. One approach attempts to measure the amount of mining required for an individual EV. The answer changes, however, depending on whether we measure the weight of metals once they have been refined or also include the enormous quantity of waste produced in the process of mining. It also matters whether we assesses the material demands of EV production in isolation or compared with the raw materials—including, of course, fossil fuel energy—needed to manufacture and operate a traditional vehicle. The response can likewise change dramatically depending on the size and type of electric mobility. An electric SUV consumes a much greater volume of material inputs than does a smaller sedan or e-bike. An electric bus is even more resource-intensive to manufacture, but we might think about the metals that go into it differently, knowing that many more people are served by it than by an individual car. Lastly, we might consider the full recycling potential of EV metals—even if only a small percentage of battery materials are currently recovered.

In other words, behind this seemingly simple query lie all the complexities and dilemmas of the energy transition—and of how we all, individually and collectively, move around the world.

As a first cut, let's take a look at a 60 kWh electric vehicle, a typical battery capacity in Europe (for scale, slightly less than that of the Chevy Bolt). Averaging across battery chemistries suggests that each one of these vehicles contains around 160 kilograms, or about 353 pounds, of refined lithium, cobalt, nickel, manganese, graphite, aluminum, and copper.[101] A larger, luxury EV like Tesla's flagship Model S requires 530 pounds of refined mineral inputs for its hulking 1,200-pound, 85 kWh battery.[102] The average EV battery in the United States falls roughly between these two examples, at 70 kWh—which, by the way, is double the capacity they were a decade ago.[103]

When we broaden our perspective to include the inevitable waste involved in mining, the quantities balloon. Obtaining this bigger figure, which better captures the physical footprint of mining and its associated impacts, involves a calculation called, fittingly, the "rock-to-metal ratio."[104] This ratio varies not only by mineral but by specific deposit. According to a study conducted by USGS geologists and Apple supply chain experts, obtaining a single metric ton of nickel requires, on average, 250 metric tons of ore and waste rock. A metric ton of copper requires 513 metric tons of ore.[105] A metric ton of lithium from hard rock—the deposit type of all of Australia's major projects, which supplies 37 percent of global demand[106]—requires a whopping *1,634 metric tons* of ore and waste rock.

In the chapters that follow, we will consider this ratio in the context of brine deposits like Chile's, which involve mining salty, subsurface water rather than hard rock. But suffice it to say that 95 percent of the brine evaporates into the dry, hot desert air. Going back to the luxury Tesla model, researchers at MiningWatch Canada, an NGO focused on holding the industry accountable, estimate that producing a single one of these vehicles requires 40.7 metric tons of solid mine wastes and 3,400 liters of wastewater—in addition to the hundreds of pounds of materials that actually end up in the battery.[107]

When we think about the environmental impact of any product, it is inevitably a comparative exercise, relative to not consuming the product at all or to a less impactful alternative. Here, the relevant comparison is between the material needs of electric transportation versus those of traditional vehicles with internal combustion engines (ICEs). At this point, it is useful to distinguish between *stocks* and *flows*. This binary, formalized in late nineteenth-century economics but applied to social and natural systems of all sorts, captures the difference between a snapshot in time versus change over time.[108] As defined by Irving Fisher in 1896, "food in the pantry" is stock, whereas the movement of food into the pantry—say, after a trip to the supermarket—is flow. Flow, by its nature, is measured over some duration of time—a day, a month, a year.

These concepts better equip us to analyze the conundrum of comparing the material requirements of an electric vehicle with those of an ICE vehicle.[109]

Let's start with stocks: the materials embodied in each type of vehicle. The IEA estimates that 210 kilograms, or 463 pounds, of "critical minerals" go into the components of a typical EV: battery (the vast majority of this figure), electric motor, and car body. According to the same measure, the engine, power train, and body of an ICE vehicle requires 35 kilograms, or 77 pounds of metals.[110] So far, EVs look much more materially intensive than traditional cars. One key caveat is in order. Because the IEA is only looking at critical mineral inputs, it excludes a huge portion of the materials that go into making both traditional and electric cars—namely, the roughly 2,000 pounds of steel and several hundred pounds of aluminum that make up most of the body of either type of car.[111]

Even with this caveat, EVs are significantly more intensive in minerals than their traditional counterparts—and require six times more of the critical minerals prone to supply disruptions than ICE vehicles. But this conclusion changes when we take into account the ongoing flows of energy—specifically, fossil fuels—needed to power a gas-guzzler. The average ICE car consumes around 15 metric tons of oil over its lifetime—71 times the quantity of minerals embodied in an EV.[112] This of course does not account for the total volume of mined material: Including the 40.7 metric tons of solid waste and 3,400 liters of liquid waste makes an EV much more comparable to an ICE car, even accounting for the vast quantities of gasoline the latter gobbles up.

But there is a critical difference: The metals that do end up in EVs are recyclable, which could, over time, produce a "feedstock" of recovered materials that replaces extraction. The fuel that powers a car can only be used once.[113] At the moment, however, the promise of the "circular economy" remains exactly that: a promise. Activating the reusable potential of electric mobility will require stringent policies and massive new investments in recycling capacity.

There is, of course, another crucial variable to consider: emissions.[114] This is likewise less straightforward to measure than it might seem at first glance. EVs do not produce tailpipe emissions (although, like any road vehicle, they do generate localized tire and brake pollution). And, if they run on carbon-free energy, EVs do not contribute to climate change at all while they are being driven. But things get more complex when we recognize that energy systems are nowhere near fully decarbonized: The electricity powering the battery might be generated from dirty fossil fuels, and there are life cycle emissions of producing the EV, from mine to factory. The extraction and processing of metals—including those used to make EVs and charging infrastructure—contribute a substantial 10 percent of the global greenhouse gases that warm the atmosphere.[115]

The latest research shows that even accounting for both of these sources of emissions, ICE vehicles absolutely contribute more to global warming than do EVs.[116] The gap between the emissions of each widens the cleaner the energy sources—and likewise decreases the dirtier the grid that powers the battery and the energy sources that power battery production in the first place. In fact, if 100 percent of the electricity used to produce batteries and recharge the vehicle comes from coal power, the life cycle emissions of electric and traditional cars are comparable.[117] (As a corollary, the more progress made in decarbonizing the energy system, the less carbon would be emitted across the life cycle of an EV.) The larger the EV, the higher its material inputs, its life cycle emissions from production, and its electricity-related emissions. A large e-SUV powered by a typical American energy mix is only slightly less emissions-intensive than a compact, fuel-efficient traditional car. Some scholars have even suggested that models like the hulking electric Hummer might actually negatively impact climate mitigation efforts, as it uses a huge quantity of raw materials that would otherwise help produce more mass-market EVs, thus delaying electrification of the nation's fleet as a whole.[118]

Nevertheless, we can decisively say that in terms of helping confront the climate crisis, EVs beat ICE vehicles. Electric cars, however, are not a panacea,[119] and must form part of a broader tool kit of more climate-friendly, less mining-intensive, and more equitable transportation options. The primary driver for lithium demand is the passenger electric vehicle. By that token, reducing the centrality of individual EVs in the quest for zero emissions would lessen the pressure on lithium markets—and on landscapes and communities, of course. That would mean more mass transit, more walkable (and bikeable) cities and suburbs, and more housing density.

Confronting the United States' love affair with the personal automobile presents plenty of obvious challenges, from powerful vested interests to consumer habits so entrenched that we might consider them core to American national identity. But so, too, does the prevailing path forward. It will be an enormous feat not only to produce at least 200 million new electric vehicles by 2030,[120] but also to retire all the traditional cars. This reflects a more general conundrum of mainstream approaches to the energy transition. In an economy based on growth and profits, it is much more palatable to talk about producing new technologies and harnessing new energy sources than it is to suggest banning the incumbent technologies or energy sources that are the cause of the climate crisis in the first place.

THERE IS NO ASPECT OF THE ENERGY TRANSITION THAT BETTER illustrates the dilemmas of extraction than electric mobility. As societies decarbonize, the majority of demand—from 50 to 60 percent—for energy transition minerals will emanate from this sector alone.[121] For the mining industry, this marks a "momentous change" and bears the "good news" of a "fresh source of value" and an "era of reinvention" for extractive firms.[122] For affected communities, the moment is less auspicious: Between 2010 and 2024, there were 835 allegations of human rights abuses across eight important transition mineral sectors (bauxite, cobalt, copper, iron ore, lithium, manganese, nickel, and zinc).[123]

Contra the CEOs of major mining companies, extraction isn't just a set of profitable assets or lucrative new markets. It is much more than the sum total of mine sites in the world or a subset of economic activity. Extraction is fundamentally a political question and an arena riven by conflicts—between Global North and Global South, between states and firms, between communities and corporations, between workers and their bosses. And it would be hard to find a country more shaped by those conflicts than Chile.

CHAPTER 4

Lithium for Chile

On July 16, 1972, Salvador Allende, president of Chile and Latin America's first democratically elected socialist leader, addressed a large crowd of Chilean youth in front of a sleek, low-slung structure punctuated by a single minimalist tower. Months prior, the building had buzzed with the chatter of dignitaries from 131 countries who had gathered for the third-ever international meeting of the United Nations Commission on Trade and Development (UNCTAD).[1] In form and function, the edifice embodied the promise of Latin American modernism. This promise found expression in everything from manual workers' inclusion in architectural decisions to the use of domestic construction materials, a strategic choice in the context of suffocating US-backed economic sanctions and blockades.[2]

The occasion commemorated the first-year anniversary of the country's nationalization of the copper sector, a holiday called the Day of National Dignity. As Allende explained, centuries of foreign control over the nation's "essential" resource wealth had had profound effects, impeding the very ability of the "Chilean masses ... to feel truly human."[3] In an otherwise lofty speech, Allende's language turned visceral when he described the long reign of transnational capital, which had ruled by "digging its relentless claws into our soil," "hoarding... the riches extracted from the bowels of our land," and in the process gaining not only economic profits and political influence but control over the very "conscience" of Chileans.[4] For Allende, nationalizing the country's copper was much more than an economic policy. Owning the natural resources that colonial powers had for so long used to exploit Chile's people provided a new, material basis for working-class power: "We have not bought our dignity; we have conquered it through popular struggle. They won't be able to crush us."

Just as copper was central to Allende's vision of democratic socialism, so, too, did it prove pivotal to the coup that deposed him on September 11, 1973. Nationalizing the mines brought the Chilean government into direct confrontation with the mines' foreign owners. Prior to nationalization, US companies controlled 80 percent of Chilean copper production. Those exports in turn accounted for the same percentage of the country's foreign exchange earnings.[5] Shortly after Allende won election in 1970, President Nixon had vowed to "make the economy scream."[6] When Allende seized the property of American mining firms, Nixon had his pretext. Adding insult to injury, Allende's government charged the companies $774 million as restitution for "excess profits," more than canceling out compensation for their assets.[7] The punishment was swift and severe. In response to Allende's affront, the US government withheld bilateral aid, downgraded the country's credit rating, influenced debt negotiations with multilateral banks, and indirectly provided funds to a truckers' strike that drove the Chilean economy to a halt.[8]

Economic chaos provided an opening for dictatorship. Upon taking power, General Augusto Pinochet commandeered the UNCTAD building as his regime's headquarters, transforming a monument to Third World solidarity into the war room of neoliberal reaction.[9] From this perch, the dictatorship sold off hundreds of state-owned companies and returned the expropriated operations of US-based multinational companies like Dow Chemicals and Firestone to their prior owners.[10] In the case of copper, Pinochet kept the previously nationalized mines under state control—but he made sure to reimburse the mining companies that Allende had kicked out of the country.[11] Such compensation was one of many tools to lure foreign capital back to extractive enterprises. A series of decrees and laws established exceedingly favorable conditions for foreign investors in the copper sector, with dramatically reduced tax and royalty rates and new protections for private mine owners.[12]

As part of his mission to make Chile desirable for investors, Pinochet also kneecapped mine workers. On October 19, 1973, the very same day that the military junta declared its plans to reprivatize large swaths of the Chilean economy, the "Caravan of Death" stopped in Calama, a mining town in the Atacama Desert.[13] The soldiers of this terrifying unit, which patrolled the country by helicopters, detained and subsequently assassinated twenty-six people. Most of the dead were workers in the enormous Chuquicamata mine.

The massacre at Calama was the result of a cold political calculus. Organized workers posed a threat to Pinochet's political project. When the general took power, Chilean workers were more likely to belong to a union and more likely to go on strike than in any other country in the region.[14] When Allende was still in office, rank-and-file miners agitated for worker control of production, clashing not only with state-appointed managers but also with their union leadership.[15]

Under Pinochet's repressive regime, copper miners kept their radical ardor alive. In 1983, the 26,000-member Confederation of Copper Workers went on strike, despite having had their trade federations and union meetings declared illegal.[16] The copper miners' work stoppage was the first national one under Pinochet's rule. It shut down three of the four state-owned mines in the northern desert that, combined, produced a million metric tons of copper.[17] As Thomas Miller Klubock, a historian of Chile, observed, the 1983 strike exemplified "copper miners' central role in the resurgence of civilian opposition" to Pinochet's regime.[18] Perhaps that's because their dignity was at stake.

PROTECTING PRIVATE PROPERTY. COURTING FOREIGN CAPITAL. Attacking unionized labor. In all of these ways, Pinochet's interventions in the mining sector follow textbook definitions of neoliberalism. On a basic level, neoliberalism is the belief that markets should be free from interference. It follows that key economic decisions should be made by investors, entrepreneurs, and consumers—not governments, workers, or communities. Both supporters and critics of free markets point to Chile as a marquee example. That these policies were implemented by a brutal dictatorship is either an inconvenient fact or damning evidence.

The details of Pinochet's approach to resource extraction unsettles this easy understanding of Chile as a neoliberal paradise.[19] Governments of countries with large oil or mining reserves tend to take a keen interest in those sectors, even if their leaders profess a commitment to the principle of laissez-faire. Revenues from natural resources, whether in the form of leases, royalties, or direct sales, generate state income. Certain natural resources are also often seen as strategic from a national security perspective. In the case of Chile, Pinochet's regime not only retained, but actually expanded, the role of the state in the mining sector. He simply did so in a manner that encouraged more private investment.

Over time, the reforms first adopted under Pinochet dramatically expanded the presence of foreign multinationals in Chile's mining sector. Today, state-owned Codelco accounts for just a quarter of Chile's copper output.[20] But what is perhaps more notable is that Pinochet established Codelco in the first place—even as he privatized almost everything else. Instead of reprivatizing the copper mines that Allende had nationalized, Pinochet consolidated them into one state-owned enterprise. He did so to appease the more nationalist wing of the military, which was suspicious of selling off a sector as strategic as copper.[21] The military brass also had a direct material interest in the mines: Revenues from copper sales financed about a quarter of the military's budget.[22]

This curious mix of foreign capital and state control also prevailed in the nascent lithium industry. On January 1, 1979, Decree No. 2886 declared lithium a strategic state-owned resource to be used in the national interest.[23] The regime gave Chile's nuclear agency the right to stockpile lithium, a key ingredient in thermonuclear weaponry, and required its sign-off for any legal act pertaining to the element.[24] The decree also, and most consequentially, banned new leases for lithium mining.[25] Any companies that already had rights to mine lithium would retain them, but no new leases would be issued.

The unusual structure of Chile's contemporary lithium sector is the ongoing legacy of this Cold War–era decree. Despite the fact that the country holds nearly a third of the world's lithium reserves and produces 20 percent of the global supply, Chile's lithium industry remains in the hands of just two multinational companies, both of which were lucky enough to own concessions predating the ban. These two companies—Albemarle and SQM—control all lithium extraction on the vast Atacama Salt Flat.

The mineral potential of the Atacama Desert salt flats had been recognized in the early 1960s, when William E. Rudolph, geologist for the Anaconda mining company, was hunting for new freshwater sources to process copper and stumbled upon lithium-rich brine instead.[26] But it wasn't until 1974, soon after Pinochet's violent coup, that lithium development began in earnest. That was when Pennsylvania-based Foote Mineral Co. noted "a change in the political climate" and became interested in Chile's lithium resources.[27] The origins of lithium mining in Chile, in other words, are inseparable from the dictatorship.

Less than a year into the new regime, a delegation consisting of Foote's president, its manager of international marketing, and its chief geologist headed to the northern desert. They were accompanied by a geologist from the Chilean state geological agency. The timing was auspicious. Chile's lithium had been discovered but not yet exploited. A new dictator, friendly to US corporations, had just taken power. And since lithium had not yet been declared "strategic," there were few if any barriers to entry into the sector. The lithium frontier was wide open for corporate extraction. It was fitting, then, that Foote's company magazine referred to the Atacama Salt Flat as "lithium El Dorado" and recounted the delegation's journey in the style of a colonial-era chronicle:

> *From San Pedro to the southern part of the Salar, where the brine had been found, was a long haul, three hours of careful driving. Much of the distance, about 100 kilometers (60 miles), they bumped and rattled along in a Chevy pickup truck over salt flats and only slightly improved sandy terrain. But if the so-called road was rough, the view was unusually picturesque, as if to compensate for the riders' discomfort. On their left, the Andes mountains towered some 19,000 feet above sea level, and every so often a snow-capped smoking volcano rendered the scenic panorama even more striking and surrealistically beautiful.*[28]

The effort of traversing the challenging terrain proved more than worthwhile for Foote. The brine they tested had a lithium concentration of 1,500 ppm—five times higher than the company's deposit in Silver Peak, Nevada—positioning the location as a "world champion in lithium resources."[29] With this tantalizing discovery in hand, Foote and Chile's state development agency, CORFO, entered into negotiations that would result in the nation's first contract to explore and extract the mineral via a joint venture.[30] Over the next several decades, Foote's agreement with the Chilean government, its Atacama lithium mine, and its Silver Peak mine were acquired by Albemarle, which continues to operate the facilities today.

The other lithium mining operation in the Atacama Salt Flat, SQM, also owes its presence there to the dictatorship. The firm had been nationalized by Allende; Pinochet privatized it.[31] A series of subsequent buyouts and transfers made SQM the sole proprietor of lucrative lithium assets that conveniently predated the 1979 ban on new leases.[32]

At the time of this writing, Albemarle and SQM continue to enjoy what is in effect a legally sanctioned private duopoly. Paradoxically, the strength of the companies' ties to the country's lithium sector—the decades of physical investments and contract negotiations—gives the state an advantage. Both corporations have paid out too much in the sunk costs of mining equipment and political pressure to simply step away from their valuable lithium assets. State officials have made some use of their bargaining chip. They have wrung the two firms for a larger cut of revenues, while also attempting to attract additional lithium companies to the countries' many salt flats. But in stark contrast to Allende's radical takeover of the copper industry, successive Chilean governments have resigned themselves to the enduring presence of Albemarle and SQM.

This status quo has not gone uncontested. The gap between the palpable potential of public control and the reality of corporate dominance has provoked lithium nationalism. This is the recurrent dream of extracting resources not for global export or corporate profits, but for Chile—as a fount of development and, in Allende's stirring language, dignity.

⸻

FOR RESEARCHERS LIKE MYSELF, IT CAN BE DIFFICULT TO OBSERVE the inner workings of extractive economies: closed-door negotiations between ministers and executives; complex formulas to allocate state revenues and corporate profits; volatile commodity markets; remote extractive frontiers; proprietary control of the most basic information; limited regulatory oversight and democratic accountability. These features form a breeding ground for corruption and regulatory capture.[33] They also hinder the basic tasks of scholarly investigation:

accessing sources, verifying facts, collecting documents, and triangulating across diverse perspectives.

Undeterred, I've searched for cracks in what Franz Kafka called *The Castle*. Wandering the endless hallways of this edifice of opacity, I've often been drawn to the mid-ranking bureaucrats who populate its many cubicles. Neither elected officials nor high-level ministers, these unsung functionaries implement decisions made by others—and command an intimate, workaday knowledge of otherwise abstract concepts. At their desks, amid the reams of dry memoranda and calendars of endless meetings, they experience firsthand the messy encounter of regulation and reality, the fine art of corporate evasion, the limits of government authority, and, on occasion, the unexpected moments when the powerful can be held to account. They are also pulled in multiple directions by competing centers of political gravity. In their quiet way, then, these bureaucrats personify, even humanize, the grand forces of history in all their complexities, contradictions, and changes.

Or so I told myself when I decided to trek across Santiago to visit Chile's nuclear agency, located on the slopes of a hill in a residential area of the tony Las Condes sector of the city. Since the 1970s, the agency has retained a crucial, albeit somewhat obscure, role in the country's lithium industry. In a holdover from the Cold War era, any legal act pertaining to lithium requires the agency's approval, including renewals of or revisions to the contracts for the two large-scale mines on the Atacama Salt Flat. Meeting with nuclear bureaucrats gave me an oblique way to enter the enigmatic world of lithium. And oblique, I've found, is often best.

As I walked from the bus stop, a long row of ranch-style, single-family homes with the requisite bright green, manicured lawns stretched along my left. To my right, an enormous, privately owned soccer field. The great blue sky was cloudless, the streets quiet save for an occasional car or the faint staccato of a garden sprinkler. When the agency's campus came into view, its domed reactor building and modernist offices transported me to the to US version of the 1960s, a cinematic montage of a nuclear laboratory superimposed on the architecture of suburbia. The soaring Andean Mountains that formed the scene's backdrop were the only reminder that I was in Chile.

After a brief screening by military guards, I was greeted by my guide. Felipe Mujica, the nuclear agency's senior industrial officer, had spent almost four decades in the mining industry, specializing in automation and communications technology, before joining the nuclear agency. He was used to mediating between the public and private sector.[34] As we sat down at a long conference table, Mujica captivated me with an endless stream of tales that moved fluidly across Chile's many histories of extraction—fables that, regardless of the century or decade in question, ended with the same moral.

He recounted the era of copper nationalization under Allende and Pinochet's efforts to woo back foreign capital, pausing for a moment to recommend *The Shock Doctrine*, Naomi Klein's bestseller on "disaster capitalism" that devoted substantial attention to Pinochet's coup and regime.[35] He then traveled farther back in time, to the late nineteenth-century War of the Pacific. Nominally fought between Chile, Peru, and Bolivia, this conflict was in reality a proxy battle on behalf of British nitrate companies.[36] Next came the devastation wrought by the German invention of synthetic nitrates in the early twentieth century, a discovery that wrecked the economy of the Atacama Desert—home to the only naturally occurring nitrate deposits of sufficient concentration to mine.[37] As he spoke, I thought of the buried bodies of those disappeared by Pinochet's regime and interred in the northern, arid expanse. So many ghosts haunt this extractive frontier.

For Mujica, all these episodes illustrated the national tragedy of an extractive economy. As Chile's lithium exports rose in global prominence, this tragedy risked repeating itself. Although Mujica noted the ecological impacts of lithium extraction (referring to the process of evaporating water in a desert as "contradictory"), he was speaking as a technocrat, not an environmentalist, and was most concerned about the state's limited capacity to monitor and regulate the sector. He saw this capacity as undermined by a lack of even the most basic knowledge about the activities of the two firms that controlled all lithium extraction in the country—a legacy of Pinochet that had left bureaucrats "terrified" and unable to see the state as a regulating body.

The anthropologist James Scott coined the phrase "seeing like a state" to describe the ways that states use maps, statistics, and other tools that survey, standardize, and measure to turn the messiness of everyday life into the moldable clay of governance.[38] Pinochet selectively dismantled state capacities. During the dictatorship, the military saw a boon in spending, while social services like housing, healthcare, and education were put on the chopping block.[39] As we saw with the establishment of Codelco, the dictatorship did intervene in the economy. Beyond copper, there were generous subsidies for the forestry industry and public R&D to help the salmon sector.[40] But the goal here was to encourage investment and protect private property—not to regulate capitalists. Lithium exemplifies Chile's inability to see like a state. The nuclear agency, despite its expansive legal mandate, had neither a laboratory to test lithium samples bound for the container ships departing Chile's ports nor a shared database with the customs agency to ensure that export quotas were not being exceeded.

Just weeks before our conversation in February 2019, these lacunae in lithium governance had made international headlines. An internal audit at the nuclear agency revealed "significant errors" in the databases tracking Albemarle and SQM's physical exports and their contractual quotas.[41] The discrepancies between the nuclear agency's database and the custom agency's database revealed a pattern of excess shipments over a period of thirty years (1984–2015), spanning lithium's evolution from a little-known industrial input to an essential ingredient for the electronics and auto industries. For regulators and reporters alike, the key question was whether the companies' practices represented intentional fraud or an innocent oversight. The nuclear agency proposed an investigation to get to the bottom of it.[42] But the investigation never took place.[43] And the very fact that it took thirty years for the discrepancies to come to light underscores the trademark opacity of extractive sectors: mining in peripheral regions with limited government presence and rare media scrutiny; hard-to-track physical shipments from mine to refinery, refinery to port, port to ship; number crunching at the customs house, painstakingly calibrating contents between contract and container.

As it turned out, the database mismatches were just the tip of the iceberg of a tense drama between a government dependent on mineral exports and the mining companies that control the production, logistics, and even basic information in a strategic sector.

><

"CHAOS." "A GIANT DISORDER." THE STRONG WORDS SENT SLIGHT ripples across an otherwise calm face. I was talking to Patricio Aguilera, who served as the nuclear agency's executive director from November 2015 to October 2018.[44] We were seated across from one another in a Starbucks tucked among the government buildings where he had spent his decade-long career in the Chilean state.

Aguilera directed the agency during a particularly critical period. With the EV transition picking up momentum, lithium had acquired a new global importance. At the same time, Albemarle and SQM's actual and alleged corporate misbehavior put lithium mining in the political spotlight in Chile. The growing market for a previously minor export, combined with increasing consciousness of its impact on the environment and mounting awareness of complex and shady corporate dealings, meant that bureaucrats and citizens alike began demanding major reforms. To that end, then president Michelle Bachelet's center-left government established a top-level National Lithium Commission that assembled representatives of the public and private sectors, labor, Indigenous communities, and international experts for six months of research, site visits to the Atacama, and deliberations on the future of lithium in Chile. The resulting report, published in January 2015, outlined a Goldilocks governance model: minimize the ecological harms and economic inequities of this extractive sector and maximize its benefits to the public good.[45] The mining sector would have to pay more for the privilege of extracting the country's lithium, and Chile would invest the resulting funds in technological innovation. In other words, the report laid out a path for Chile to escape the trap of extraction and vault itself into the value-added chemical and manufacturing processes downstream of mining. Central to this vision was the report's final recommendation: a state-owned lithium company.

This vision of lithium for Chile—environmentally friendly and economically dynamic—stood in ever sharper contrast to reality. The years stretching from 2014, when the National Lithium Commission first met, through 2019, when the findings of the nuclear agency's audit of Albemarle and SQM were made public, were punctuated by one lithium-related scandal after another.

While the audit was still ongoing, the nuclear agency denied Albemarle's request for a tripled export quota. Despite Albemarle's concerted lobbying, already wary government officials remained skeptical that the company could triple its output without extracting additional brine in a region already under severe water stress.[46] It didn't help the firm's case that they refused to release data that the state had requested on the size of their lithium reserves.[47] An even bigger flare-up concerned a subject of direct material interest to the state: cash. In 2021, the state development agency, CORFO, brought an arbitration against Albemarle for allegedly underpaying its royalties to the state by $15 million.[48] Initially Albemarle denied these charges, but after three years, in April 2024, it entered into a settlement agreement. That agreement did not include any admission of wrongdoing. But it did note that there was a discrepancy between CORFO's and Albemarle's respective calculations of the royalties owed, and that the payment of $15 million was intended to align Albemarle's payments with the exact amount that CORFO had claimed was due.[49]

The controversies swirling around SQM were even more serious. The company was already infamous for its links to the bloody Pinochet dictatorship, family nepotism, and illegal trading among its various holding companies.[50] Overlapping with the commission's work and Aguilera's tenure, the Chilean public learned that the company had sent illicit payments to former and current politicians from across the political spectrum, including President Bachelet's Socialist Party.[51] It was ultimately revealed that SQM had made almost $15 million in illegal political contributions (a polite phrase for bribes) over seven years. The company's massive lobbying effort paid off, resulting in weakened environmental oversight and reduced fines in the case of regulatory violations.[52] In January 2017, the US Securities and Exchange Commission fined the company $15 million for the infractions pursuant to a criminal complaint, while the US Department of Justice fined the company another $15 million in a parallel civil action as part of a deferred prosecution agreement (which ended in 2020). But Chilean prosecutors ultimately settled for a mere $4.2 million, only a third of which went to the state.[53] The rest was donated to foundations chosen by the firm.[54]

Extractive sectors are notorious for corruption, but SQM's scandals were so many it boggles the mind. In addition to the illegal campaign financing, SQM was accused of massively underpaying royalties owed to the state, tax fraud, registering mining and water rights that belonged to the state agency CORFO, violating labor law, and tampering with the environmental monitoring system.[55] (Most if not all of the proceedings initiated against the company except for those alleging labor law violations were terminated or suspended—which only provoked more public outrage.) Despite these many scandals, on January 17, 2018, CORFO and SQM signed a new agreement that tripled the company's lithium quota and extended its lease to 2030.[56] In late April, the deal was approved by the nuclear agency, despite officials' initial misgivings.[57]

Widespread concerns about corporate corruption incited its historical nemesis: resource nationalism. Regulators might have been willing to sign off on the deal, but the Chilean people were not. An outraged group of trade union confederations and left-wing elected officials formed a Lithium for Chile movement that demanded nationalizing the company.[58] On January 29, 2018, just two weeks after the agreement had been finalized, Lithium for Chile organized a protest in the capital.[59] The next day, resistance erupted along the salt flat. The Council of Atacameño Peoples organized a blockade of CH-27, the main highway in northern Chile.[60] Discontent spread to Congress, where lawmakers shared the public outrage and nationalizing impulse. Chile's lower house of Congress voted to urge President Bachelet to reject the contract and establish a state-owned lithium company; in October of that year, the body voted in favor of nationalizing SQM.[61] These votes were effectively symbolic, but they nonetheless stamped an official seal on popular indignation.

Amid the swirling scandals and demands for expropriation, one question was on everyone's mind. Why would the government sign a contract with a firm that was at the center of so many legal disputes and was universally perceived to have betrayed public trust? The answer reveals much about the power relations that structure resource extraction in places like Chile.

Until the ink was dry, the contract was by no means a certainty. Eduardo Bitran, executive vice president of CORFO and one of the government's two chief negotiators, had threatened to both terminate SQM's prior contract and force the company to pay restitution to the state, above and beyond its outstanding debts, as compensation for committing "moral damage" and discrediting a state institution.[62] But once the contract was signed, both Bitran and Aguilera, the other chief negotiator, asserted that the contract marked a major, even historic, advance in the economic benefits that a Global South government had been able to wrest from a multinational corporation.

How should we interpret these contradictory statements? Do they represent the post hoc justifications of embarrassed bureaucrats? Or did government negotiators outmaneuver their corporate counterparts, winning major concessions?

The Chilean economy, and in many ways the state itself, relies on export-oriented mining and agriculture. Barring a deeper change to that model, foreign investment is a political necessity. An earlier generation of Global South leaders turned to expropriation as a path out of dependency, but changes in the architecture of the global economy have made this path much riskier. Free trade agreements, like the one Chile signed with the United States in 2003, empower investors to sue national governments over policy decisions that threaten profits.[63] The threat of legal action, combined with the state's deep fiscal reliance on extractive sectors, tightly binds regulators' hands.

And yet: Chile had some power over SQM. Like any mining company, SQM had outlaid substantial, site-specific physical investments in lithium mining for decades. Their brine pumps and evaporation ponds, all customized to the particular depth and density of the Atacama reserves and to the exceptional intensity of the sun beating down on the high Andean plateau, had cost the company over $2 billion, with an additional $1.4 billion planned by the end of 2024.[64] These investments were designed to maximize extraction and therefore profit. But they also amounted to enormous sunk costs, tethering SQM in place and motivating the company to offer concessions, including higher royalties, that might ensure fruitful future production and sales. SQM's conundrum is an example of what economist Raymond Vernon famously dubbed the "obsolescing bargain" of resource extraction: The longer that any mining or fossil fuel firms operate in a given country, the more their negotiating position erodes.[65] Chile, in other words, lacked the power to escape extractive capitalism but had the leverage to negotiate better contracts.

In my conversations with Aguilera and Bitran, both negotiators underscored their achievements. Compared with prior agreements, the 2018 SQM contract (and the 2016 Albemarle contract it was modeled on) substantially increased the total revenues each company paid the state. Aguilera reckoned that the economic benefits "between SQM and Chilean society" were now split evenly.[66] The increased royalty payments would flow not only to the state's general budget, but also to regional and municipal governments and Indigenous communities. SQM would additionally contribute funds for a new Clean Technologies Institute. In addition, any refined lithium that the company sold within Chile's borders would receive a 25 percent discount to incentivize a domestic battery supply chain.

In our interview, Bitran emphasized that the new royalty rate was "the highest in the world."[67] To underscore the point, he used language that resonated with the region's long history of resource sovereignty and the growing movement to nationalize lithium. As he had put it during a prior radio appearance, "With a tough, strong negotiation . . . we have managed to recover lithium for Chile."[68] But extractive investment is a double-edged sword. State leverage emanates from the very same source as corporate power: mutual, yet asymmetric, dependency.

As our conversation unfolded, Bitran tacked between confidence and defensiveness—the sword's two edges. When I pushed him on how he could even negotiate with a firm guilty of "moral damage," he asserted he had no choice. As he explained, not renewing SQM's lease wouldn't have forced the company out of the country; it simply would have limited their operations to "extracting potassium," which they also have rights to.[69] He also didn't see full expropriation as a viable option, given the hefty sum ($5 billion) dictated by the constitution. In direct response to the congressional lawmakers who called on President Bachelet to reject the contract, he fired back: "What is the alternative? What do you propose? What could you have done that would have been better for the country?"[70] His questions were heavy with historical baggage and unfulfilled promises.

A THOUSAND MILES TO THE NORTH, THE CONFLICT OVER LITHIUM was far from settled.

The new dispensation may have stabilized the industry, sent more money to state coffers, and guaranteed local communities a piece of the economic pie. But in the Atacama Desert, on the front lines of lithium mining, the industry continued to cause local environmental and social harm—and provoke contention. At the heart of the conflict is a seemingly technical question: Is brine water?

At corporate conventions and in interviews with lithium executives, the people I spoke with wanted me to understand that brine is emphatically not water.[71] "Important to make a difference between what is freshwater and what is brine."[72] "There's been a lot of talk about water, of course we extract brine."[73] And, most simply, "Brine is not water."[74] SQM's green initiatives website, Sustainable Lithium, proclaims that brine isn't water and that "it is not suitable for human or animal consumption."[75] The emphatic tone in which my sources expressed this statement suggests that it isn't only, or primarily, a scientific claim, but a normative one. If, as lithium company personnel insist, brine is not water, then it does not merit the same protection as water. At a deeper level, it is not as valuable or important as that life-sustaining liquid.

As a corollary, lithium companies claim that their operations have zero impact on freshwater. Speaking at an exclusive corporate conference in Santiago in 2019, Ellen Lenny-Pessagno, then Albemarle's top manager for Chile and now the firm's global vice president of government and community affairs, issued the industry's standard talking points on this issue: "We have essentially no impact on freshwater."[76] Appealing to the ethos of the green capitalists in the audience, she said, "We are using passive solar energy to concentrate the brine," a process she described as "very natural" and using no chemicals. (In fact, the process of producing lithium carbonate from brine does use chemicals, specifically calcium hydroxide and sodium carbonate.[77])

Brine pumping, Lenny-Pessagno continued, cannot affect water, since "freshwater doesn't mix with brine" when pumps remove brine from the nucleus of the salt flat. She then made the bolder argument that extracting pushes freshwater upward, creating new surface lagoons. Thus, this executive not only asserted that lithium extraction doesn't damage the environment, but more optimistically asserted that it "improve[s] the environment." Most emphatically, Lenny-Pessagno asserted, "While we produce lithium, what we really produce is sustainability," invoking a vision of healthy ecosystems in northern Chile to zero-emissions vehicles at the other end of the supply chain.

Lenny-Passagno and her executive colleagues are using "water" and "freshwater" interchangeably to mean drinkable freshwater. But they are not synonymous. As one research article on the subject points out, the distinguishing feature of water is not whether it is directly drinkable, but rather its capacity to act as a solvent that carries nutrients and other elements to cells and play liquid host to "vital chemical reactions."[78] From estuaries to the ocean to the world's many hypersaline lakes, salty water is itself part of the earth's biosphere. It is this life-supporting function of brine that SQM dismisses: "In the core of the salar [the Atacama salt flat] there is only a salt crust and there has *never been any flora or fauna*. Nor has any element of *environmental interest* been recognized" (emphasis added).[79] Even as scientists are busy identifying the microscopic beings that populate global desert ecosystems, the lithium company's blunt, confident negation of these efforts and their findings raised another question: What counts as life, and, just as importantly, as life worth saving?

This question ricocheted across my field sites, from Chile to Nevada to Portugal. It surfaced amid mining plans threatening to render a wildflower extinct, to decimate already endangered sagebrush habitat ("the largest and most threatened ecosystems in North America"[80]), to destroy the site of the US government's brutal massacre of Paiute people, and to contaminate a river that supports agropastoral livelihoods. Of course, accelerating climate change is also wreaking havoc on biodiversity, Indigenous lands, and agricultural harvests.

Zooming out to a planetary scale, the urgency of the energy transition only intensifies with each passing year, as do the conflicts along its supply chains. But for those on the front lines of the expanding lithium frontier, the two sets of sacrifices don't cancel out. Rather, they compound one another.

><

THE CHILEAN STATE ITSELF DOES NOT RECOGNIZE BRINE AS A FORM of water. This regulatory gap is an artifact of Pinochet's 1981 Water Code, which established a market for water, resulting in a uniquely privatized and unequal water system that favors large corporations in water-heavy industries such as mining and agriculture.[81] It should not be surprising that the exclusion of brine from the official definition of water has, in recent years, complicated the state's attempt to regulate lithium mining.[82]

Copper stands out as by far the thirstiest of the sectors in the northern desert, with copper companies owning almost 50 percent of the water rights in the Atacama Salt Flat basin. Lithium companies, however, receive a double benefit from the legal framework. According to their contractual quotas, the two companies together can use 264 liters per second of freshwater and extract 2,142 liters per second of brine.[83] They thus own significant water rights (10 percent of freshwater rights in the basin, while all households combined hold 2 percent[84]), yet the brine they extract is not regulated as water.

With the help of the intense sun, 95 percent of the water contained in the brine is sucked up into the air. Ingrid Garces, a professor of chemical engineering at Chile's University of Antofagasta and an expert on the lithium industry, calculates that for every ton of lithium produced, 2 million liters of water are evaporated—none of which is considered water under Chilean law.[85] And if and when any of these companies exceeds its contractual quota, as is alleged to have occurred, the problem is even worse.

Although the Chilean state hasn't budged in its definition of lithium brine as not-water, it has shown more interest in regulating the sector's impact on the environment in recent years. In 2016, Chilean regulators sanctioned SQM for illegal actions that threatened the delicate ecosystem of the salt flats, including tampering with the alert system of its freshwater monitoring wells, overextracting brine, and failing to report declining populations of the desert's carob trees.[86] In response to the threatened sanctions, SQM agreed to implement a "compliance program" consisting of new monitoring systems. But the company also asserted that any harm it had committed was "marginal." In 2016 and 2017, the General Water Directorate (DGA), which manages Chile's water, declared the two rivers that serve the Atacama Salt Flat basin to be "exhausted."[87] In 2018, the same agency issued a prohibition on using groundwater for extraction in the Atacama Salt Flat.[88] And in 2022, the Superintendency of the Environment (SMA) opened a sanctioning procedure ("procedimiento sancionatorio") against Albemarle, SQM's neighbor on the salt flat, for overextracting brine as well as for failing to comply with the early warning system by immediately reducing extraction levels, threatening to impose nearly $5 million in fines.[89] That same year, a different government agency sued Albemarle and two copper mining companies that operate in the Atacama for causing "serious, permanent and irreparable deterioration of the aquifer, of the Tilopozo plains, of the fauna, and of the life systems and customs of the Peine Indigenous Community."[90] In December of 2024, this lawsuit ended in a negotiated agreement requiring all three companies to restore the water system, remediate the environment, and compensate Peine.[91]

Despite the state's escalating efforts to rein in mining, northern Chile remains a massive extractive zone. One key reason is government reliance on mining revenue, which tilts the scale in companies' favor by taking government's most powerful enforcement tools, such as revoking the permits required to operate, off the table.[92] But time and again, when I asked regulators why the newly spirited enforcement actions had failed to curb extraction, they pointed to a seemingly technical culprit: the lack of objective data on environmental impacts. Rather than carrying out their own monitoring operations, the state relies on corporations' voluntary compliance and self-monitoring. The system of self-monitoring presumes corporate good faith. But corporations maximize value, not virtue.

Powerful firms not only extract lithium but control—and hide— crucial information about their operations and their environmental impacts. This fact puts bureaucrats in a bind: How can you regulate what you do not know? Carolina Díaz, an environmental biologist who coauthored a Chilean government report on the Atacama Desert's fragile water system, was adamant that corporate prerogatives pervert scientific inquiry.[93] A data point: SQM's contract stipulates its right to review government agency studies prior to publication.[94]

Díaz and I were chatting in the offices of her environmental consulting outfit, Amakaik. I asked her thoughts about lithium mining in the Atacama Salt Flat. She replied bluntly: "My opinion is that it isn't sustainable at all. But I don't have the data to prove this. That's because all the data is in the hands of private companies." And she added, "If you don't have your own data, it's difficult to oversee" the companies being regulated.

Díaz complemented her concern about the lack of government data with concerns about the quality of private data. She listed a number of problems. For starters, mining companies collect data for specific purposes, such as complying with regulatory requirements. Each firm also uses its own methodology, designed by whichever private consultancy it contracts for the purpose. Each only measures freshwater, brine, and flora and fauna in the *part* of the basin in which it operates. And so on.

According to Díaz, this collection of partial and inconsistent data leaves the state unable to independently verify the most basic aspects of their own environmental management plans, for example, whether SQM is reducing its use of brine. More generally, the state's de facto decision to delegate governance to corporations makes it more difficult to assess the environmental status of the salt flat and the broader ecological and water systems in which it is embedded. The number of actors demanding access to the region's waters—lithium and copper mining operations, agriculture, tourism, Indigenous communities—requires a comprehensive management program.[95] Such holism remains elusive in a system where the state relies on individual corporations.[96]

Even in an imagined world of perfect information, other hurdles stand in regulators' way. As Mónica Musalem Jara, a regulator at Chile's water agency, told me: "There is no doubt that it is a single system: freshwater and brine."[97] But she lamented the "total regulatory disorder" that reigned over this holistic hydrological system—exacerbating water scarcity in the desert.

THIS REGULATORY DISORDER, BOTH SYMPTOM AND CAUSE OF THE dominance of extractive capital over the rugged landscape of the Atacama Desert, has prompted local backlash.

Conflicts began in the 2000s, when residents filed complaints against SQM with national water, environmental, and health agencies. The mining camp was releasing its sewage directly into the surrounding environment, they alleged, and the mining operations were drawing freshwater illegally from unauthorized wells.[98] The ensuing protest prompted mining companies to think more carefully about how they distributed benefits in the hopes of diffusing, or better yet preempting, local tensions.[99] In 2012, Rockwood (later acquired by Albemarle) reached an agreement with Peine that inaugurated the practice of sharing a percentage of royalties with a directly affected community. In 2016, Albemarle (which had by then purchased Rockwood) negotiated a similar arrangement with the Council of Atacameño Peoples, which represents all eighteen of the Indigenous communities that ring the Atacama Salt Flat. Albemarle now channels 3.5 percent of its mining royalties to local projects—a sizable sum totaling $10 to $15 million annually (based on 2022 production levels).[100] Following in Albemarle's footsteps, SQM committed to investing $10 to $15 million annually in sustainable development initiatives in Atacameño communities.[101]

These royalty-sharing agreements are a form of what's known as corporate social responsibility. Corporate social responsibility is an umbrella concept that covers everything from company-funded soccer fields and schoolhouses to corporate promotion of causes ranging from Indigenous rights to women's empowerment. These practices gelled in the early 2000s.[102] By that time, multinational mining companies had increased their presence in the Global South, responding to looser regulations designed to attract foreign investment. Predictably, the combination of more mining and weaker governance resulted in human rights abuses and environmental impacts, which began to take a reputational toll.

Fearing a backlash, in 2002 some of the world's largest mining corporations founded the International Council on Mining and Metals under the banner of "sustainable development."[103] The companies jointly committed to a form of extraction that would mutually benefit community and corporation.[104] In Chile, Albemarle and SQM have embraced this vision, touting inspiring stories on their websites of a newly built community center and cooperatively owned vineyards.[105] But assessing the overall impact of the millions of dollars disbursed through royalty sharing agreements would require objective information and governmental oversight. Both are in short supply.[106]

The consequences of corporate social responsibility go beyond its stated aims. One effect is to divide its residents between those who benefit from the largesse and those who do not. The vineyard, for example, has provoked discord between the farmers participating in the program and their neighbors over a familiar point of tension in the Atacama: water access.[107] Sometimes corporate overtures backfire: The Atacameño council rejected SQM's entreaties, prompting the company to approach each of the eighteen communities, one by one, to negotiate individual agreements.[108] And in a handful of cases, corporate social responsibility initiatives have actually provided resources for communities to resist the mine's influence.

This last situation is how Francisco Mundaca came to run an environmental monitoring unit funded by Albemarle. When I first met Mundaca, a civil engineer specializing in hydrology from the community of Toconao, he was glad the lithium company was paying for crucial training to teach Atacameño community members how to monitor "water and biotic" impacts.[109] He was less sanguine, however, about whether the resources provided were adequate to the task: the funding, for example, did not cover physical equipment. Mundaca also spoke of a deeper challenge. How, exactly, would the community members responsible for auditing the environmental toll of lithium mining maintain autonomy from the lithium company financing the monitoring?

Later that same day, I saw Mundaca again. He was one of the speakers at an educational event—"Extractivism and Indigenous Territory"—organized by the Council of Atacameño Peoples in March 2019. But before I could satisfy my curiosity about how Mundaca would navigate his company-funded role in a discussion critical of lithium mining, I witnessed a community trying to wrest its power back from the mining companies.

I entered the squat, whitewashed adobe building on San Pedro's main square, the Plaza de Armas, through its curved archways. I was early, wanting to make sure I had a front-row seat. By the time the program began, the small community center was packed, with every seat taken and many attendees standing. For this tourist hub, the crowd was unusually diverse. In the audience I saw residents of Atacameño communities; those who made their living as tour guides, artisans, or service workers in the booming hospitality industry; and even some foreigners—the group that usually predominated in every other social setting I had experienced in the town.

I felt their rapt attention as Sergio Cubillos, then the Council's twenty-nine-year-old president, began to speak. Cubillos hailed from Peine, the village that was the first to negotiate a royalty distribution agreement with Rockwood (later acquired by Albemarle). A village with a history of "vexed" relations with both the lithium and copper industries, Peine has borne the brunt of the water impacts of resource extraction.[110] At the same time, residents have become highly dependent on the mining sector for jobs, with a majority of working-age adults either employed in the lithium industry or in mining-related services.[111] But residents of Peine have been vocal about the impacts of extraction, despite their economic dependency on the mining industry.

Cubillos's opening remarks set the tone for the rest of the event: He declared the topic of the conversation to be "extractivism"—which, as he noted with a nod to the diverse constituencies in attendance, "threatens tourism, agriculture, and Atacameño culture." Most importantly, he wanted to discuss "how to combat it."[112] Cubillos already had a reputation for taking a stronger stance on mining than his predecessors in council leadership. Growing up in Peine, Cubillos came to understand mining's "impact on the social fabric," with an economy based on the cash nexus of wages displacing one centered on communal labor, agriculture, and herding. This shift initiated before he was born. Starting in the 1970s, drought conditions begun to make pastoral livelihoods difficult. Over the decades that followed, intensified copper mining further exacerbated water scarcity. Many families that had once grazed sheep, llama, and goats in verdant pastures gave up herding entirely.[113] Then lithium mining came along, desiccating the landscape even more.

Cubillos was part of a generation of young leaders radicalized by these changes, having participated in road blockades and a weeklong hunger strike targeting SQM.[114] The trigger for that particular action was Chile's latest deal with the company—but the deeper cause was the long-standing pattern in which the government failed to consult Indigenous communities prior to extractive projects, despite legal requirements that they do so.

"No more companies. No more extraction."[115] By the time Cubillos took the floor in San Pedro, this was his position on lithium mining. Since the late 1990s, the Atacameño people had legally recognized territorial rights in the Atacama Desert.[116] But without any form of state-mediated consultations, individual Atacameño communities negotiated directly with the mining corporations, creating a situation that sowed divisions within communities just as it pitted them against one another.[117] As the new president of the council, Cubillos was committed to ending this cycle.

As Cubillos explained, insofar as there was no formal process for consulting Indigenous peoples, no regulatory framework to prevent environmental impacts, and no recognition of the Atacameño people's rights to water and territory, the Atacameño council could not accept any new lithium extraction on the Atacama Salt Flat. It would moreover remain vigilant in monitoring the two existing mines, launching lawsuits or protests when necessary.

After Cubillos gave his opening comments that night in San Pedro, the meeting's attendees heard from a series of the council's own experts, including Mundaca. Mundaca's work was funded by Albemarle. But the sentiment of anti-extractive resistance was palpable in the room, and Mundaca stayed true to his scientific and political principles. He roundly criticized the state's approach to governing the companies, which allowed them to self-monitor while "overexploiting" the Atacama Salt Flat, reducing vegetation, and shrinking wetlands. He directly rejected corporate efforts to brand brine extraction and evaporation as environmentally friendly, referring to their process as "mining water": a threat to the very basis of life in the desert.

At first, I was taken aback by Mundaca's bold stance, given the source of his paycheck. But zooming out, things fell into place. Local resistance—the reality of it and the fear of it—was the reason the mining company had negotiated agreements with Atacameño communities in the first place. From a corporate perspective, these agreements served their function. They provided fodder for investor-pleasing publicity and persuaded enough residents of the companies' good intentions to weaken the prospects of a unified community front against extraction. But they did not address the basic power relations at stake or bring back the once-lush pastures and the livelihoods they supported—and so the potential for conflict remained. Corporate social responsibility can greenwash, but it can also provide grist for new grievances, feeding into the very processes of protest it was intended to prevent.

><

AT THE END OF THE MEETING, CUBILLOS RETURNED TO THE STAGE, accompanied by the council's lawyer, Juan Carlos Cayo. In tandem, the two men launched a heady critique of the role of extractive industry in dispossessing the Atacameño peoples. Together, they deconstructed the foundations of Western thought. Cayo described mining as a "process of colonization" that attempts to sever nature and culture into a mutually opposed binary rather than treating them as part of a unified "cosmovision" of *"patta hoiri,"* Mother Earth in Kunza (the traditional language of Atacameño peoples).[118] Cubillos spoke of the sacred mountains that safeguard the watershed and with it, the Atacameño communities.[119] Using the language of reciprocal care, Cubillos invoked residents' responsibility to the smallest of life-forms: The "beings that live off of the salt water" are our "little brothers" (*hermanos menores*) and they "must be protected." Cubillos contrasted the richness of "ancestral knowledge," which had long understood the water scarcity of the region, with the paucity of official data on mining's impact on water and the moral hazard of self-monitoring firms. The result, he declared, was that the Atacama had been transformed into "a zone of water sacrifice."

Not everyone in attendance found this rousing rhetoric convincing. Several audience members questioned the Indigenous leaders' commitment to protecting the salt flat. Cubillos pushed back: "The enemy," he stated "is not us. It is not you, the inhabitants. It is the state, and the lack of auditing and enforcement." But the concerns kept coming. Referring to prior agreements between lithium corporations and communities, one member of the audience asked: "Are you going to keep negotiating the salt flat in exchange for money?" The question put Cubillos in a tricky spot, given the reality of pre-existing mining projects and agreements and the looming threat of an expanding extractive frontier: "We [the council] have decided to not negotiate any agreements with companies. The agreements that exist, were implemented by [former] leaders." Cubillos had no choice but to acknowledge the conflict: "I know there are concerns. That's why we are doing these talks (*charlas*). I share your worries."

However much he tried, Cubillos could not change history. He could not undo the decisions of prior leaders, the sequelae of which were social division and distrust. He could only hope to forge a new path forward on the basis of collective knowledge, the defense of territory, and the shared commitment to the protection of water and life in all its forms.

Such a future would constitute a sharp break from the past. In Chile, as in the rest of Latin America and the Global South more broadly, extraction traces its origins to violent colonial encounters. These encounters dispossessed native peoples, destroyed socio-environmental lifeworlds, and accumulated vast riches for European empires. They also designated entire landscapes as disposable in the name of power and progress. These landscapes are extractive frontiers, the physical places where nature and capitalism meet—producing profit for some and harm for others.

CHAPTER 5

The Return of Resource Nationalism

In the best-case scenario, resource extraction is a means to economic development, not an end. The policymakers and economists who promote mining envision dense ecosystems of investments, sectors, and skills: complex configurations that capture more value for the originating country. These countries can then use the windfall to catapult their societies to new levels of innovation, income, and consumption. That's in theory. In practice, extractive economies are prone to path dependency. Most states that rely on oil and mining for the bulk of their revenue have done so for a very long time, in many cases since before they were free from the chains of colonial rule. Overcoming this inertia is extraordinarily difficult.

From this perspective, the most ambitious element of Chile's 2018 contract with SQM was not the higher royalty rate, but rather its underlying vison of Chile as a high-tech green superpower.[1] The contract represents an assertion that the only thing stopping Chile, a country rich in copper, lithium, and wind and solar energy, from joining the ranks of industrialized economies is a policy environment that encourages local investment and R&D.[2]

So many countries across the Global South share these aspirations.

Chile's experience offers both cautionary tales and glimmers of hope. For years after the contract with SQM was signed, the much-vaunted Clean Technologies Institute the company was required to help fund remained unbuilt. The first attempt, in 2021, resulted in a Congressional Investigation into irregularities and conflicts of interest,[3] with Chile's Supreme Court ultimately annulling the contract that had been awarded to a consortium of foreign universities. At long last, in April 2023, a new contract was awarded to a group of Chilean universities and the Institute is finally taking shape.[4] Attempts to woo battery makers with preferentially priced lithium similarly suffered many years of false starts.[5] But in July 2023, the Chilean government finally selected its first recipient for discounted lithium: BYD, the Chinese battery and EV powerhouse on a global hunt for "strategic access" to raw materials.[6] The $290 million plant would move Chile one link up along the supply chain by producing cathode materials, the immediate step after the lithium carbonate already produced in the country. Full-scale production could be next: BYD has committed to building a raft of new battery and EV plants across the Global South and Europe, from Thailand to Mexico to Hungary.[7] Months later, the government secured a second investment from another Chinese company, Tsingshan Holding Group, which committed to a $233.2 million plant to produce lithium iron phosphate using discounted domestic lithium.[8] Along with new "value chains" and the "transfer of knowledge," officials touted the several hundred jobs that both investments would generate in the desert region of Chile's far north.[9]

Clouds soon blotted this sunny future. A year after the deal was secured, BYD announced it was indefinitely delaying construction, ominously referencing "uncertainties" and "complications." No specifics were given, but the cooling off of global lithium markets and slowing growth in EV sales were likely culprits. As of the time of writing, plans for the project are still on hold.[10]

Foreign investment as a path to economic development makes sense on paper. Reality does not always comply. Even if both battery chemical plants move forward as planned, industrial upgrading address only part of the problem of extraction in places like Chile. Employment could be a form of compensation for communities caught in the crosshairs of lithium and copper mines—places that have long suffered the slow violence of contamination and water scarcity.[11] But for Indigenous organizations and grassroots environmental groups, the possibility of a paycheck does not directly address, let alone repair, ecological harm. For them, getting to something that feels like justice would require a more direct confrontation with the forces first unleashed by colonial conquest, then brutally restored by Pinochet's coup, and only moderately tamed by the subsequent years of democracy.

Just such a confrontation occurred in 2019.

THE 2019 MASS UPRISING IN CHILE AND THE PIVOTAL EVENTS THAT followed unfolded amid a spate of protests that rocked the world, with eruptions of discontent in Hong Kong, Tunisia, Ecuador, Lebanon, Argentina, Egypt, Iraq, and more. The grievances and targets varied, but participants consistently rallied against forms of austerity, corruption, and repression that worsened economic inequality and subverted democratic representation. Little did protestors—or the governments they battled—know that a pandemic, geopolitical conflicts, and inflation were on the horizon.

Those three developments made for a more challenging terrain for grassroots protest, and most of the 2019 movements dissipated and demobilized. But in Chile, the tide of change was unusually strong, having swelled for decades before a seemingly minor event—an increase in the subway fare—catalyzed months of demonstrations. As millions poured into the streets, Chilean elites tasted the fear of revolution.

Suddenly, everything was at stake. That included the country's deeply entrenched model of resource extraction.

For Chile, like so many other countries reliant on resource exports, the energy transition has presented a fork in the road for the entire economic and social order. Across the Global South, the old model of extraction controlled by foreign multinational firms, and countries trapped in the snares of dependency, has breached the limits of social tolerance and political viability. The global race to mine newly "critical" minerals could entrench dependency and exploitation—or it could provide an opening to remake the global economy, with all its harsh inequalities and devastating externalities, from the ground up. Meanwhile, the combination of accelerating climate catastrophe, uneven energy transition, and mounting geopolitical tensions has generated a new playbook of threats and opportunities. Fresh strategies are needed.

From Indonesia to Bolivia, ambitious political leaders in the Global South see development opportunities in newly essential commodities and technologies, and resurgent social movements have sought to redefine the social contract of resource extraction.

Nationalization still offers a powerful tool to challenge the continued dominance of multinational corporations over resource sectors. But while the strategy remains relevant in Latin America and across the Global South, resource nationalism has limits of its own. State ownership doesn't eliminate the environmental impact of mining, nor does it automatically empower the communities most affected. And the promise of public stewardship also contains the risk of entrenched reliance on mining. By more fully incorporating resource extraction into the workings of the state, resource nationalization can impede, rather than facilitate, the transition to a less extractive economy.

There are few places on earth where activists and policymakers have grappled with the multifaceted harms of extraction as did Chile in the early years of this decade. There, a radical idea took hold. This was the moment to finally achieve both equitable development and ecological sustainability, while prioritizing resource sovereignty and democratic participation alike. Whether these goals were complementary or incompatible was an open question. The answer held global ramifications. In Chile, visionary advocates did everything they could to find out.

The country's path to this unusual amalgam included explosive protests, a watershed election, a constitutional defeat, and ongoing policy experimentation. The story reveals much about what it takes to transform extraction—and the tremendous obstacles such efforts face.

THE PROTESTS FIRST ERUPTED IN OCTOBER 2019. AN INCREASE IN metro fares provided the initial spark for high school students to jump turnstiles and sabotage equipment in subway stations across Santiago.[12] Soon the movement had expanded to encompass a long list of social groups and grievances, from economic inequality to entrenched patriarchy. At times, over a million people filled the streets to chant, "It's not about 30 pesos, it's about 30 years," a slogan that captured the scale of protesters' ambition. This was a movement to dismantle neoliberalism and deepen democracy.

The uprising shook Chile's power structure to its core and achieved several key victories. The most important of these were the convening of an assembly to rewrite the country's constitution, which still reflected the priorities of the Pinochet dictatorship, and the election in 2021 of the nation's first truly leftist administration since Salvador Allende came to power. President Gabriel Boric also represented a new political generation: at thirty-six years old, he was Chile's youngest president ever.

On the campaign trail, Boric proclaimed, "Lithium is the mineral of the future."[13] He also warned that this future was at risk of being held hostage to the past: "Chile cannot make the historic mistake of privatizing resources again."[14] He pledged to establish a national lithium company. But Boric also acknowledged that public ownership, in and of itself, would not eliminate the harms of extractivism. During the massive celebration of his victory, speaking before tens of thousands of people packed shoulder to shoulder on the wide Avenida La Alameda, Boric asserted, "To destroy the world is to destroy ourselves. We don't want any more sacrifice zones."

Frontline communities and foreign investors anxiously awaited more concrete news of the administration's plans. In April 2023, a year into his administration, Boric finally unveiled the government's national lithium strategy.[15] As expected, the blueprint included a state-owned lithium company. But in a surprise to both corporate leaders and leftist dreamers, Boric did not plan to expropriate the assets of either of the two incumbent producers, SQM and Albemarle. Both companies would retain their existing contracts. Any future contracts, however, would take the form of public-private partnerships: joint ventures between lithium companies and a to-be-established state-owned enterprise.

Boric's blueprint cited Allende as an inspiration, but his approach was more conciliatory toward extractive capital than anything Allende had proposed. In another sense, however, the strategy involved a major innovation. Boric pledged to protect 30 percent of the salt flats from lithium mining by 2030, and he promised that all new lithium mines would use extraction techniques that minimized environmental impact.[16] He also committed to direct dialogues with the Indigenous communities that "coexist with the salt flats." In poetic language, Boric asserted: "These salt flats and lagoons are not just lithium, they are people, they are communities, they are the water of the desert, they are biotechnologies and other minerals, they are the home of ancient cultures, and they are witnesses of the past that we will preserve today for a better future."

Latin American leaders from earlier eras did not typically consider Indigenous perspectives or ecological protections when announcing their plans to nationalize extractive sectors. Boric, however, was faced with a powerful wave of Indigenous and environmental resistance to large-scale mining in Chile and across the region. This resistance had reshaped public policies. In Ecuador, the 2008 constitution recognized the rights of nature and expanded the right to prior consultation. Subsequent court cases in Ecuador have limited or even prevented extraction on those grounds, most recently blocking a copper mine in March 2023.[17] Several other countries have passed legislation or referenda restricting or banning oil extraction or mining, whether at the subnational (Argentina, Guatemala) or national (Costa Rica, El Salvador, Honduras, Panama) level.[18] Nor could Boric ignore the scientific evidence of damage to salt flat ecosystems or the prior government pronouncements declaring the Atacama Desert watersheds "exhausted."

The blueprint's emphasis on sustainable, socially conscious governance sat in potential tension with its imperative to "accelerate the exploration of the salt flats," with the aim of tapping into Chile's "enormous potential." According to Boric, the goal wasn't growth for its own sake. Instead, increased mining revenues would pay for social services and public infrastructure. In short, lithium could provide "a more dignified life for everyone."[19] Boric's words, with its allusion to Allende's Day of National Dignity, were no accident. In the classic register of resource nationalism, Boric linked state involvement in a strategic extractive sector with ordinary Chileans' well-being. As the president put it, "No more mining for the few."[20]

Was this possible? Could public policies both limit and expand extraction? Attract foreign investment and increase the role of the state? Ensure mining-funded dignity for all and protect the most directly affected communities and landscapes? These questions, and their stark trade-offs, were by no means unique to Chile. Resource nationalism is back on the march around the world—and so are challenges to it. These developments have reverberated across the extractive zones of the global economy, shaking the material foundations of the energy transition.

MORE THAN A DECADE BEFORE BORIC'S ELECTION, ON APRIL 1, 2008, Bolivian president Evo Morales decreed the "industrialization" of lithium resources in the country's Uyuni Salt Flat to be a "national priority." The goal, Morales proclaimed, was to foster "economic and social development" in the Potosí region where the deposit is located.[21] Morales tasked the state-owned mining company with creating a new public entity to carry out this order. In 2010, Morales's more detailed plan for developing lithium as a strategic state sector made clear that multinational firms would be entirely excluded from R&D, lithium extraction, or the production of lithium compounds.[22] Foreign companies could only participate in downstream production—for instance, manufacturing cathode materials or batteries. The government finally established Bolivia's state-owned lithium company, YPL (*Yacimientos de Litios Boliviano*), in 2017.

In Mexico, President Andrés Manuel López Obrador convened Congress in April 2022 to consider several dramatic changes to the energy and mining sectors. Declaring "the lithium is ours," in an explicit reference to the country's 1938 nationalization of oil, López Obrador secured congressional approval for granting lithium new legal status.[23] The amended mining law recognizes lithium as a matter of "public interest" and part of the "patrimony of the nation" and bans contracts or concessions for all lithium reserves.[24] In August of that year, López Obrador established a state-owned lithium company called Lithium for Mexico (LitioMx for short) to explore and extract the mineral, as well as to "administrate and control" the value-added supply chains downstream of mining.[25] Mexican state officials also joined their counterparts in Argentina, Bolivia, Brazil, and Chile in calling for coordinated lithium governance.[26] Commentators dubbed this nascent dialogue the beginnings of a lithium OPEC, conjuring Western worries of producer cartels and supply disruptions.

This new wave of lithium nationalism is not limited to Latin America. At the end of 2022, the Zimbabwean government banned the export of unprocessed lithium-bearing ore. The stated aim was to stimulate a domestic lithium-processing industry—an aspiration that is becoming reality as Chinese companies invest in both mines and processing plants.²⁷ The governments of Namibia, Tanzania, and Ghana followed suit.²⁸ These African policymakers were emulating Indonesia, which implemented similar measures for raw nickel exports beginning in 2014, incentivizing the growth of nickel processing and even battery manufacturing within the country.²⁹ This trend is truly global. According to Verisk Maplecroft, a leading risk analytics and consulting firm, between 2019 and 2024, over a third of governments around the world implemented new measures to increase state control of mining and energy sectors.³⁰

The international business community's response to such plans has been swift and predictable. Headlines like "Chile's Plan for State Control in Lithium Dismays Business," "Mexican Mining Industry Under Threat from Sweeping New Regulations," and "Africa Gears Up to Keep More of the Profits from the Lithium Boom" warn investors about the risks to their bottom lines and supply chains.³¹ But the headlines also depict a shift in resource governance as a fait accompli. When it comes to resource nationalization, official declarations are just the beginning of a slow and uncertain process of building state capacity and reigning in corporate power. And these days, the inevitably tense negotiations are no longer limited to governments and firms. Communities want a say, too.

"BORIC'S PLATFORM IS TOTALLY CLEAR," GONZALO GUTIERREZ told me matter-of-factly as he reached for a bound copy of the report produced by the National Lithium Commission, a body on which he had served.³² He saw the current government as picking up where former president Michelle Bachelet had left off. For Gutierrez, the goals were self-evident: to maximize Chile's benefit from its lithium wealth while simultaneously protecting vulnerable landscapes and communities. The means were likewise obvious: state ownership and regulatory muscle.

I was speaking with Gutierrez in April 2022 in his new office at the

Ministry of Mining, where he now served as the chief adviser responsible for the lithium sector. The task of converting lofty campaign promises into facts on the ground fell on his shoulders.

Despite Gutierrez's insistence on the "clarity" of Boric's program, questions soon outnumbered answers in our conversation. This was understandable given the context. When we spoke, the Boric administration had been in power for only a month and a half. It was confronting the unenviable combined forces of a pandemic, inflation, low growth, a legislative minority, and a right wing that retained significant power. The constitutional convention had not yet completed its work, let alone put the new text to a popular vote. But the uncertainty surrounding the basic definition and core functions of the national lithium company Boric had promised on the campaign trail reflected more than the challenges of a newly installed government. Nationalizing lithium would require nothing less than changing the balance of power between the state and multinational firms.

The Atacama was, in Gutierrez's words, a "zone of savage extraction." His visceral language recalled Allende's references to the "relentless claws" of capital and the "bowels of our land." Only a strong state could rescue Chilean society from such snares.

Not everyone was convinced that state-led mining was the answer. Despite Boric's promise of "direct dialogue," Indigenous groups' response to his government's national lithium strategy ranged the gamut. The Colla people, whose ancestral territory encompasses the Maricunga Salt Flat, expressed skepticism.[33] For its part, the Council of Atacameño Peoples, which represents the eighteen communities that live around the Atacama Salt Flat, rejected the plan entirely.[34]

Indigenous opposition to his lithium blueprint was exactly the outcome that Boric had wanted to prevent. His emphasis on dialogue had been deliberate: When those directly affected from a policy are excluded from decision-making, protest becomes more likely.[35] Participation is a particular sticking point for Indigenous communities. Since the late 1980s, established international norms have held that

Indigenous peoples have a stake in policies or projects that threaten their territory, culture, and livelihoods.[36] This principle is at once reparative and preventative; an acknowledgment that violent dispossession is both a bloody history to atone for and a potential future to forestall. Chile has signed and ratified the main international convention on Indigenous prior consultation and established official procedures to implement this right. But in practice the process is rarely applied.[37]

CHILE'S CONSTITUTIONAL ASSEMBLY FIRST CONVENED IN JULY OF 2021. Radical environmentalists made up almost a quarter of the elected body, representing 38 out of 155 delegates.[38] For these "eco-constituents," as they called themselves, the historical paradigm of resource nationalism was at once relevant and outdated. Relevant, because after all these centuries, Latin America remained an exporter of raw materials. Natural resources therefore remained at the center of political economy. Outdated, because political economy needed its complement of political ecology. They knew this from practical experience. Most of the eco-constituents were actively involved in specific struggles to defend ecosystems and communities from extractive industries, whether open-pit copper mines or monocrop avocado plantations.

¡Las aguas robadas, serán recuperadas! (Stolen waters, will be recuperated!)

The staid plenary floor of Chile's constitutional assembly was suddenly alive with the chants of the eco-constituents. This grand *hemiciclo*, a high-ceilinged semicircular room adorned with paintings depicting Latin America's nineteenth-century wars of independence, is located in an equally elegant white building that had once housed Chile's Congress, replete with Corinthian columns, neoclassical porticoes, and lush gardens. Seated next to me was Cristina Dorador, a renowned expert on the microbial ecology of the Atacama Desert. It was April 2022, during the final stretch of drafting the new constitution. Dorador, one of the eco-constituents, had allowed me to accompany her that day to give me a glimpse of the proceedings.

Moments earlier, Dorador had rushed me past a skeptical guard at a security checkpoint and into the thick of action. When we entered, Juan José Martín Bravo, coordinator of the convention's ambitiously titled Committee on Environment, Rights of Nature, Natural Commons, and the Economic Model, presided from the podium. He was presenting the committee's sprawling proposal, which touched on everything from food sovereignty to glacier protection to economic planning.

As I followed Dorador to her assigned seat, Martín Bravo read proposed Articles 23–31 to the assembled crowd. The first of the articles, all of which addressed "the constitutional status of minerals," was penned in the familiar vocabulary of resource nationalism: the Chilean state ought to have "absolute, exclusive, inalienable, and imprescriptible dominion" over all minerals in its territory. But the subsequent articles departed from this venerable tradition. As he continued to speak, Martín Bravo, a twenty-six-year-old climate activist, relayed the committee's more innovative proposals: that the state-led development of the sector should be guided by social, democratic, and environmental criteria. Mining would be excluded entirely from protected natural areas.

It was during the next presentation, given by Carolina Vilches, also a member of the environmental committee, that the chants broke out in defense of water. Vilches hails from Petorca Province in central Chile, a flash point in the larger conflict between agribusiness and water access.[39] She has seen firsthand the deleterious impacts of thirsty, large-scale avocado plantations, which produce the green-fleshed fruit for export to Europe and Asia, on small farmers' livelihoods.

The environmentalist delegates were connected by a web of water. Like several of her colleagues in the *hemiciclo* that day, Vilches is a member of the Movement for the Defense of Water, Land, and the Environment, an organization that was founded in 2010 in Petorca but now links activists across the country.⁴⁰ Such networks respond to a stark injustice. Chile's water system is notoriously unequal and privatized. A mere 2 percent of the country's water resources goes to human consumption. The forestry sector uses a shocking 59 percent, while the export-oriented agricultural industry uses 37 percent. Mining uses officially account for 1.3 percent of terrestrial freshwater resources, but this figure is deceptively low, since Chile's mining sectors increasingly depend on water produced by desalination plants.⁴¹ The desalination plant in Antofogasta, which serves BHP's Escondida mine 170 kilometers away in the Atacama Desert, is the largest in the Americas and one of the largest in the world.⁴²

Lithium mining uses much less freshwater than copper. But as we have seen, the sector unquestionably extracts and evaporates enormous quantities of salty water. In one of their more audacious proposals, the eco-constituents aimed to banish that industry practice. As members of the environmental committee spoke from the podium, Dorador guided me through her printout of the proposed articles in whispers. We were nestled among the other eco-constituents, desks adorned with banners one might see at an anti-extractive protest ("*Salares = vida*"/ salt flats = life). In a hushed tone, she told me that "we"—the eco-constituents—"were able to get the *humedales* (wetlands) included in the proposal, in order to exclude the salt flats from mining." Indeed, right below the main paragraph regarding limitations on mining was a standalone sentence: "Wetlands will be excluded from all mining activity"—including those of the Atacama Desert.

I immediately realized the implication of this proposal. It would amount to a ban on lithium mining in Chile.

⋈

THIS BOLD GAMBIT TO BAN LITHIUM MINING IN CHILE DID NOT make it past the plenary floor. By a slim margin of five, the entire package of environmental clauses failed to garner the necessary two-thirds supermajority. The prohibition of mining in wetlands turned out to be one of many sticking points. There were simply too many radical notions for the likes of center-left Socialist Party delegates, whose votes were essential for any of the more ambitious proposals to move forward.

Members of the environmental committee went back to the drawing board. Two weeks later, after multiple rounds of internal deliberations and savvy vote whipping, the committee's platform garnered the plenary's support, sending a raft of new articles into the draft constitution. The delegates voted to strengthen the role of the state in the ownership and value-added development of mining sectors; to recognize water as "essential to life," prioritizing the human right to water as well as its role in ecosystems above all; to establish new rights to a healthy environment and access to "environmental justice"; to require mining companies to repair environmental harm; to ban mining in glaciers and protected areas; and to empower the state to declare other water-vulnerable areas off-limits from extraction. If ratified, these constitutional articles would transform extraction in Chile.

The draft constitution offered the most anti-extractive approach to resource governance in global history. The mining sector nevertheless breathed a sigh of relief.[43] Their worst fears had not been realized. The convention ultimately didn't approve articles to nationalize and expropriate all mining projects or to exclude mining from all wetlands. The former prospect had especially riled the industry. The president of the country's association of mining companies described the idea as "barbaric."[44] According to Sergio Bitran—a Socialist Party politician and, ironically, former mining minister under the Allende government—nationalization would amount to a "delirious return to the past." The mainstream business press meanwhile framed the proposal for nationalization through the lens of "country risk" and its desirable opposite, "country and resource reliability."[45]

But the barbarism had been kept at bay. The high-ranking personnel in the most coveted corner offices slept soundly. As we spoke in an elegant conference room in Albemarle's headquarters in Las Condes (nicknamed "Sanhattan," a portmanteau of the country's capital and the center of global finance), Ignacio Mehech, vice president of external affairs and the country manager for Chile, took the long view: "We have been in Chile for forty-two years, through many changes in government, and we'll be here at least twenty more."[46] His colleague Marcelo Valdebenito, manager of community relations, chimed in, noting the "long-term institutional time frame" of government relations, which were structured by a twenty-seven-year contract the company signed in 2016. He emphasized Albemarle's "alignment" with Chile's new model of sustainable development.

In this narrative, the current government's program had, in effect, realized the company's own vision, which preceded not only Boric's election but the cataclysmic social uprising from which it issued. Those messy events receded from view as the two corporate executives reassured me, and perhaps themselves, that the administration "isn't here to expropriate or nationalize." They told me that Albemarle was in fact "enthusiastic" about the opportunities for a joint venture with a state-owned company. Above all, the company wanted to "continue collaborating" with the state.

Chile's progressive government finds itself caught in a trap familiar to countries of the Global South. Take too hard a line with multinational companies—whether through regulatory interventions or nationalizing threats to the sanctity of private property—and risk capital flight and disinvestment. Take too diplomatic an approach and watch the country's resources—natural and monetary—drain out to the benefit of companies and consumers elsewhere.

These tensions are exacerbated when a state company is relatively new to a particular extractive sector. Bureaucrats and activists alike told me that the Chilean state lacked the knowledge to properly regulate brine extraction in the salt flats—let alone become directly involved in extracting the resource. As undersecretary of mining Willy Kracht told the press: "We don't have the time we would need to learn as a country without the support of a strategic partner."[47] In other words, in the near term at least, Chilean state officials foresee the necessity of "joint ventures" with multinational lithium companies. As the Boric administration confronted the challenges of lithium nationalism in practice, the president's bold promise to never repeat the "historic mistake of privatizing resources" faded into the familiar moderation of "public-private partnerships." Seen in this light, Albemarle's jingoistic promise to "continue collaborating" synthesized, and sanitized, the power relations at stake.

Government officials, then, were both cautiously optimistic about the transformative potential of this moment in Chilean history and all too aware of how greater state involvement in such a critical extractive sector of could go wrong. Navigating these dilemmas was an everyday reality for Pedro Glatz Brahm, a top adviser to the minister of environment. I managed to catch Glatz Brahm on his lunch break in a noisy Chinese restaurant in Santiago's historical downtown during a brief respite in his day of otherwise endless meetings.[48]

While Glatz Brahm had his doubts about whether a state-owned lithium company could drive innovation in a market already dominated by a handful of large firms (which, among other things, benefited from economies of scale), he was more concerned about the questions not being asked. With a certain intensity, he ticked them off: "Are we ready to reduce lithium extraction? To limit how much we export? If we can't answer these, and if we don't know how to do so within the global economy, what exactly are we doing?"

Glatz Brahm, a committed environmentalist, is skeptical of the possibility of greening a fundamentally extractivist development model. But he wasn't opposed to all lithium extraction, in principle. Ultimately, it mattered to him what the lithium was being used for. As he put it: "It isn't a left-wing project to provide raw materials for [individual passenger] EVs." Furnishing the extractive inputs for public transportation, though, felt like a more noble cause—a more socio-environmentally rational use of harmfully mined materials. Glatz Brahm mused about the possibility of using trade agreements and supply contracts as tools to achieve this end. "It's better to negotiate with e-bus companies than Tesla," he asserted. While his talk of contractually obligated public-benefit uses for lithium strikes me as aspirational, it is perhaps not much more so than the idea of Chile establishing a state-owned lithium company engaged in cutting-edge research. Given the urgent nature of the climate crisis, it may not be feasible to build ecosocialism in one country alone. It's perhaps more practical to repurpose global supply chains by subjecting them to new principles: minimize extraction, maximize public benefit.

><

RECHAZO. THIS SPANISH WORD FOR THE ENGLISH-LANGUAGE NOUN "rejection" or the first-person "I reject" is nearly an onomatopoeia—its very sound imparting harsh finality. On September 4, 2022, Chileans voted by a large majority to reject the ambitious constitutional proposal that delegates had so painstakingly crafted. This was the outcome that left-wing delegates, along with activists in a wide range of social movements and political parties, had feared for months, even as they organized throughout the summer to salvage the possibility of victory. The loss nevertheless stung.

The delegates and their civil society allies had spent the fourteen months leading up to the referendum focused on the text itself. Conservative political forces, which had been relatively underrepresented in the constitutional convention, channeled their political energy toward generating public opposition. Their message was amplified by the oligarchic economic groups that own most of Chile's print and television media, as well as by viral memes that flooded WhatsApp and Facebook. Many of these memes included fabricated or otherwise false information about the constitutional text or process. Meanwhile, the forceful showing of left parties and social movements in the elections for the convention delegates may have led them to overestimate their depth of support among the public, especially given that election's relatively low turnout.

It didn't help that the draft constitution had become a barometer of support for President Boric, who, like many of his progressive colleagues across the region, had seen his popularity nosedive as inflation eroded people's spending power. His lack of a congressional majority made it nearly impossible for the administration to advance key planks of its agenda. As September approached, centrist and center-left politicians and pundits joined the right in criticizing the constitution for being too radical. Among the many examples they marshaled to make their case were the environmental limitations on mining and the expansion of Indigenous rights.

But even as the draft constitution failed, Chile has not reverted to the status quo ante. Through their arguments and advocacy at the constitutional assembly, grassroots activists and their allied delegates shifted the Overton window by introducing new ideas into the national discourse and establishing a new set of expectations for progressive resource governance. Localized struggles along an extractive frontier, so often relegated to the geographic and political margins, captured national attention. Meanwhile, the Boric administration continued to implement a lithium strategy that bore the traces of the eco-constituents' most visionary ideas even as it dashed their hopes.

⸺

"IF THEY DON'T WANT TO LISTEN TO US, IT'S TIME TO SPEAK MORE strongly."[49] On January 8, 2024, eight months after Boric called the *salares* the home of ancient cultures and the water of the desert, and just four months after Chilean voters rejected the new constitution, the Council of Atacameño Peoples declared that the time for the President's lyrical odes to socio-natural harmony had ended. Now was the time of antimonies: contracts versus consent; development versus democracy.

The precipitating event involved the first contract signed under the banner of the government's new lithium strategy. Codelco, the state-owned copper company, and SQM had formed a partnership that would extend SQM's contract for three decades in exchange for Codelco gaining a sizable equity stake in the firm's Atacama operations. Codelco would acquire majority ownership and managerial oversight, while SQM would retain veto power. The corporation, in other words, accepted reduced control to ensure its future operation.[50] This could be seen as a perfect distillation of the obsolescing bargain between resource-rich states and extractive firms—and, viewed from a certain angle, a victory of progressive governance.

There was one pesky detail. The discussions that produced the agreement had originally included the Council of Atacameño Peoples—until suddenly, they didn't. What had started as a "tripartite" dialogue had quietly mutated into a bilateral negotiation.[51] The Indigenous council only learned of the memorandum of understanding from media reports. That the feeling of betrayal was familiar did not render it less painful.

The council's response was unflinching. After a series of escalating communiqués, the council made good on its threats. On January 9, Atacameño leaders called for protests. By the next day, more than five hundred had gathered to block six different areas along public roads. Organizers had strategically chosen these locations to inflict maximum inconvenience on SQM's lithium mines. According to the press, demonstrators prevented the ingress and egress of "workers, supplies and lithium," forcing SQM to halt operations.[52]

Council leaders called off the disruption after a meeting with the minister of mining, who promised a visit by the president himself, the council's top demand.[53] By that point, SQM's mine had suspended its operations for six days. It's telling, though, that for at least three days after the occupation officially disbanded, protesters from Socaire, one of the eighteen communities the council represents, continued to hold the line.[54] The next week, residents of the Toconao community decided to block the access road again.[55] Members of both communities remained staunchly opposed to any extension of SQM's presence on the salt flat and unconvinced that a meeting with Boric would do anything to address their concerns.

Even amid moments of relative unity, extraction divides communities. Not everyone protests—and not everyone thinks that the protest should end.

⌖

IN MARCH 2024, NEARLY A YEAR AFTER THE BORIC ADMINISTRAtion first launched its national lithium strategy, the government released a map. Maps, as we have seen, are better understood as projections of desires and dominion than as neutral descriptors of geography. This map projected the future of lithium in Chile and, given the country's enviable endowments, the world. The Boric administration identified sixty-eight salt flats viable for extraction.[56] Of these, officials flagged two, Atacama and Maricunga, as "strategic." The official reasoning was that the deposits were the country's largest and likely the most productive, but the "strategic" designation also meant that only ventures with majority state ownership would be awarded contracts. Another twenty-six salt flats would be subject to much looser regulation, allowing corporations to take the lead without public sector participation. A separate list of twenty-seven *salares* were included in a network of protected wetlands.[57]

Progress is in the eye of the beholder. This survey reserved by far the largest and most profitable lithium reserves in Chile for majority state ownership. It also conserved one-third of salt flats, as promised by Boric. And it aligned both of those objectives with a third: the dramatic expansion of lithium mining in Chile.

That's one way to look at the map. Another is to observe how it crystallizes relations of economic and political power. Corporations not only retain but expand their presence. State-led extraction does not threaten private assets, but in effect protects them. Chilean scientists and social movement activists also questioned the criteria used to distinguish between protected salt flats and those open for corporate business.[58] For example, Antonio Pulgar, a lawyer at Chile's oldest environmental law firm, noted that flamingo nesting habitats were not considered, and salt flats home to species existing nowhere else in the world are slated for new mining. Pulgar also worried that the rush to mine the now-expanded lithium frontier would move full speed ahead, while the regulations and resources needed to protect fragile wetlands would be deferred—or simply neglected altogether amid a new extractive frenzy.

Each viewpoint contains a truth. The first recognizes the real influence of both resource nationalism and environmentalism in shaping resource governance in Global South countries. The second concedes the enduring power of the world that colonialism and capitalism created.

In fits and starts, in advances and reversals, societies like Chile are trying to find their place in the emergent green economy. This means reckoning with extraction and, ideally, moving up the ladder of economic complexity. On the other side of the global divide, dominant states are likewise vying to attract investment in renewable energy technologies. But these Global North governments have another, more perplexing goal. They don't just want high-tech manufacturing or cutting-edge research and development. They want domestic mines to provide the minerals that their downstream sectors rely on. For American and European policymakers, international trade has proven an unreliable source for critical materials. This is the new era of green dominance.

PART III

GREEN CAPITALISM

Tiehm's buckwheat, Rhyolite Ridge mine site, Nevada

CHAPTER 6

Green Dominance

"We can't compete with the Asians on cost. So, what we want to compete on is the value proposition, which is: We're offering a cleaner, greener alternative."[1]

So said Peter Handley, the head of the European Commission's Raw Materials Unit, when I met with him in Brussels to discuss the EU's new goal of bringing lithium mining to Europe. This "value proposition," Handley explained, had another goal: ensuring "resource security, which for us means long-term security of supply." Handley's logic deftly equated environmental sustainability with economic competitiveness and presented both as essential to a third concept, security. Onshoring lithium production, in other words, would protect Europe from the volatility of global markets as well as the uncertainties of geopolitics.

As I gazed up at the appropriately dreary and gray modernist facade of the EU's Directorate-General for Internal Market, Industry, and Small and Medium Enterprises, which houses the Raw Materials Unit, I steeled myself for the familiar experience of coaxing information from functionaries trained to be discrete. To my pleasant surprise, however, bureaucrats like Handley wanted to talk. They were equally eager to hear my perspective on what they regarded as the entirely novel political and economic problems of the energy transition.

Our meeting took place just two months before Italy reported its first case of COVID-19. But even before the onset of the pandemic, elites were worried about the resiliency of global supply chains, particularly when it came to so-called critical minerals. A mounting populist backlash to the political establishment on both sides of the Atlantic, China's vertiginous and seemingly unstoppable ascent, dramatic turnovers in the American White House, the increasingly intense consequences of climate change—all of this had shaken policymakers' faith in their ability to maintain what they were now calling "supply chain security." Subsequent events, key among them Russia's invasion of Ukraine and its effects on energy and raw materials markets, only reinforced the sense that policymakers needed a new approach to the global economy.

In this context, EU officials had begun to see the energy transition as a panacea. They realized that this transition could do much more than stem global warming and lay the foundations for a greener future. Building this future would entail new infrastructures, technologies, sectors, and trade routes. Collectively, these investments could buttress Europe's status in a turbulent world. EU policymakers specifically looked to lithium battery supply chains, from their raw material beginnings to high-tech final products, as the most strategic terrain for asserting global power.

This is geoeconomics: the notion that economic policy and national security are one and the same. In past eras, this fusion of economy and security took place in the context of total war. Today, the battlefields are supply chains and the goal is green dominance: supremacy over new energy technologies.

In one meeting after another with EU bureaucrats, I saw dreams take hold that reflected those of Chilean policymakers as if through an inverted mirror. In Chile, a country rich in lithium deposits, political elites wanted to climb the ladder of value-added production, manufacturing cathodes, battery cells and packs, and, most ambitiously, electric vehicles. In contrast, Europe already produced batteries and electric vehicles—but nowhere near as many as China. And more to the point, Europe barely had a lithium mining sector. Every one of its upstream nodes in the supply chain depended on imports.

In the European Union, policymakers settled on "onshoring" as the solution to this weakness. The US government, too, soon followed the EU's lead. In both places, onshoring meant persuading the private sector to build new lithium mines and battery factories in Global North economies currently dominated by the finance and service sectors. The $3 trillion global auto industry was an especially strategic laboratory for the type of green industrial policy that was quickly achieving consensus on both sides of the Atlantic and across the political spectrum.

From Brussels to Washington, DC, onshoring lithium battery supply chains from mine to factory had become all the rage. And that meant reversing decades of globalization encouraged by free trade agreements, "just in time" production techniques, and innovations in shipping and communications technologies. In their place would go barriers to trade, protections for strategic sectors, and incentives to source inputs domestically. Greening capitalism required the visible hand of the state.

※

WHEN IT COMES TO GEOECONOMICS, BUREAUCRATS FACE A FUNDAmental question: What is the role of the state in a capitalist economy? In their zeal to encourage new mining and industrial sectors, US and European administrators have answered by reinvigorating "industrial policy." This long-unfashionable term refers to government-led efforts to develop entirely new economic sectors, to revitalize old ones, and to coordinate the interactions between sectors. This approach departs from the decades-old consensus often referred to as neoliberalism, which sought to liberate capitalism from the fetters of regulation.

Ideological notions inherited from the Cold War tend to sharply contrast government planning with the operation of free markets, or the actions of state bureaucrats with those of private investors. But the reality of the state's role is, and always has been, much more complex than this.

During World War II, the United States mobilized its entire economy, and much of the Western Hemisphere's, to secure the raw materials and manufacturing required for combat.[2] This planning effort, which required serious state coordination, encompassed lithium supply chains. The US War Production Board mandated that all lithium ore be directed to the war effort. This directive reflected the use of lithium compounds in refining other metals, deicing planes, purifying air (including in submarines), and lubricating machinery.[3] During the Cold War, lithium took on strategic importance as an input in thermonuclear weapons.[4] In October 1950, a few months into the Korean War, the Atomic Energy Commission directly invested in the lithium supply chain with the goal of converting lithium to tritium, a radioactive isotope of hydrogen used in these weapons.[5] The $3 billion outlay was among "the greatest federal construction projects in peacetime history."[6]

In Europe and the United Kingdom, the scale of reconstruction after World War II demanded that states invest billions of dollars in rebuilding their cities and their economies. This project would have been impossible without the coordination and targeted financing of basic industry by European governments backed by the Marshall Plan. Along the way, many of these countries, including France, England, and Austria, established state-owned enterprises in infrastructure and telecommunications.[7]

A generation later, the governments of Margaret Thatcher, in the United Kingdom, and Ronald Reagan, in the United States, dismissed the idea that state agencies should strategically shape economic activity. The transformation of the British economy was dramatic. Before Thatcher came to power, state-owned firms controlled 9 percent of the country's economy; by 1997, that share had plummeted to a mere 2 percent.[8] Similarly, France sold off twenty-one national companies in 1993. That same decade, Portugal's economy went from 20 percent state-owned to 10 percent.

None of this meant that the state disappeared from the economy—even if that was the avowed goal of some right-wing ideologues. In the United States, industrial policy lived on in the Pentagon, particularly in the aerospace industry.[9] But more generally, public policies across the Global North increasingly prioritized favorable conditions for private investment, under the assumption that the benefits of economic growth would "trickle down" to ordinary people. What was lost was a holistic, birds-eye view of the economy and the role of public involvement in key investment decisions.

Today, this kind of thinking is back. The European Union, its members states, and the US government have embraced a suite of policies to induce investments in lithium mines, battery plants, EV factories, and recycling facilities.

Industrial policy involves a delicate dance of disciplining and courting capital. The dramatic growth of battery and EV manufacturing in China provides an excellent example. Public policies required foreign firms that wanted to operate on Chinese soil to establish joint ventures with Chinese companies. State subsidies, meanwhile, favored domestic battery production and vehicle assembly and levied onerous tariffs on imports.[10] Yet a third strategy deployed a mix of administrative penalties and selective tax credits to push automakers to rapidly electrify their fleets, ensuring a domestic market for the end product of the lithium battery supply chain.[11]

Policymakers in contemporary Europe and the United States are now playing catch-up with China. They, too, see the wisdom in selecting strategic sectors for government support and protection. The United States has adopted a combination of stiff tariffs and mineral sourcing requirements to jump-start a US supply chain. The European Union, in a bid for even greener dominance, has imposed sustainability requirements on battery production as well as a ban on the sale of traditional cars after 2035.[12] These directives aside, American and European governments offer firms more carrots and brandish fewer sticks than their counterparts in China. Their goal is making the desired investments more profitable and less risky. Sweeteners include tax breaks; producer and consumer subsidies; loans, grants, and prizes; direct public investment; R&D support; and fast-tracking and other means of deregulation.

Whatever form it takes, industrial policy admits that capitalism doesn't always function as advertised. Sometimes, crucial industries aren't profitable enough to attract investment. Other times, they are beset by coordination challenges, with missing links in their supply chains. Path dependency—a phenomenon in which actors stick with status quo practices even when circumstances shift—is another issue. From a firm's perspective, changing products and production lines is costly. But change, both rapid and holistic, is precisely what the energy transition requires and what industrial policy is designed to encourage.

In the case of batteries, the problems start upstream. The lithium market has been plagued by volatile cycles of over- and undersupply—and, as a corollary, by dramatic swings between low and high prices. From 2018 to 2020, market supply for lithium outpaced demand, as mines ramped up in response to an expected takeoff in the EV market that did not materialize (with the key exception of China). This market glut depressed prices and dampened financiers' interest, slowing the development of lithium mines (again, with the exception of Chinese firms and state agencies).[13] The conditions were ripe for a tighter market. When consumers in European and American markets began expressing more interest in electric vehicles, the market was out of balance again. This time, prices shot through the roof.

Ominous headlines warned of a "looming supply shortage" and a "stalled" EV revolution. Pundits asked, "How long will the lithium supply last?"[14] The media coverage also made it clear that more was at stake than market fundamentals. This was a matter of the geoeconomics of lithium: "The US fell behind"; "China is winning"; "Europe is on the rise."[15]

At issue was twenty-first-century green dominance.

◦───◦

THE SEEDS FOR THIS SHIFT TOWARD INDUSTRIAL POLICY WERE planted in 2008. Confronted with a financial crisis that could be attributed, at least in part, to deregulation of financial markets, policymakers began to question their faith in untrammeled markets. In the United States, foreclosures skyrocketed and Lehman Brothers collapsed. After the most acute phase of the crisis had passed, other problems came into view. Occupy Wall Street brought public attention to yawning inequality and corporate capture of government; the Tea Party triggered the return of right-wing populism. Both phenomena, as opposed as they were, troubled the political consensus for unbridled capitalism.

The commodity boom was also a problem. Even as economies in the Global North teetered on collapse, the global appetite for everything from copper to soy to beef boosted the economies of resource exporters in the Global South, especially in Latin America. China's rapid growth and proliferating factories accounted for much of the demand, but other emerging economies clamored for their own share. That contrast threw Western hegemony into doubt for the first time since the 1970s. The great economic powers of the Global North suddenly found themselves competing with China for market access and paying more for what they did manage to import.[16]

The feeling of déjà vu was palpable. American and European elites hadn't sweated this much since the oil shock. But they now saw China, rather than OPEC petrostates, as the primary threat. And this time, instead of oil, they wanted access to the bevy of "critical minerals" necessary for new energy technologies.[17] Specifically, they wanted rare earth elements. These metals, which include neodymium, lanthanum, and yttrium, are essential to a wide range of electronic devices and green technologies, including solar panels, wind turbines, and EV motors. Despite their name, rare earths are not rare. Several countries have technically and financially viable reserves, and ongoing exploration will surely discover new deposits.[18] They do, however, tend to exist in low concentrations where they are present.

Perhaps more importantly from a geoeconomics perspective, the vast majority of rare earths have consistently emanated from a single country—the polar opposite of a diversified, resilient supply chain. From the 1960s to the mid-1990s, that country was the United States. During those three decades, the Mountain Pass mine in California was the world's single largest source of these elements.[19] Now that country is China, which currently produces over 70 percent of the global supply.[20] Aside from questions of access, the shift has generated new concerns about the environmental costs of rare earth mining. In China, rare earth mining and refining operates according to standards that are notoriously lax, to devastating ecological and social effect. The mines produce extensive soil and water pollution due to acid chemical leaching, feature uncontrolled waste pits, and have been linked to "cancer villages" with unusually high rates of the disease.[21]

The Chinese government was aware of both the reputational problems and international leverage associated with its rare earth mines. Between 2000 and 2010, state officials reined in extraction and imposed export quotas in response to environmental and health crises in mining regions.[22] Then, in September 2010, the Chinese military disrupted a shipment of rare earth elements to Japan following a dispute in the contested waters between Taiwan and Okinawa. The international press framed the incident as an "embargo." A market panic followed. In response, Obama administration officials and members of Congress embraced the language of "green nationalism,"[23] arguing that the United States should onshore rare earth mining and recycling on the grounds that domestic sourcing is "environmentally superior" to Chinese imports. They did so despite the fact that Mountain Pass was shuttered in 2002 for environmental contamination.[24]

These events set the stage for renewed attention to critical minerals in the Global North. The December 2010 publication of the US Department of Energy's (DOE) *Critical Minerals Strategy*, followed by the European Commission's first catalog of critical minerals in 2011, only reinforced a sense of a cataclysmic shift in resource policy. Although neither the United States nor the European Union had yet labeled lithium as "critical," the DOE noted that lithium's status would likely change in the near future: "Lithium is the only key material that shifts into a higher criticality category from the short to medium term."[25] The observation proved prescient.

IN THE UNITED STATES, THE PROCESS OF ONSHORING BATTERY SUPply chains began with a seemingly technical classification. In 2018, the US Department of Interior added lithium to its list of critical minerals.[26] The "critical" part of the label doesn't refer to the absolute or relative scarcity of the resource in question. There wasn't suddenly less lithium in the earth's crust or waters. Instead, "critical" signals geoeconomic status. It means that government officials view the mineral as relevant to national security, essential for economic functioning, and prone to supply disruptions.

The designation unleashes political powers and investment opportunities. Once a mineral is included on this special list, it becomes easier for either the executive branch or Congress to expedite mining permits or offer tax breaks to the mines that produce it.[27] Which is exactly what happened next. In September 2020, President Donald Trump issued Executive Order 13953, "Addressing the Threat to the Domestic Supply Chain from Reliance on Critical Minerals from Foreign Adversaries and Supporting Domestic Mining and Processing Industries."[28] The executive order directed agencies to speed up the permitting process and take other actions that might increase mineral production. The same month, DOE's Argonne National Laboratory partnered with Albemarle on a project exploring advanced brine-processing methods.[29]

A vision began to gel. Witness, for example, Senator Lisa Murkowski's "American Mineral Act," first introduced in May 2019 with support from both sides of the political aisle and announced at the Benchmark Minerals Summit, a closed-door gathering of corporate executives and government officials in DC. As Murkowski put it, "Our reliance on China and other nations for critical minerals costs us jobs, weakens our economic competitiveness, and leaves us at a geopolitical disadvantage."[30]

US officials also cited ethical concerns with relying on imported minerals. Francis Fannon, Trump's assistant secretary of the Bureau of Energy Resources in the State Department, drew attention to the "serious issues" plaguing the mines providing inputs for the energy transition. The issues he referred to are familiar to anyone with knowledge of extractive sectors: human rights abuses, environmental degradation, and political corruption. Speaking before yet another Benchmark Minerals event, an EV Fest in May 2020, Fannon warned that these blemishes threatened the fledging EV market, potentially "[staining] a whole industry."[31]

Looking back on these remarks, it's easy to read them as an early instance of a now routine, and patently bad faith, Republican attack on electric vehicles. But Fannon was upbeat about the green future, emphasizing his "optimism" about the growth in "clean energy technologies." Instead, he worried that a few corporate bad apples in the mining sector might provoke a "backlash" from consumers and investors alike. This Trump official was in fact promoting EV supply chains—so long as they were built here at home, where there was "a long, earned history of responsible mineral development," or as a second best, friend-shored from the jurisdictions of similarly "responsible" country partners.

President Joe Biden expanded these policies. When it comes to lithium, it seems, support for onshoring is bipartisan. Just one month after his inauguration, Biden signed the Executive Order on America's Supply Chains, requiring a sweeping one-hundred-day review of supply chains for "critical and essential goods." Two of the four goods specified were "high-capacity batteries, including electric vehicles" and "critical minerals and other identified strategic minerals." The resulting report recommended expanding the domestic mining of lithium and other critical minerals to build a lithium battery supply chain "from soup to nuts"—as one government official put it—"from sustainable mining and processing to manufacturing and recycling."[32]

A flurry of policy activity followed, several involving Argonne National Laboratory and the Department of Energy. The administration's actions invoked the Defense Production Act, a law dating to the Korean War that establishes executive authority over "critical and strategic materials" that are "essential to the national defense."[33] During Biden's first year in office, these institutions and powers provided loan guarantees, underwrote R&D for corporations, financed feasibility studies, and promoted the environmental credentials of particular extraction techniques.[34] Representatives from the mining industry saw such moves as a clear "signal" of the administration's commitment to domestic mining.[35]

For Trump, onshoring lithium offered a way to counter Chinese power. Biden shared this goal and added another: By investing in the energy transition supply chain, Biden signaled his commitment to combating climate change. In other words, not just dominance—green dominance. Whatever the immediate political calculus, it has become clear that supply chain security offers an increasingly rare bipartisan appeal. The 2021 Infrastructure Investment and Jobs Act, passed with support from both parties, allotted $6 billion (of $550 billion) to lithium battery–related investments.[36] Among other things, the bill funds geological mapping of critical minerals; streamlines the federal permitting process for mining critical minerals; and establishes grants, prizes, and federal programs to incentivize battery recycling and materials recovery as a means of ensuring "supply chain resiliency."[37]

At this point, events began to accelerate. In August 2022, Congress passed and Biden signed both the Inflation Reduction Act (IRA) and the CHIPS and Science Act. The IRA contained the most expansive industrial policy aimed at the civilian economy yet seen in US history—and the first with a green complexion. The bill included new incentives across the battery supply chain, from mining to manufacturing, as well as consumer subsidies for both EV purchases and home energy storage. It also established an estimated $660 billion in tax credits for "advanced manufacturing," which includes the production of electrode materials, battery cells, and battery modules and the extraction of critical minerals.[38] The CHIPS and Science Act—with the acronym standing for Creating Helpful Incentives to Produce Semiconductors—contains $52 billion in inducements for manufacturers to produce chips in the United States.[39]

While the bills mostly offer carrots, they also include some sticks. To take full advantage of the manufacturing incentives, for example, companies must abide by prevailing wage and apprenticeship requirements. More onerous, however, are the surprisingly stringent sourcing requirements for EV components and battery minerals. The CHIPS and Science Act limits the ability of firms that take the funds from investing in China or "other countries of concern." For an electric vehicle to qualify for consumer rebates under the IRA, increasing percentages of the "critical minerals" contained in its battery would need to be sourced either from the United States or from a country with which the United States has a free trade agreement, starting with 40 percent in 2024 and reaching 80 percent in 2026. The vehicle must also be assembled in North America. Any EV produced with minerals or other components originating in or processed in "a foreign entry of concern," including China, is excluded from the consumer rebate program.

A green fortress was being built. And no castle is complete without a moat. In May 2024, Biden dramatically increased tariffs on Chinese imports of technologies and their mineral inputs, among other goods "vital for America's economic future and national security."[40]

Here, too, Biden followed in Trump's footsteps in targeting China, even as he focused geoeconomic escalation more specifically on the energy transition and other high-tech sectors.[41] Tariffs on imported Chinese batteries went from 7.5 to 25 percent; "critical minerals" from 0 to 25 percent; semiconductors from 25 to 50 percent; EVs from 25 to 100 percent. Economists broadly agree that trade decreases by double the rate of tariff increases, such that any tariff rate above 50 percent is technically a ban—and a 100 percent tariff is a ban plus a political statement.[42] In this case the statement was clear. The means to fighting climate change—green dominance—had become an end in and of itself. What that in turn implies for the prospects of saving the planet remains to be seen. But thus far, the signs are not auspicious.

When Trump returned to the White house, he threatened to dismantle government support for EVs, while simultaneously asserting that the US should "dominate" critical minerals, even floating the idea of building mineral refineries on Pentagon military bases.[43] In US politics, the critical minerals consensus has proven more durable than climate action.

ON THE OTHER SIDE OF THE ATLANTIC, EU POLICYMAKERS WERE likewise developing a multifaceted "critical raw materials" policy.[44] In Brussels, as in Washington, policymakers desired self-sufficiency in energy transition minerals. But in Europe, bureaucrats have paired the dream of resource security with sustainability. It is in Europe, then, that the possibility of a truly green capitalism has been put to the test.

In the European Union, officials have relied more on publicly funded innovation, regulatory standards, and targeted subsidies than on the uncapped tax breaks so prominent in US industrial policy.[45] In part, this reflects prohibitions on deficit spending. The EU cannot slash revenue now in hopes of triggering a windfall later.[46] This fact has ruffled trans-Atlantic alliances. The US tax breaks attract European green capitalists, who get more bang for their investment buck by setting up shop (or mine) in the United States rather than in France or Germany.[47] But while the European Union can't offer what one expert has called "bottomless mimosas"[48] for industry, it can provide a commitment to green practices and a greater sense of policy stability compared with the whiplash that characterizes US national politics.

Sustainable supply chains start with "responsible" mining, which has a geoeconomic logic of its own. EU policymakers see sustainable extraction and ethical production as the West's comparative advantage—the one terrain on which their economies can outperform China.[49] Officials bet that simultaneously securing and greening lithium supply chains would give their firms a market advantage in a sector dominated by their Chinese counterparts.

The European Union may not be able to issue tax credits, but public money is still flowing to firms. In 2017, the European Commission established the EU Battery Alliance with a goal of incubating a battery supply chain across the continent. Under the Battery Alliance's umbrella, the EU earmarked €925 million on battery R&D between 2021 and 2027 via its innovation fund, Horizon Europe.[50] Another key EU institution, the European Investment Bank, has loaned billions to battery factories and cathode plants; a zero-carbon lithium mine in Germany might be next.[51] The EU's technology institute directly invested in pilot lithium mines in Spain, Germany, Portugal, and the Czech Republic and has partnered with Demeter, a private equity firm, to establish a €500 million fund to attract investment in battery materials like lithium.[52] There are similar developments at the member-state level. The German state-owned development bank, for example, has established a new €1 billion fund to make equity investments in mines in the country as well as elsewhere in the European Union.[53]

The stated aim of all this public money is to "de-risk" private investment and thus close the "financing gap" in lithium battery investment.[54] But the bigger goal remains supply chain security. In March 2024, the European Union officially adopted the Critical Raw

Materials Act, which establishes what officials hope will be a realistic path to "secure and sustainable" supplies of minerals like lithium: by 2030, 10 percent mined within the EU's borders, 40 percent processed within the EU, and 25 percent obtained from recycled materials.[55]

The reference to recycled materials is telling. For European policymakers, green capitalism is measured by the means of production—not just the ends. In December 2022, just months after the US Congress passed the IRA, the EU could boast of its own achievement: the Sustainable Battery Regulation.[56] The law requires battery manufacturers to incorporate increasing levels of recycled content and to provide labels disclosing the batteries' carbon footprint. Eventually, batteries will be subjected to life cycle emissions targets.

In the EU, then, security is complemented with circularity. This malleable concept can refer to anything that "closes the loop" of economic production: recycling, reuse, or repair; using materials, energy, and water efficiently; and eliminating waste, including by converting scraps into feedstock. Environmentalists have long promoted the goal of a fully circular economy. But viewed from a different angle, circularity also offers a route to supply chain security. Reducing the amount of new material throughout the manufacturing process in turn decreases the EU's "dependency on materials from third countries" and buffers against the threat of "potential disruptions," in the regulation's own words.[57] Circularity would help EU officials achieve "strategic autonomy," a keyword of EU politics that moves deftly between the domains of security and economy and now links both to sustainability.[58]

Peter Handley, the head of the EU Commission's Raw Materials Unit who we met at the beginning of this chapter, ticked off the myriad reasons for onshoring lithium mining: solar trade wars; volatile lithium markets; the specter of instability roiling Latin American exporters ("Chile or Bolivia, one day it's the most reliable supplier, next day in chaos").[59] He and I spoke in December 2019, and Handley, of course, had no way to predict the impacts of a prolonged pandemic, market shocks, and multiple wars on commodity prices. But his tone was foreboding nonetheless: "There is a risk that we will lose our whole value chain... with massive economic consequences."

Onshoring, in other words, meant "control," as Joanna Szychowska, the head of the EU Commission's Automotive and Mobility Industries Unit, told me. For this reason, she insisted, building a self-sufficient supply chain in Europe was "as much an economic project as political."[60]

But could Europe control the world?

At least at the time of this writing, the answer would appear to be no. Onshoring is happening in Europe, but many of the lead firms are Chinese. CATL, headquartered in Fujian Province and the world's largest battery maker, built a 14 GWh battery plant in Thuringia, Germany, to more efficiently supply this crucial component to European automakers in the area, including BMW.[61] A second CATL plant is currently under construction in Debrecen, Hungary.[62]

CATL's press statements announcing their new plants smoothed over any perceived tensions between Europe's onshoring goals and a Chinese entrant to the market. Parroting the EU's own policy language, CATL's promotional materials framed their investments as part and parcel of the EU commission's own ambition of "localizing innovative battery technology to drive the growth of the region's EV industry" and "building a sustainable Europe."[63] In announcing the Hungary plant, in particular, CATL directly aligned itself with such EU initiatives as the Sustainable Battery Regulation. And, speaking directly to the commissioners' concerns about the political fallout of deindustrialization, CATL emphasized that its German plant would create over 2,000 jobs.[64]

German and Hungarian officials and European automakers alike welcomed the news of these plants, raising a difficult question: Would the European pivot away from "dependence" on China be possible without investment on the part of Chinese firms?

THE VISION OF A WEST FULLY DECOUPLED FROM CHINA MAY BE A chimera. But such fantasies are motivating real changes on the ground. US and European efforts to onshore battery supply chains have produced concrete results in the form of new domestic lithium mines. One of these is Nevada's Thacker Pass, a claystone deposit that, once completed, will be the second lithium mine on US soil. The project uses a novel technique to extract lithium that involves adding sulfuric acid to a liquefied slurry of clay.[65] The mine is owned by Canada-based Lithium Americas. In January 2021, the US Bureau of Land Management approved the company's environmental impact assessment (EIA) and granted it a "record of decision," enabling the mine to advance from the planning stage. Thacker Pass benefited from the regulatory fast-tracking encouraged by Trump's executive order on critical minerals, which sped up the public hearing and permitting processes.[66]

In his comments to the press after the permit was issued, Lithium Americas president and CEO Jon Evans echoed the emerging geoeconomic consensus on critical minerals, telling reporters, "Thacker Pass has the potential to provide ... lithium chemicals critical for establishing a strong domestic lithium supply chain."[67] Evans's colleague Alexi Zawadski, president of the company's North American operations, emphasized the Thacker Pass mine's claims to sustainability. He explained: "We recycle a lot of our water. We actually generate carbon-free energy from our process, and we'll have an excess that we'll sell to the grid."[68] His comments were ironic, given that in Jujuy, Argentina—where his company then operated a lithium mine[69]—Indigenous communities have criticized lithium mining for its water usage.[70]

Thacker Pass is just one of many mines planned for a veritable US lithium boom. Over one hundred projects in the western states alone have either begun the permitting process or have received initial financial backing.[71] Of course, given the speculative and risky nature of the mining business, only a subset of these will succeed. But the number of proposals is still striking.

One factor enabling the lithium rush is the 1872 General Mining Law, which governs extraction on public lands, where the vast majority of US mining projects are sited.[72] This law contains no environmental or water safeguards or requirements for community consultation or consent—and was explicitly designed at the time of its passage to transfer Indigenous lands to white settlers.[73] Although a patchwork of other regulations at the federal and state levels address some of the shortfalls of the 1872 law, it remains the primary rule for mining on public land. It allows mining companies to stake claims on that land and commence the process of prospecting without permits, and it does not require mining firms to pay any royalties to the government.[74]

The Inflation Reduction Act imposes no new regulations on the mining industry, while showering firms with generous support. Mining executives were rationally effusive in the days after President Biden signed the bill into law. Evans, of Lithium Americas, was "delighted"; his company got to work on plans for its next lithium mine in the United States even before Thacker Pass broke ground.[75] In March 2024, Lithium Americas' executives had reason to be even more delighted: The Department of Energy approved a $2.26 billion loan, covering over 75 percent of the capital costs of the Thacker Pass mine. As with all DOE direct loans, the financing provided Lithium Americas with more favorable interest rates and flexible repayment schedules than any private financial institution would offer.[76]

The timing was particularly auspicious for Lithium Americas, as months of lower commodity prices for lithium had begun to spook investors, stalling some projects and shifting the mood from "euphoria to despair" in the words of one lithium CEO.[77] Lithium Americas' stock price rose as soon as the DOE loan was announced. Public policy—and public money—had ironed out the wrinkles between extractive and financial capital. But the contradictions between green industrial policy and green capitalism, and between sustainability and security, run deeper than this.

※━━━━━※

THE LITHIUM RUSH HAS PUT STATE AND LOCAL BUREAUCRATS IN A particularly hard spot. In late 2016, when Bradley Crowell first assumed his role as Nevada's chief environmental regulator, he never expected that lithium would be so central to his job—or to the evolving politics of the energy transition. But as he explained when we spoke in the fall of 2021, his position as director of the Nevada Department of Conservation and Natural Resources thrust him into the fraught collision of "energy supply chains versus protecting landscapes and habitats and species."[78]

Crowell was no stranger to beltway politics. His seventeen years working in DC included stints as an assistant secretary at the Department of Energy, an adviser to Senator Sheldon Whitehouse, and a legislative advocate for the Natural Resources Defense Council. His appointment at Carson City returned him to the state where he was born and raised. For state-level bureaucrats like Crowell, the signal from the White House was clear: America needed to "[shore] up the critical mineral supply chain" and do so in a "sustainable and responsible" manner.

The problem was a total lack of federal guidance as to what "sustainable and responsible" meant in practice. Staying aligned with the White House while managing tensions among "stakeholder groups"—the ubiquitous, anodyne term encompassing corporations, rural communities, Indigenous tribes, and environmental advocates—presented a day-to-day challenge for Crowell. At the same time, he and everyone working for the state government felt pressure to boost Nevada's tourist-driven economy, which had been devastated by the pandemic. (Mining accounts for a surprisingly small percentage of Nevada's employment and share of the state's GDP.[79]) Promoting mining projects was not at all in his department's purview, but Crowell saw the potential for a "circular economy of lithium in Nevada"—in which lithium is mined, batteries manufactured and recycled, and their materials recovered, all within the state's borders—that could simultaneously create jobs and reduce mining-related harm. And all of it could happen at home, "in America," reducing the carbon footprint of the electrified economy. For all these reasons, Crowell saw a US renewable energy supply chain as a "no brainer."

Persuading skeptical members of Indigenous reservations, other rural communities, and their allies in environmental advocacy groups, however, was another story. As Crowell told me, his department sought to "get the message out there" that the new green economy was "a great opportunity that we should seize." The message sounded familiar. I had heard it countless times in White House press releases and at industry conventions; it circulated seamlessly from the federal government to the state and local levels and traveled back and forth across the blurry line between the public and private sectors. But as in so many of the conversations I have had with the government officials promoting mining, a cloud hovered at the edge of his otherwise sunny optimism. As protests and lawsuits took aim at the lithium boom, Crowell wondered "how much the Biden administration is willing to buck the far left" in its pursuit of a clean energy supply chain.

Over at the Nevada Division of Minerals, head administrator Mike Visher agreed that Nevada, with its vast underground resources and predictable "regulatory environment," was "uniquely positioned" to benefit from a mining-intensive energy transition.[80] Just as important, onshoring was the ethical thing to do: "We know we have to have these minerals... shouldn't we take advantage of an asset in a place that's heavily regulated, versus turning a blind eye to it happening overseas in a Third World country. It's an inconvenient truth. That's what's occurring now with a lot of key battery materials. In the Congo, the conditions are horrific. No one wants to be part of that." His positive attitude toward domestic mining befits his position. Unlike

Crowell's department, the Division of Minerals doesn't so much regulate mining projects as "assist companies" who are actively exploring opportunities in the state by providing them with information on mining claims and the permitting process.[81]

Visher nevertheless foresaw multiple potential obstacles for a lithium boom in Nevada, all of which emanated from two fundamental facts: "The resources are where the resources are" and mining those resources "is not a neutral activity." Visher warned that a "NIMBY attitude" threatened to slow down the construction of a made-in-America supply chain. But Visher also worried about regulatory capacity. Politicians talk about speeding up the time frame to open new mines. What is missing, Visher told me, is the "money and resources" to hire more bureaucrats, whether at federal agencies like the Bureau of Land Management or state ones like his Division of Minerals. Visher sees a contradiction between the onshoring imperative and the widespread suspicion of the administrative state: "There isn't a lot of impetus to expand the size of the federal government." Instead, "Everyone thinks you can just make things more efficient."

This mentality extends to battery and EV companies, who believe you can simply "flip a switch" and secure the mineral inputs to "[produce] the widgets." No one seems to understand that the permitting time frames for the mining projects that feed the factories "are years, not months." Visher also sees companies across the supply chain, from mine to battery plant, simultaneously facing more public pressure on transparency and sourcing and demands from shareholders to maximize returns. Wherever the buck stops, he says, the energy "transition will come at a big cost.... No one wants to acknowledge that everyone is going to bear some of that burden. They just don't want it to be them."

Well, not everyone exactly. Visher thinks that the costs of the energy transition will ultimately fall on less organized groups, "the consumer or taxpayer." Lithium companies, however, seem poised to profit.

CHAPTER 7

Green Mining

It was June 2019, and I was at the posh W Hotel in Santiago, Chile, for the first day of the 11th Annual Lithium Supply & Markets Conference. Conference-goers couldn't have known it at the time, but that year marked a turning point for the industry. A future of high market demand and supportive public policies lay just over the horizon. The EV revolution was finally kicking into high gear—and lithium would be one of the most sought-after elements in electrifying transportation around the world.

None of this—not lithium's takeoff, not the pandemic, not the Great Power race to green dominance, not Russia's invasion of Ukraine—was knowable in 2019. Instead, discussions centered on what might seem, in retrospect, an unexpected subject. At every corporate lithium convention I've attended, attendees have fixated on a particular theme, ranging from the geopolitics of critical minerals, to the rise of green industrial policies, to the challenge of delivering enough supply to meet market demand, to the pressures of addressing ESG (an acronym for financial strategies sensitive to environmental, social, and governance risks, shorthand for either green or greenwashed investments, depending on who's talking).

Back in 2019, the theme was a question: Was lithium a commodity? This might seem a strange question for a room full of capitalists to ask themselves. If a commodity is "a substance or product that can be traded, bought, or sold," lithium certainly fits the bill. But conference participants had a more specific meaning in mind. Here, as in the pages of the business press, commodity meant a raw material: an input for further processing and production, whether extracted or harvested. Copper and beef, oil and soy, lumber and nickel—these are commodities.

Commodity markets fundamentally rely on nature, whether it takes the form of mineral-rich ores in the earth's crust or the specific weather conditions that produce a particular crop. At the same time, commodities are alienated from nature. Traded as a bale of cotton, a barrel of oil, or a ton of copper, commodities are bought and sold in abstractions of measurement units and prices that erase the physical differences between units. The price for a bushel of soybeans isn't for a specific bushel of soybeans, but rather a hypothetical bushel of soybeans that could come from anywhere. As Javier Martínez de Olcoz Cerdan, a managing director at Morgan Stanley, put it during that 2019 convention, "a commodity is a product that you don't care where it is produced."[1]

Before he offered that pithy definition, it was clear that Martínez planned to be provocative. His opening line, "Last year some people told me that many people wanted to kill me at this conference," elicited hushed chatter and nervous laughter. He proceeded to explain that lithium was a commodity just like any other, or at least in the process of becoming one.

This comment sparked intense debate. The major lithium companies rejected Martínez's basic contention that lithium was a commodity. Instead, they saw it as a "very bespoke product": a highly customized chemical optimized to meet the varied and technical specifications of their customers, especially battery makers.[2] Lithium deposits take varied forms, from hard rock to soft clays to liquid brine—and quality varies widely within each of these categories. Bolivian brine resources, for example, contain high levels of magnesium, an impurity that must be removed to produce battery-grade lithium chemicals—one reason that country's lithium sector has developed more slowly than that of its neighbors. Neither the people who produce lithium nor the people who buy it, in other words, see lithium as a homogeneous product.

At stake in the question of commodity status was whether lithium's price would be determined by commodity markets or by closed-door negotiations. As a representative of Morgan Stanley, an investment banking company, Martínez thought in terms of commodity markets. Surveying the state of the lithium market, Martínez conveyed his optimism that prices for a ton of lithium carbonate, at that day selling for $10,800 per metric ton on the Chinese spot market, would continue to decline as new supply was brought online. He predicted that prices would likely settle down to around $7,300 by 2031.[3] His forecasts about pricing trends turned out to be wrong, at least so far: rather than smoothly floating downward, lithium prices have been dogged by persistent volatility, hitting the dizzying high of $80,000 per metric ton in late 2022 through early 2023 before crashing again.[4] But in his assessment that lithium is slowly but surely on its way to becoming a fungible commodity, Martínez appears to be correct.

Historically, the lithium market has been dominated by long-term contracts between mining companies and downstream purchasers, called offtake agreements.[5] Such contracts fix prices ahead of time, providing security to buyers and sellers. Offtake agreements are not totally insulated from broader market dynamics. They usually contain a mechanism to periodically adjust the contract price in response to the going rate in the world's main spot market, based in China. But to analysts and investors, the prevalence of such long-term arrangements signaled lithium's status as an "immature" commodity, compared with such established commodities like oil or copper.

Lithium is now firmly on its way to adulthood. A major growth spurt came during the boom of 2022–2023. Understandably, mining companies wanted to cash in on the bonanza, prompting them to embrace flexible contracts with variable rather than fixed pricing schemes, subject to more frequent adjustments.[6] For buyers, of course, high prices are bad news. Buyers turned to "futures" contracts, or agreements to trade a given quantity of a commodity at a set price and on a specific date, as a hedge against volatility. Since the supply and demand for raw materials rarely matches, such financial instruments in theory help balance the market over time.[7]

These two trends—variable pricing and future contracts—make a persuasive case for lithium's status as a commodity. The combination has also made it possible for lithium to finally step out onto the floor of the worlds' premier commodities exchanges. For instance, the Chicago Mercantile Exchange (CME) established a futures market for lithium hydroxide in May 2021.[8] For the first few years, the exchange was quiet—but trading began to take off in the spring of 2023, and volume continued to increase in 2024.[9]

Converting lithium from a specialized product to a generic commodity means that lithium companies must relinquish some control. This was exactly the future that lithium companies had sought to avoid. On the stage of that 2019 convention, when the London Metal Exchange (LME) announced its own intentions to launch a lithium futures market, executives from three top firms spoke in unison. The vice president of Albemarle refused to cooperate: "We view this market as a specialty chemicals market... for us, an index price goes against that strategy... our intent is we will not be providing price information to the index." SQM's vice president reiterated that "lithium is a specialty chemical not a commodity." The vice president of Tianqi echoed both of them, stating, "We agree, all our customers have different specifications, at the moment an index can be challenging... if it's not done right, it can be misleading as well."[10]

Lithium executives may have lost the battle over lithium's commodity status. But that is only one of many tensions roiling the industry. Ongoing price volatility continues to act as a wedge between mining companies and the financiers they hope to attract. Geopolitical headwinds are segmenting global trade in unpredictable ways. Meanwhile, the environmental and human rights concerns that continue to swirl around their core product present a somewhat counterintuitive profit opportunity. If lithium is on the way to becoming a more generic raw material, then hawking "green" or "ethical" lithium is one way to stand out from the crowd.

RAW MATERIALS MARKETS ARE NOTORIOUSLY FICKLE. IN THIS sense, lithium looks like a classic commodity. Over the prior six years, lithium's price has experienced multiple dramatic reversals, spiking only to vertiginously fall. One reason for commodity volatility is what economists call "inelasticity." As the word suggests, this condition describes either a supply that can't expand quickly to meet new demand (an inelastic supply) or, conversely, a market in which consumers don't change their behavior in response to changing prices (inelastic demand).

The markets for raw materials, especially extractive sectors, are often rigid on either side of the equation. It takes a long time, often more than a decade, to open a new mine. Mineral production can't be ramped up quickly, even if there are lots of eager buyers. This means prices can climb quite high without dampening demand. On the flip side, the difficulty of calibrating supply to demand can produce market gluts and crashing prices. Mines are easier to finance when prices rise—but there's no guarantee of a market for that output once the mineral is ready to be sold. The demand side, too, faces constraints: If an industrial process requires a particular mineral, manufacturers can't just replace it with something else when prices increase. Manufacturers tend to swallow the cost rather than exit the market, thus keeping prices high.

Lithium's volatility is iconic. US Global Investors, which publishes an annual "Periodic Table of Commodities Returns," awarded lithium the title of "most volatile" commodity in the decade between 2013 and 2022.[11] In 2024, the International Energy Agency (IEA) also singled out lithium prices as the most erratic of all the critical minerals it tracked.[12] Some of this reflects the simple mechanics of commodity price cycles. Depressed prices reduce profitability and deter investment, which eventually takes a toll on supply, which in turn renders the available lithium more valuable, encouraging new exploration and eventually pushing prices down again—rinse and repeat. But it also reflects the fluctuations of public policy. Demand for EVs, and thus for their supply chains, is contingent on governments' fickle support for climate action. Politics is another source of market volatility.

Whether you see high prices as good or bad depends on where you sit along the supply chain. Tight markets are good news for lithium producers.[13] In a January 2023 presentation to investors, Eric Norris, the president of Albemarle's lithium division, stated, "Pricing needs to remain elevated in order to support the incentives required to take on those investment risks."[14] The perception of "need" may be relative: Albemarle's 2022 profit margin of 65 percent was over *four times* the mining industry average of 15 percent.[15]

Governments of exporting countries like Chile likewise benefit from high prices—as do their societies, potentially, depending on the terms of the country's contracts with multinational mining companies and the uses to which the state puts the resource rents. But after any boom is an eventual bust, and producer countries' vulnerability to market fluctuations can mean budget austerity and social suffering in times of low prices. For precisely this reason, many Global South governments with significant deposits of transition-related minerals are attempting "downstreaming": linking their raw material sectors to higher-value, and more economically stable, nodes on the supply chain, such as processing and manufacturing.

Those who purchase lithium, meanwhile, have an obvious and

opposing interest in cheaper raw materials. Given that the vast majority of lithium is destined for batteries that power passenger EVs, the most relevant downstream sector is the auto industry. The automotive sector has in recent years been buffeted by a variety of supply chain woes, from semiconductor shortages to record shipping costs. But for EVs in particular, batteries are the most expensive component. In the words of energy analyst Ahmed Mehdi, "raw material price volatility can make or break battery economics."[16]

During the lithium surge of 2022–2023, prices got so high that battery producers explored substitutes. The costly lithium that Albemarle executive Eric Norris framed as essential to attracting investment instead drove manufacturers to explore cheaper battery chemistries. Some of these recipes, such as one involving lithium iron phosphate, still include lithium, but they eliminate the need for costly nickel and cobalt inputs. Another set of options scraps lithium altogether, with sodium as the top contender among these. Chinese firms are again taking the lead in innovation. In October 2024, CATL revealed a new sodium-lithium battery pack; Chery, an automaker owned by the municipal government in Wuhu, its first customer.[17] This "hybrid" battery optimizes across multiple parameters, taking advantage of sodium's affordability and lithium's energy density.[18] BYD, the world's largest EV company, likewise has reported progress in diversifying away from lithium, with an initial foray into sodium batteries for stationary storage on energy grids.[19]

This is what economists call "demand destruction": when demand for a good, in this case, lithium, falls in response to persistent high prices. But car manufacturers are generally not yet ready to give up on lithium, which they still prefer for powering EVs.[20] And ironically, two years of declining prices for lithium, and thus for lithium batteries, have now called sodium substitution plans into question.[21]

Amid all this market turbulence, some car companies are reviving an old approach: vertical integration. In January 2023, General Motors invested $650 million in Lithium Americas to help develop the

Thacker Pass project in exchange for "exclusive access" to the mine's phase 1 production and the "right of first offer" to phase 2 production.[22] In October 2024, GM deepened its relationship with the lithium miner, establishing a joint venture that gives the car company a direct ownership stake in Thacker Pass.[23]

These moves escalated a trend that had been a few years in the making, with automakers taking increasingly aggressive moves to secure their lithium supply. Their tactics ranged from establishing long-term offtake agreements with lithium companies to direct equity investments in mining projects.[24] Automakers engaging in these practices hope to ensure their access to minerals and to reduce their exposure to the volatilities of commodities markets, even as they tie their fates more closely to the output of specific mines.

The return of vertical integration is a curious development. For decades, major multinational corporations have focused on untangling their core operations from the mines, mills, and feeder factors gobbled up by their predecessors. The approach feels like a throwback, harkening back to Henry Ford's investments in steel mills and coal mines to supply the raw materials for his sprawling auto empire. The extractive inputs of the energy transition pose a potent challenge to the economic logic of free trade, globalization, and spatially dispersed supply chains.

While financial institutions seek to render lithium a tradable, homogeneous commodity, both buyers and sellers cling to specificities: customized battery chemistries; secure, exclusive supply streams; and sustainable lithium, shorn of any associations with conflict or contamination.

Lithium branded as sustainable offers benefits to buyers and sellers. For battery and EV makers, virtuous inputs buttress reputational capital. For mining companies, claims to corporate responsibility can command a "green premium" for their product. Financial institutions are taking notice. Benchmark Minerals, the top price reporting agency for battery metals, now publishes a separate "sustainable lithium" price, which uses an index of seventy-nine indicators to calculate the going rate for ESG-friendly lithium.[25] Similarly, by issuing "green bonds," lithium companies like SQM and Livent have accessed loans on more favorable terms.[26] Investors who purchase such bonds accept lower interest rates in exchange for greening—or greenwashing—their portfolios. In this arrangement, lithium firms claim to be "green" because their product is an input for electric mobility—even though the loans are used to finance resource extraction, with all the environmental harms that can entail.

In so many ways, then, the lithium sector and the battery and EV production it enables have become a laboratory for the possibility of capitalism without carbon. Green capitalism transforms sustainability from an ethical sensibility to a valuable asset. To understand how this has happened, let's go back to Santiago in June 2019, where lithium entrepreneurs had gathered to chart their course toward a still uncertain future.

AS I SAT AND LISTENED TO LITHIUM CAPITALISTS SAY, ONE AFTER the other, that lithium is no ordinary commodity, I began to think there was more at stake than market control or proprietary information—something more philosophical, or existential. Lithium, they seemed to say, was not tainted like other extractive commodities, with their myriad associations with water contamination, human rights violations, and military coups. In fact, lithium was not an earthly matter at all, but a lofty chemical, calling to mind a pristine laboratory setting rather than an enormous open pit, rickety piles of sludgy tailings, or the toxic sublime of multicolored evaporation ponds that mar the salt flat of the world's driest and oldest desert.

In the shared imagination of the lithium industry, lithium was not some base industrial metal. No. Lithium was a critical ingredient in the clean technologies that would enable a zero-carbon economy, one of so many "sustainable economy materials," per Tesla's savvy neologism. What I sensed was an anxiety about whether and how to repackage extraction as an environmentally friendly endeavor. In other words: Could mining be green? The implications extended to the entire global economy. If mining is an exceptionally destructive activity, then the prospect of benign extraction offered hope for a truly green capitalism.

"Sustainable sourcing" is now an industry mantra across the EV supply chain. It's nothing new for corporations to (claim to) address social and environmental concerns about the impacts of their products as a way to protect their brands. But the EV market has another wrinkle. Consumers who purchase EVs are responding to public policies that encourage them to switch from traditional internal combustion engine vehicles, with the ultimate goal of meeting zero-emissions targets. The entire point of electrifying transportation is to eliminate fossil fuels from the sector. As a privileged tool in the climate action tool kit, EVs are imbued with an aura of virtuous consumption. When you go electric, you are buying a product that helps save the planet. Such green consumers might think twice about purchasing an EV if its battery materials were tainted with allegations of toxic pollution or forced labor.

This, at least, is what industry representatives and observers want to talk about when I ask them about automakers' increasing attention to "sustainable sourcing" as they embark on electrifying their fleets. Just as noteworthy is that the mining companies are making similar commitments—promising, in effect, to clean up their own act. While mining companies have long been concerned about local perceptions of their operations and have developed a sophisticated set of tactics to mitigate local protest, it is a newer phenomenon for these firms to broadcast their green and ethical bona fides to audiences far from the sites of extraction. The parallel pivots in the auto and mining industries are related. As auto companies signal their preference for "sustainably sourced" metals, mining companies compete with one another to project the image most compatible with EV makers' efforts to appeal to green consumers, investors, and regulators.

This complex interplay between sustainability and corporate competition is a quintessential example of what political economist Stefano Ponte calls "green capital accumulation."[27] In this dynamic, companies' strategic management of sustainability has become a means of increasing their market power and, ultimately, their profits. Lead firms—in this case, consumer-facing multinationals like car companies—are more concerned about reputation than are their suppliers, who tend to be much less publicly visible. At the same time, lead firms have leverage over their suppliers. They have the power to force the firms they purchase materials or components from to take sustainability seriously—or at least look like they are—and absorb the costs that that entails. Hence the proliferation of mining companies boldly promising to meet climate targets, reduce water use, embrace the circular economy, and more directly engage Indigenous leaders and organizations.

As car companies exert more control over their supply chains, they are also directly investing in sustainability initiatives in novel ways. Volkswagen organized a visit to the Atacama Salt Flat to investigate mounting concerns about water use.[28] BMW commissioned a team of scientists to study the same and to propose new sustainable extraction techniques.[29] Mercedes-Benz, BMW, and VW published a suite of statements touting their practices and assuring the public of their sincere interest in sustainability and ethics.[30] In language indistinguishable from that of global advocacy campaigns, VW announced: "The raw materials for our electric batteries must be extracted under sustainable conditions. We must therefore do everything possible to ensure that the extraction of lithium does not harm people or nature."[31]

THESE SECTOR-WIDE SHIFTS IN CORPORATE STRATEGY SURFACE IN individual lives. Franziska Killiches leads the Raw Materials and

Environment Team in Volkswagen's Sustainability Management Department, the latest iteration of a position she has held at the European auto giant since 2019. A glance at her résumé reveals valuable experience in various German government entities, all related to the thorny policy area of extractive industries.[32] A classic case of the "revolving door" from the public to the private sector, she arrived at Volkswagen equipped with an insider's view of strategic state agencies.

Less than a year after she was hired by Volkswagen, Killiches found herself on a twenty-hour journey from Wolfsburg, the company's headquarters, to the northern reaches of Chile.[33] "The ground is hard as stone. Every drop of water evaporates immediately," she observed, a "first impression" of the Atacama Desert that is as old as Europeans' initial encounters with the landscape nearly five hundred years ago.[34] Killiches had arrived with a clear mission: to paint "our own picture" of the lithium that is mined in Chile before making its way into her company's car batteries. For Volkswagen, such firsthand scrutiny was now essential. Scientific research, NGO reports, and media coverage had drawn attention to lithium's impact on the desert's fragile water system. The "accusation" was crystal clear.[35] But was there "anything to it"?[36]

Lithium is just one of a growing number of high-risk raw materials that get special attention from Volkswagen.[37] From cobalt to cotton, the company assesses the "probability and severity of human rights and environmental risks" of specific inputs alongside the more vaguely defined risks associated with their particular country of origin. Assessing risks is, by nature, an exercise in comparisons. Analysts conjure a murky spectrum of far-flung locales, each more or less dangerous for the humans who live there—and more or less threatening to the reputations and the profits of the corporations that do business in them.

The exercise of assessment is complicated by the structure of global supply chains. As of 2024, when Volkswagen's most recent

"Responsible Raw Materials Report" was published, the corporation "did not directly source any battery raw materials" and instead purchased battery cells "from suppliers which are themselves up to several supply chain steps away from the raw material origin."[38] More precisely, as Killiches explained in an interview with the Swiss-German newspaper *Der Bund*, mining occurs "up to nine supply chain steps" away.[39]

Volkswagen's long supply chains illustrate a more general reality. For decades, major corporations have sought materials that they could buy reliably and at low cost. In the process, they have created multilevel networks of upstream extractive, processing, and manufacturing suppliers that span the globe. The very complexity of these networks creates zones of opacity, shrouding the links between corporations with recognizable brand names headquartered in the Global North and the relatively obscure mining companies operating along the peripheries of the world economy. This opacity has long benefited executives and investors. But today, in a world of new reputational risks and volatile geopolitics, these same corporations aim to "shed light," as Killiches put it in the same interview, on the darkness.[40] Hence her "fact-finding expedition" to the "lithium desert" of Chile.[41]

The expedition was just one example of Volkswagen's evolving tool kit of risk mitigation techniques. For supplier firms, these include a contractually obligatory code of conduct, "sustainability training and workshops," and audits, buttressed by a "supply chain grievance mechanism" for corporate whistleblowers or affected community members to share allegations directly with the auto group for further investigation.[42] But with suppliers operating in tens of thousands of discrete locations, such tools are inevitably limited. The surest way to reduce risk is to rein in the sprawl of raw material suppliers.

Volkswagen has made its first move to source lithium directly, signing a contract for the "environmentally friendly lithium" that Vulcan Energy Resources aims to produce from its brine deposit in Germany's Upper Rhine Valley. The move ensures the car company at least five years' worth of supply beginning in 2026, when the mining project is planning to enter commercial-scale production.[43]

Volkswagen was the third automaker, after Stellantis and Renault, to strike a deal with Vulcan. The company uses a direct lithium extraction (DLE) method to filter lithium out of geothermal brine, ultimately producing, they claim, a "Zero Carbon Lithium" that "harness[es] renewable geothermal energy to drive lithium production, without using evaporation ponds, mining or fossil fuels" in its operations.[44] Beyond the promise of green mining, Vulcan offers European carmakers geographic proximity in a world of geoeconomic realignments, facilitating Volkswagen's efforts to build a European supply chain from mine to factory—a goal that dovetails neatly with the European Union's onshoring ambitions. Geoeconomics does, however, sometimes collide with geopolitics: In late 2022, Volkswagen was forced to delay its plans to construct six battery plants by 2030 because of the spike in energy prices, and therefore operating costs, caused by Russia's invasion of Ukraine.[45]

For the time being, then, Volkswagen remains dependent on lithium—and many other materials—sourced from around the world. Which brings us back to the Atacama, where the company's efforts to assess the precise reputational risk posed by lithium's impact on water have been bedeviled by our now familiar culprit: the lack of a "consistent hydrological model."[46]

Just like Chilean regulators, Atacameño community leaders, and environmental activists, Volkswagen saw the absence of a coordinated water management and monitoring system as a major source of the problem. But unlike these critics, the company did not look to the Chilean state as the agent to fill the vacuum of governance. Instead, corporate managers have faith in the power of corporate responsibility. Specifically, Killiches and Volkswagen are hanging their hopes on the Responsible Lithium Partnership, a voluntary, multi-stakeholder initiative that "seeks to promote sustainable development and improved natural resource management" in the Atacama.[47] The partnership was convened by the German government's development agency, GIZ—where Killiches had worked for over three years[48]—and funded by Volkswagen, Mercedes Benz, the chemicals giant BASF, and Fairphone, a mission-driven cell phone company using "fair and recycled materials."[49]

As I later learned in interviews with GIZ officials, the partnership was a true collaboration between the German government and multinational corporations, who shared a "worry" about lithium, a "high-priority" raw material that was also the site of local conflict and dueling social perceptions in Chile.[50] On the surface, this was mining—and capitalism—at its greenest and most ethical, optimizing not only its own operations but also compensating for the severe deficit in state capacity. Or at least that was the image the partnership sought to portray.

A key question for participants and critics alike is whether an effort coordinated by a German government agency and financed by the corporations that ultimately purchase the lithium simply reproduces the pattern of privatized governance that prevails in extractive zones like the Atacama. As GIZ's on-site official told me, in that desert region there is a "strong and constant" level of contact between mining companies and communities—a material reality that itself has caused "internal divisions" in the social fabric. For this official, the multi-stakeholder approach is different and potentially better because "everyone has a voice." The partnership isn't pegged to a specific mine, the official emphasized, but rather addresses the "cross-cutting theme" of water management.[51]

In my conversations with corporate staff and agency officials, I had a strong sense of an earnest mission. They seemed to truly believe in their employers' professed benevolence, even showing enthusiasm for their role in helping car companies responsibly produce a consumer good now enlisted in the fight against climate change. But as soon as sustainability becomes essential to corporate branding, it loses its ethical or environmental meaning. Instead, it becomes a commodity, bought and sold on the market like any other.

A MENAGERIE OF RISK CONSULTANTS, SUSTAINABILITY ANALYSTS, and industry certification agencies now offer their services to extractive, battery, and auto firms that seek a competitive edge in "responsible mining." Green and ethical branding, in other words, has itself generated a market opportunity for all manner of entrepreneurs.

Take Harrison Mitchell, who in 2008 had the prescience to cofound RCS Global, a "proven leader in data-driven ESG performance" that envisions "a world where natural resources are produced, traded, and transformed in a way that generates sustainable positive impacts on people and planet."[52] The company retains twenty-nine employees in its Better Mining team alone and consults for eight of the top ten auto giants, as well as mining, battery, and electronics companies. Before moving into the consulting market, Mitchell worked for Global Witness, a large international NGO that campaigns against human rights violations and environmental degradation, particularly in extractive sectors.[53] This background gives him special—and quite valuable—insight into the movements targeting mining companies.

I encountered Mitchell in late 2020 at another iteration of the Lithium Supply & Markets Conference, where he was leading a panel on "Responsible Sourcing of Lithium."[54] I was immediately impressed by his granular knowledge of global advocacy—and savvy ability to draw connections between the world of do-gooders and that of profit-seeking corporations. Mitchell attributed the flurry of corporate attention to sustainable sourcing to NGOs, specifically to Amnesty International's 2019 call for the production of "ethical" batteries within five years. The challenge built on Amnesty International's 2016 report with the NGO Afrewatch, "This is What We Die For," which exposed horrific human rights abuses in the cobalt mines of the Democratic Republic of Congo (DRC) that provided crucial raw materials for cell phone and EV batteries.[55] While the underlying report primarily focused on addressing human rights abuses in the DRC, it also alluded to violations of Indigenous rights in Latin America and the emissions of coal-powered battery plants in East Asia—realities that could "undermine [the] green potential" of EVs.

Mitchell saw Amnesty's statements and reports as emblematic of broader trends in the politics of extraction, with lithium as the next "big focus."[56] He described how "responsible sourcing" concerns tended to diffuse from one extractive node to another, potentially encompassing "fifteen to twenty raw materials." At the 2020 meeting, Mitchell warned attendees about the inevitability of more stringent regulation, citing the EU as the vanguard (the body's Sustainable Battery Regulation was released two months later and adopted in 2023). And he noted the increasingly vocal concerns of investors and customers, who in turn were encouraged by the "media environment." The result was a "trend ... in one direction ... more scrutiny on supply chains, sustainability, and responsibility." All of that, of course, also meant more clients for outfits like RCS Global, a firm poised to help legacy auto companies and mining multinationals adopt better practices—or, at the very least, protect their reputations.

RCS Global itself operates in an increasingly competitive market. While firms operating along the EV supply chain try to outdo one another on the terrain of sustainable sourcing, consultants and certifiers likewise rival one another, promising ever-more rigorous forms of analysis and auditing that will ultimately increase their clients' reputational capital. The entity that has commanded the most respect from journalists, academics, and NGO professionals is the Initiative for Responsible Mining Assurance (usually referred to by its acronym, IRMA).[57] Indeed, RCS Global helps its clients align their operations with IRMA's standards, ostensibly to prepare for an eventual audit by one of IRMA's two licensed auditing firms.

IRMA's credentials rest in part on those of its executive director, Aimee Boulanger. Before joining the initiative over a decade ago, Boulanger spent many years in the world of NGOs like Sierra Club and Earthworks. She described her work in these organizations as "classic community organizing."[58] She supported directly affected communities in their efforts to resist extractive capitalism, whether they were "fighting a new mine" or calling attention to "water issues at an existing mine." This experience was crucial to her first major challenge when she was hired as an IRMA staff member: "building trust." As Boulanger noted, it was hard enough to establish trust between the "Big Greens" (mainstream, professionalized environmental NGOs, often headquartered in Washington, DC) and frontline communities—let alone between the latter and the mining companies they were so often in conflict with. For these reasons, the "multi-stakeholder" model at the heart of IRMA—wherein representatives of multinational corporations, environmental advocacy organizations, and directly affected groups dialogue directly with one another to develop a shared standard for responsible mining—took "years" to build. It remains the subject of some controversy in activist circles.

IRMA was founded in 2006, well before energy transition metals became a salient policy issue. As Boulanger explained in our conversation, its origins instead lie in an earlier moment of attention to global supply chains: the problem of so-called "blood diamonds," or more generally "conflict resources," that emerged during a series of civil wars across West Africa beginning in the 1990s.[59] In 1998, the UN Security Council adopted Resolution 1173, which sanctioned the Angolan political party UNITA for its use of diamonds to finance the country's civil war.[60] It was in this context that the CEO of Tiffany's approached Earthworks with a counterintuitive request. He wanted the environmental NGO to hold him and his company accountable and to help the firm identify "responsible" diamond suppliers. Earthworks declined, as it didn't have the in-house capacity to develop a list of "green clean mines" or to audit the sourcing decisions of end-use buyers. But the organization continued to work closely with Tiffany's to establish just such an entity.[61] Hence, IRMA.

While IRMA initially focused on the jewelry sector, by 2016 it had moved into personal electronics and, later, electric mobility. Echoing Mitchell's genealogy of sustainable lithium sourcing, Boulanger identified Amnesty International's 2016 report on Congolese cobalt as a turning point for expanding IRMA's mission. Once again, the move was driven by a query from a consumer-facing lead firm: "When that report came out, Microsoft called us." Today, IRMA works with corporations across the EV supply chain, with members including lithium miners like Albemarle, SQM, and Livent (with others, such as Lithium Americas Corporation and Piedmont Lithium, currently awaiting full approval) as well as downstream companies, such as BMW, Ford, GM, Mercedes-Benz, Tesla, and Volkswagen. BMW, the first automaker to join the group, additionally had a representative on IRMA's member-elected board, the organization's main governance body, from 2020 to 2024 (its slot is now occupied by a representative of Mercedes Benz).[62]

IRMA finds it necessary to clarify what membership in its organization does *not* mean: "an endorsement of the company," "that a mine has achieved a specific score," or "that a purchaser has sourced materials from IRMA-assessed mines."[63] These clarifications betray an understanding that firms do, in fact, frame their membership in IRMA as itself an indication of responsible practices and, implicitly, a sign of IRMA's "endorsement."

The slippage between membership and endorsement is, perhaps inadvertently, encouraged by the organization's own website, which includes a map of all "stakeholders" at some stage of an IRMA audit. When I first stumbled upon this map in January of 2022, it was called the Responsible Mining Map.[64] I noticed that it included SQM's lithium mine on the Atacama Salt Flat. The mine earned its place on the map because an IRMA-approved auditing outfit had begun its third-party assessment of the mine's operations. But considering everything I had learned about SQM, I was surprised to find it listed on a map of responsible mines. Given the preponderance of political corruption, financial fraud, contract violations, regulatory interventions, environmental lawsuits, and grassroots protests associated with the firm, labeling its Atacama project "responsible" struck me as—at the very least—questionable. A year later, the map's name had been changed to the more value-neutral Engagement Map—perhaps a tacit admission on the part of IRMA that labeling a mine "responsible" before its audit had been completed was inappropriate.

These terminological slippages provided copious marketing opportunities for SQM. From the very moment SQM joined IRMA in August 2021—several months before any assessment had commenced and when its membership was still listed as "pending"—SQM went on a public relations blitz, boasting that it would be the "first" lithium company to subject itself to IRMA.[65] (In fact, Albemarle, its corporate neighbor on the same salt flat, had initiated IRMA certification almost a year prior.[66]) SQM devotes multiple pages of its website to IRMA and has wasted no opportunity to mention its participation in the audit.

This is how industry accumulates green capital. Mining firms leverage the mere announcement of their intent to participate in a voluntary certification initiative as evidence of the sustainability of their operations. Such announcements send a signal to shareholders, civil society, regulators, and, perhaps most importantly, the powerful corporations downstream of extraction. Certifications are in turn feeding into contract negotiations between lithium companies, battery makers, and EV firms—and could one day merit a separate futures market for "green lithium."[67]

But what does it mean, concretely, for a company to take part in a voluntary sustainability assessment? Organizations like IRMA perform a difficult balancing act. On the one hand, if the barriers to certification are too high, mining firms will not participate. On the other hand, if they are too low, noncorporate stakeholders—in this case, frontline, labor, and advocacy groups—may sound the alarm about greenwashing. And there are further complications. Mining companies like SQM and the consumer-facing lead firms who purchase mined products, whether Tesla or Tiffany's, hope to achieve different things with their certification. Consumer-facing firms want the strongest possible protection from reputational damage. In theory, they might prefer to receive an audit that reveals "irresponsible" practices like the use of child labor or the failure to consult Indigenous communities over one that papers over such harms, only to have them surface later in the media or an NGO campaign. The actual mining companies, in contrast, want to achieve the highest possible score—period. Reports of violations would not only provide fodder for activist critics, but also potentially scare off potential corporate purchasers.

These tensions are evident in IRMA's increasingly stringent requirements for corporate membership. When IRMA first opened for membership in 2019, the protocols only required that participating entities engage in a "dialogue" with the organization's other stakeholders.[68] But less than a year later, corporations "had to commit to an audit within one year"; they would be listed as "pending" until the audit commenced. Boulanger explained that IRMA tightened its requirements because of the "concern raised by the NGO Labor and Community Sectors" that membership could be "construed as commitment to independent audit" even if no such commitment had been made.

In January 2022, the organization tightened membership requirements further.[69] Companies directly involved in mining are now required to have completed at least one full audit of at least one of their mines and to have attained a score of at least 50 out of 100. If the company owns multiple mining assets, it must promise to have other sites audited within a specified time frame. The membership requirements for downstream mineral purchasers and financiers remain relatively vague. They must "*agree to encourage* mining companies to engage in IRMA" and "*communicate an interest* in sourcing materials from, or investing in, mines independently audited in the IRMA system" (emphasis added).[70]

As it happens, SQM cleared the benchmark for membership. In September 2023, the company's Atacama mine received a score of 75, which, as their press release proudly noted, is "the highest rating delivered to date." The company received positive marks for labor conditions, biodiversity protection, community support, and managing noise pollution—and lower marks for security arrangements, emergency preparedness, and free, prior, and informed consent of Indigenous peoples.

The site visit that formed the basis for SQM's audit lasted just four days.[71] Auditors spoke to only eight members of nearby Indigenous communities, hailing from just four of the eighteen communities bordering the salt flat, obviously a limited sample. Indeed, representatives of Peine, one of those four communities, explicitly declined to participate.[72] It's noteworthy that ERM conducted no interviews with environmental activists, civil society advocates, or organizers of independent workers' unions.[73] The report itself, lengthy as it is, relies heavily on SQM's self-reporting. The section on water management, one of the most contentious issues in the Atacama Desert, favorably refers more than once to the company's self-monitoring systems, but, and this is hardly surprising, it makes no mention of past revelations that the firm tampered with freshwater monitoring systems or overextracted brine.[74]

※

IRMA'S ASSESSMENT PROTOCOL IS THE STRICTEST ON THE MARKET. As Boulanger emphasized to me, no firm has ever achieved the highest score, IRMA 100, and only a handful of the world's mines have undergone the full independent auditing and public reporting.[75] Whether IRMA's willingness to issue its highest-ever rating to SQM should be read as a condemnation of the state of extractive sectors worldwide or of the green certification industry itself is an open question. Either way, the initiative's limitations reveal a deficit of binding, democratically accountable governance over resource extraction. Boulanger herself told me that "improved laws in all countries" would be preferable to voluntary initiatives.[76] But in the meantime, she emphasized, "there isn't a country in the world with laws sufficient to prevent significant harm where mining happens." In this fallen world, IRMA's defenders argue that it serves as a "template for building best practices into those legal frameworks."[77]

In theory, such best practices would involve continually monitoring extractive industries for their social and environmental harms or for their violations of national law or contractual requirements. But there is a vexing paradox at the heart of this theory of change. It is equally plausible that the existence of IRMA, and the respect the initiative has garnered in corporate, policy, and even some advocacy circles, will defer the sense of urgency surrounding enforceable laws and regulations. As a tool of "social engineering," this form of voluntary, reputation-based corporate regulation may also dampen the more militant forms of social mobilization that push governments to undertake more robust reforms in the first place.[78]

A crucial question for evaluating green capitalism, then, is whether the growing universe of voluntary, multi-stakeholder governance organizations is a second-best, temporary substitute that catalyzes states to adopt more stringent regulations, or whether these initiatives replace the state as governments in effect delegate their authority to certification outfits, corporate associations, and industry consultants.[79] In fact, states have many reasons to prefer the latter approach to reforming their own mining codes, a process that carries significant bureaucratic and political costs.

In my off-the-record conversations with officials in the Biden administration, as well as members of US Congress, it was apparent that they saw IRMA as a potential shortcut to circumvent the daunting congressional gridlock and industry pressure that has stood in the way of reforming the 1872 Mining Law. More than one of them floated the possibility of recommending or requiring IRMA assessments for mines that receive some form of government financing. Meanwhile, in Europe, officials were working with another outfit,

CERA (Certification of Raw Materials), that offers a blockchain-based "universal" certification initiative for all mining sectors and at "every stage of the value chain."[80]

The governance of mining stands at a critical juncture. Private-sector certification could provide a template for public regulation. Alternatively, precisely because it hits a sweet spot of addressing social concerns, avoiding the "sticks" of binding laws and bypassing the legislative process, certification could emerge as a long-term solution to the gaps in extractive governance. This risk looms larger than ever. In late 2024, the world's largest mining industry associations (including the International Council on Mining and Metals) joined forces to push for the "consolidation" of four major certification schemes. In response, the NGO Public Citizen has convened a global coalition of more than twenty community, environmentalist, labor, human rights, and Indigenous groups in opposition to the industry effort.[81] In a public statement, they warned that merely combining already weak and voluntary standards is tantamount to greenwashing and will merely "quicken the race to the bottom."[82]

While industry and centrist policymakers see benefits in privatized governance, movements on the ground are pushing for more transformative, and democratically accountable, changes. These range from moratoria or bans on certain mining activities, to proposals for public or community ownership, to recognizing the rights of Indigenous peoples and nature, to holistic regulatory frameworks that consider the ecological and cultural value of landscapes alongside the mineral wealth they contain, to escaping the trap of extractive models of development altogether. And these visions are intertwined with the social mobilization that has effloresced across the extractive frontiers of global capitalism.

It is to this vibrant world of Indigenous and environmental activism that we now turn.

PART IV

BEYOND GREEN CAPITALISM

Peehee Mu'huh protest camp, Thacker Pass mine site, Nevada

CHAPTER 8

Resisting Green Extractivism

Smack in the middle of the sweltering afternoon of a historic heat wave cloaking western Europe in 2022, I meet Aida Fernandes in a surprisingly bustling small café. The café is located on what you might, with some poetic license, call the Main Street of Covas do Barroso, if only in comparison with the even narrower cobblestone streets that meander off in all directions. Inside, Fernandes's neighbors are escaping the intense temperatures by drinking cold bottles of Sagres or fighting off the sweaty doldrums with a strong coffee. Conversations are voluble and animated, punctuated by the episodic banging of the espresso machine. Nelson, Fernandes's husband, sits with one group of people at the table next to us. Another group hovers by the bar. When the chatter grows too loud for us to hear each other, we move outside. Hotter, but quieter. While we are speaking, one of Fernandes's several dogs wanders up to greet us.

Fernandes wears a wide-brimmed straw hat. Her arms are tanned from working on the farm and spending afternoons with her family by the river. Her rootedness to this part of Portugal has a material foundation: She was born and raised in Covas, but she has also been farming the land that Nelson had inherited from his father for nearly half her life. They raise cows and pigs and sell the meat to local butchers; they eat the rest of what they grow, an impressive array that typically includes maize, potatoes, beans, and seasonal vegetables. This form of small-scale agriculture is in keeping with the foodways of the northern reaches of the country. As more than one banner I saw throughout my visit proudly proclaimed, the region was among the first in Europe that the United Nations recognized as a heritage agricultural site, specifically citing its "agro-sylvo-pastoral" farming style that integrates cropland into forests.[1]

It is this place-based livelihood and the social relations it supports that Fernandes fears is directly threatened by Savannah Resources' plan to open a 2½-square-mile open-pit lithium mine. The mine would be sited on the mountain just across the Covas River from the main part of the village. Fernandes worries that the mine means "losing a big part of Covas. Losing the river. Losing the land."[2] Referring to my visit, she said "Now you come and see just mountains; after you go, you will see one big mine." It isn't just the physical footprint of the transformation that frightens her. It's the permanent, irrevocable fact of Covas being converted into an extraction site: "For me, the biggest scare is it could change forever. The landscape. They'll destroy the water. Things will never be the same. And not for better."

In her view, the mine and her farm, the mine and her community, are incompatible. Only one can prevail.

THE EUROPEAN UNION'S POLICIES TO PROMOTE ONSHORING HAVE opened up a new transnational lithium frontier in southern Europe, stretching from the austere expanses of Extremadura—Spain's poorest region, with a violent history steeped in the conquest of Muslims and of Indigenous peoples across the Americas—to Galicia, with its snowcapped peaks and rugged coast—and across the border to northern Portugal. In Cáceres, Spain, where a medieval city forms a testament to the area's Moorish and Roman past, one frequently encounters the *"No a la mina"* sentiment, whether in the form of posters distributed by the local group Save the Mountain or conversations like the one I had with Rosaura, a server at a café just off the main plaza. She described the region in which she was born and raised as being reduced to a "zone of exploitation" where valuable resources are removed to be sold elsewhere, leaving a trail of poverty. In Galicia, I saw the telltale *"Non á mina"* placards taped to the window of a humble neighborhood café.³ But it was just over the border, in the neighboring northern Portuguese municipalities of Montalegre and Boticas, where the village Covas do Barroso is located, that I saw antimining posters everywhere I went: *"Não à mina sim à vida"* (No to the mine/ yes to life); *"Não minas o teu futuro"* (Don't mine your future); *"Agua e vida: não queremos perder a nossa"* (Water and life/ we don't want to lose ours).

Fernandes is one of the leaders of a group opposing the Mina do Barroso lithium project. As such, she is one member of a loosely knit, global front of resistance: a cross-border and multi-scalar patchwork of frontline organizations, transnational networks, and advocacy NGOs who are stalling the grinding expansion of the planetary mine.⁴ Other land-intensive and contaminating sectors—fossil fuels, agribusiness, logging—have increasingly encountered similar opposition. Resisting such projects means confronting multinational corporations, global investors, and powerful states. The perils of doing so are substantial. Across the globe, "land and environmental defenders" risk untimely death for simply airing grievances, attending activist meetings, and engaging in peaceful protest.⁵ And the mining sector is by far the worst offender: Of the nearly two hundred environmental defenders killed in 2023, twenty-five were slain for opposing mining projects (the logging industry came in second, accounting for five murders).⁶ And as multiple advocates told me, this is in all likelihood an undercount.

The movement against mining has been particularly strong in Latin America, where for over two decades corporations' attempts to open new iron ore, copper, and gold projects have increasingly met lockstep opposition. Latin American activists, especially those among the region's Indigenous and environmentalist movements, have developed a name for what they see as a model of economic development rooted in colonial conquest but now operating at unprecedented spatial and market scale: *extractivism*.[7] More recently, as lithium projects have expanded across the Andes and into Brazil and Mexico, and as copper giants repackaged themselves as climate saviors, this loosely networked movement took on a new target: *green* extractivism. Hailed by extraction's defenders as providing critical inputs for the energy transition, its opponents describe this style of mining as a greenwashed form of dispossession and contamination.

More and more, though, I hear echoes of grievances I first encountered over a decade ago—in my research on conflicts between communities and mining companies in the Andean highlands and Amazonian lowlands—in locales far removed from Latin America. Whether in villages in the Atacama, cafés in Covas, or Indigenous reservations in Nevada, anti-mining activists tell me similar stories of their attempts to counter the power of transnational corporations who claim to be solving the climate crisis or protecting the national interest. As I traveled from Chile to northern Portugal to the US Southwest, a geography distinct from the familiar map of nation-states began to shift into focus, revealing more in common than first meets the eye. These are the extractive frontiers of green capitalism, and they are multiplying.

The strategies that governments and corporations have embraced to manage their supply chain risks have generated their own frictions. As I moved from one planetary periphery to another, I witnessed the stirrings of a force that held the potential to challenge powerful states and firms. Protests against lithium mining are pushing open the boundaries of climate politics, revealing tensions within environmental movements. Most ambitiously, these protests call for an energy transition with global supply chain justice at its heart.

Ultimately, anti-extractive activists are forcing us to address an uncomfortable, but necessary, question: What does it mean to defend people and the planet from extraction—when others frame this same extraction as necessary to save people and the planet?

><====><

ANTI-EXTRACTIVE MOVEMENTS CONSTANTLY INVOKE THE INCOM-patibility of mining and life. The global network to which United in Defense of Covas do Barroso, the organization Fernandes helped establish, belongs, is called Yes to Life, No to Mining. Mining versus life: It sounds abstract, even philosophical. But from the Atacama Desert to Covas to Nevada, the invocation is rooted in quite practical concerns about water consumption, access to land, and the uneasy relationship between extractive industries and place-based sectors like agriculture or tourism. Locales where movements against mining form share such "water-reliant livelihoods."[8] An analysis of EJAtlas, a global database of environmental conflicts, reveals concerns about water degradation to be at stake in the vast majority of such disputes.[9]

But a reliance on water alone can't account for the intensity of specific mining conflicts or explain why some communities rise up to resist and others do not.[10] Opposition movements are pervasive in both arid and wetter regions, with fears of the sector's consumption and contamination prevailing in each, respectively.[11] What makes water a flash point for conflict is its social, political, and cultural context. Affected communities are more likely to engage in high-intensity mobilization campaigns against mining projects when they imbue water with specific meaning and, crucially, when they are not substantively consulted about mining plans.

The Thacker Pass project in northern Nevada has all the characteristics to produce a perfect storm of intense local opposition. Nevada, like the rest of the southwestern United States, has seen historic drought conditions, setting the stage for competing claims to an increasingly scarce resource. Vulnerable habitats overlap with and border the potential lithium mine, and many area residents make their living in the water-reliant ranching and agricultural sectors. The proposed mine additionally intersects with the unceded traditional lands of the Northern Paiute and Western Shoshone peoples, including the site of a mid-nineteenth-century massacre by the US calvary and locations for holding ceremonies and gathering medicinal plants.[12] The Indigenous activists I spoke with described a tribal consultation process they viewed as vastly inadequate given the mine's potential impacts. The lack of substantive engagement with tribal members' concerns stirred painful collective memories, recounted across generations, of centuries of violence, extraction, and environmental harm at the hands of US government agencies, settler colonists, and corporations.

The energy transition is not a peaceful bridge between fossil fuels and renewable energy, but a crucible where past, present, and possible futures collide. My journey to Thacker Pass took me through a landscape that surfaced these simultaneous timelines. I began in Las Vegas, where I immersed myself in the world of green capital, attending the 13th Annual Lithium Supply & Markets Conference in a casino on the strip. Next was a night in Goldfield, an appropriately named outpost of Nevada's early twentieth-century gold mining boom, now rehabilitated as a kitschy ghost town made spookier by the absence of any visitors amid a global pandemic. The following morning, I set out for Rhyolite Ridge, in the Silver Peak Range in the state's southwest, where Australian company Ioneer has proposed a mine that has occasioned a zero-sum conflict between lithium and a wildflower. Reno, my next stop, is home base for Great Basin Resource Watch (GBRW), an environmental group working in alliance with Indigenous organizations and tribes to oppose Thacker Pass.

Surreal sights punctuated my trip north. Immense white playas floated atop the Great Basin, the remnants of an ancient sea that covers hundreds of thousands of miles of the western United States and Mexico. There were the austere peaks of the Wassuk Range followed by the towering dune of Sand Mountain, beige and bright at the same time, and the menacing arc that futuristic black planes traced overhead as I passed the Fallon Naval Air Station. In Reno, I visited the Silver Legacy Casino, which featured a soaring, life-size re-creation of a silver mine shaft that wrested imaginary metals from the earth. Unlike actual mining equipment, this one featured shiny lights and music. Everywhere I went, I saw extraction: the history of it, the reality of it, the potentiality of it, and the jangly, carnivalesque sound of it.

In Reno, I met John Hadder in GBRW's cramped offices. The walls were adorned with hydrological maps and posters featuring the Dann sisters, Western Shoshone leaders who had organized to reclaim their people's land from the Bureau of Land Management to protect it from the harms of nuclear testing. Tall, broad, with serious eyes, an easy laugh, and long gray hair pulled back in a ponytail, Hadder recounted his life's journey from inorganic chemistry to environmental activism. Like that of the Dann sisters, his path into activism included a firsthand encounter with the impacts of nuclear testing on Native communities. His background in studying natural systems had given him an appreciation for nonlinear change: A seemingly minor stream of waste can, for example, through feedback loops and threshold effects, dramatically change ecosystems and the species and livelihoods they support.[13] Hadder brings this perspective to every environmental impact statement (EIS) he reads. The devil is quite literally in the details.

GBRW has been monitoring the harms of hard rock mining since 1994. When Hadder joined the organization in 2006, he and others in what he described as the state's small environmentalist community thought that mining must surely be on its way out. The industry nevertheless kept finding new places to dig, especially for gold and silver, precious metals with toxic impacts. Now they look for places to mine "critical" metals like lithium and vanadium.

The pace and variety of new extractive projects means it's impossible for one small organization to scrutinize them all. Hadder wants me to understand, too, that GBRW isn't against extraction *tout court*—a position he doesn't see as tenable. Even so, through its work with directly affected Indigenous communities, the organization has moved closer to a generalized critique of mining and the broader system of extractive capitalism of which it is a part. Hadder spoke of an "extraction and waste mindset" that would rather tear up landscapes than find ways to systemically reduce mining. This mindset is deeply embedded in state politics. Mining occupies a privileged place in Nevada's constitution, and a revolving door between industry and the political establishment has thus far protected the sector from more robust environmental regulation and more progressive royalty and tax reforms. Indeed, the global mining sector considers Nevada the friendliest jurisdiction in the world.[14]

I asked Hadder why GBRW had decided not only to oppose the Thacker Pass mine, but also take the Bureau of Land Management to court for approving the project in the first place. Hadder detailed several interconnected concerns connected to a rushed permitting process. The mine was approved in the final months of the first Trump administration, when officials' enthusiasm for "critical minerals" projects prioritized speed over accuracy. Hadder described the project's environmental impact statement as "one of the worst" he'd ever seen.

Geophysicist Steve Emerman, a consultant who provides expert support to frontline communities facing down extractive projects, offered more detail on what made the Thacker Pass environmental statement so "slapdash" and "reckless."[15] Emerman had penned a seventy-six-page technical report for GBRW that explored a specific but crucial aspect of mine safety: how the mine will store its waste, especially the tailings left over after the economically valuable mineral is removed from surrounding ore. Tailings pose several safety risks, from groundwater contamination (mining waste may contain hazardous chemicals and/or metals) to uncontrolled discharge if the waste breaches the containment system. In 2019, 272 people were killed by an avalanche of toxic mud in Brumadinho, Brazil, when the tailings dam of the Córrego do Feijão iron ore mine failed. Although a particularly severe case in terms of its human toll, the catastrophe at Brumadinho is symptomatic of a broader pattern in which "tailings facilities ... are failing with increasing frequency and severity," according to a comprehensive report on the topic.[16]

At Thacker Pass, Emerman was dismayed at a fundamental categorical error in the Water Pollution Control Permit issued by the Nevada Division of Environmental Protection. The agency labeled the mine's waste pile a "dry stack" despite its projected 46 percent water content. Mining regulators universally consider dry waste safer than wet waste because it is less likely to seep. Per Emerman's report, Thacker Pass mine "would probably have greater water content than *any tailings storage facility ever constructed*" and twice that of a conventional facility.[17]

GBRW relied on Emerman's analysis as the basis for its legal appeal of Nevada regulators granting a Water Pollution Control Permit to Thacker Pass.[18] The state environmental commission, however, granted Lithium Nevada's motion to strike Emerman's report from the appeal record. The company argued that since the report had not been submitted during the public comment period, it could not be used now to retroactively attack the decision to grant the permit.[19]

From Hadder's perspective, the obvious limitations of Lithium America's environmental analysis were exacerbated by an inadequate process of community review. The forty-five-day review process unfolded during the summer of 2020, at the height of COVID-related shutdowns. This was a moment of extreme duress—and the public health crisis was especially severe for Native American communities, which multiple studies have shown to have the highest COVID death rate of any racial or ethnic group.[20] It was in this context that the Bureau of Land Management (BLM) shifted the usual in-person public meetings to Zoom. While videoconferencing technologies might, in theory, increase public access in geographically remote areas, the technology was new to most Americans in the summer of

2020. Their use also poses a particular challenge for rural and especially Indigenous populations like those near Thacker Pass, where rates of Internet access are startling low (27.7 percent of tribal residents lack reliable Internet).[21]

These superficial consultation procedures galvanized Indigenous leaders' resistance to the Thacker Pass project. Indeed, as researchers have found around the world, a democratic deficit is itself a frequent cause of anti-extractive protest and a feature common to "high-intensity conflict."[22] This became clear to me in my conversations with Daranda Hinkey, who cofounded the People of Red Mountain, an organization of Paiute, Western Shoshone, and Bannock peoples that emerged to protect the land where the Thacker Pass mine is now being constructed.

I met Hinkey in late September of 2021, a couple of days after my meeting with Hadder. My long journey took me north from Reno, past the mining hub of Winnemucca, to nearly the Oregon border. The baroque cragginess of Santa Rosa Peak greeted my entrance to the Fort McDermitt Paiute-Shoshone Reservation. I slowly wound my way down the reservation's primary road until I found the cozy green house Hinkey shares with her partner, who had just come home from drying cowhide, and their as-yet unnamed dog, who sported a coat like a composition notebook. At just twenty-three years old, Hinkey had emerged as a powerful voice in the movement against Thacker Pass.

Hinkey is also a direct descendant of a survivor of a massacre at Thacker Pass, called Peehee Mu'huh, meaning "rotten moon," in the Numic dialect spoken by Numu (Northern Paiute) people. The name recalls a violent conflict in which Pitt River Indians killed Numu and left their rotting corpses in the shape of a crescent. It was a second massacre that Hinkey's ancestor Ox Sam survived. On September 12, 1865, federal calvary slaughtered at least thirty-one and as many as seventy Paiute men, women, children, and elders, one of the many such massacres during the years-long genocidal "Snake War."[23] It is atop this bloody landmark that the Thacker Pass mine is sited. For the Reno-Sparks Indian Colony, one of the three tribes affected by the Thacker Pass project, Lithium Americas' plans are equivalent to "building a lithium mine over Pearl Harbor, Arlington National Cemetery, or the Gettysburg Battlefield."[24]

The land holds yet more meanings and memories. Hinkey's ancestors hid from the US military in the landscape's natural caves.[25] Paiute people use the area to collect willow branches for teepee poles, obsidian for arrowheads, and choke cherries for pudding.[26] Thacker Pass, in other words, is a site of genocide, survival, and healing.

The fight against Thacker Pass became Hinkey's calling. Having been raised "very traditionally" in a close-knit family, she subsequently combined her understanding of Paiute and Shoshone customs, medicine, and knowledge of the land with the "Western science" taught in her environmental studies program at Southern Oregon University.[27] Her father had instilled a strong attachment to place and an accompanying political militancy: "One day they're going to come for our land and you gotta be ready." The warning proved prophetic. Less than a year after Hinkey returned to the reservation, Lithium Americas submitted its environmental impact statement; six months later came the BLM's record of decision.

What Hinkey learned about the environmental impacts alarmed her. The BLM's own assessment acknowledged that the open-pit mine and its related facilities would occupy nearly 18,000 acres of public land, with a "disturbance footprint" of almost 9 square miles. The mine's extractive processes would involve chemical reagents and large quantities of water and would leave behind waste in the form of rock piles and toxic streams. Its operation would threaten wildlife, including the habitat of the greater sage grouse, a bird species already in decline. She also learned that two Oregon-based members of the fringe environmental group Deep Green Resistance had already begun protesting the plans, first with the website ProtectThackerPass.org and then with a physical encampment adjacent to the proposed mine site, erected on January 15, 2021, the day that the BLM issued its record of decision, thus clearing a key permitting hurdle.²⁸ As Hinkey conducted more research, she became aware of deep regulatory deficits. For example, she discovered that the Nevada Department of Environmental Protection hasn't denied an air or water permit once in the last twenty-five years.²⁹

In May of 2021, Hinkey helped form the People of Red Mountain, and the group erected an Indigenous resistance camp just down the hill from that of Deep Green Resistance and undertook protest actions in Reno.³⁰ Establishing the People of Red Mountain was also a direct response to a rushed public hearing process combined with the inaction of her own tribal council, which had initially entered into a project engagement agreement with Lithium Americas without full dialogue with tribal members, who, understandably, had felt excluded from the process.³¹

A couple of months after my trip to Nevada, I spoke with Gary McKinney, Hinkey's cousin, a resident of Duck Valley Indian Reservation who is also active in the People of Red Mountain. He described the virtual hearings conducted by the BLM as egregiously inadequate, pointing out the irony of government officials disseminating a Zoom link when elders in his community don't have Internet. "What about their stories?" he asked. For McKinney, if the mining company isn't "going to those elders' doors," the consultation is "invalid." Or, as Hinkey had told me: "Consultation isn't just one meeting." And, just as importantly, "Consultation is not consent."

Hinkey and McKinnon's comments echoed a concern I had often encountered during my decade of research on the front lines of extraction. Too often, consultation begins and ends with the mere provision of information from company to community—information that typically emphasizes benefits like job opportunities and economic development and downplays harms like water contamination and reduced biodiversity.³²

In contrast, international law and emerging human rights frameworks emphasize the higher bar of consent. According to International

Labor Organization Convention 169, consultations should have the "objective of achieving agreement or consent." The UN Declaration on the Rights of Indigenous Peoples contains the more robust language of consultations to "obtain... free, prior and informed consent"— verbiage often referred to by the acronym FPIC. (The United States, it is worth noting, is not a signatory to either norm.[33])

In some activist circles, however, consent represents only a limited improvement. The notion of consent still carries the association that garnering agreement is the goal; it sits uncomfortably close to the corporate mission of securing a "social license to operate."

These more radical activists demand "the right to say no." Rather than assuming a cooperative outcome, this framing explicitly retains the possibility that a community might reject a proposal—veto power, in other words. The call for the right to say no reflects the growing phenomenon of an oppositional stance to extractive projects at the local level, enacted in both verbal statements and via tactics of direct action: occupations, blockades, hunger strikes, or even physical sabotage. The increasing likelihood of outright resistance to mining, alongside fossil fuel and agribusiness development, has multiple sources, from the expansion of international rights to environmental consciousness and access to information about mining's consequences to transnational advocacy networks powered by online connections. The ever-larger global footprint of mining has exposed new communities and ecosystems around the world to the threats of large-scale extraction—and affected residents are more aware about rights, impacts, and tactics than ever before.

These realities pose challenges for the energy transition, potentially pitting communities directly affected by mining for lithium, nickel, copper, and more against advocates for a rapid shift to renewable energy—or, phrased more dramatically, against climate action. They also raise fundamental questions about democratic decision-making. Who should have the authority to decide on mining projects:

the directly affected, national majorities, or, in the context of rapid global warming, some speculative international community?[34]

Making matters more complex, mining companies are positioning themselves as climate saviors, and both corporate representatives and their political allies equate opposition to a specific mine with obstruction to climate action. Government officials, meanwhile, portray anti-extraction activists as a "threat to national security," as "human bottlenecks" blocking access to critical minerals.

Some anti-mining activists nevertheless see opportunities as well as challenges. These activists told me that they believed that transition-related mining could be different from prior extractive regimes. They see the new public awareness of supply chains as an opportunity to call attention to the harms perpetrated upstream of EV manufacturing and consumption. Likewise, the proliferation of sustainability claims by firms across the supply chain potentially provides leverage—at least symbolically—to movements that contest the green credentials of mining.

Still, tensions are simmering even within the world of climate and environmental advocacy. Groups committed to an energy transition based on electrification have at times seen any pushback to lithium mining or battery supply chains as a dangerous cause of climate delay. What's more, they worry that these kinds of critiques provide grist for the forces of climate denial. Some have even suggested that criticisms of lithium mining replicate fossil fuel industry talking points. I myself have experienced this accusation many times over the course of public speaking and writing on this topic, despite my long record of promoting a rapid, just transition to renewable energy.

Opposition to mining is now coded as NIMBY: not in my backyard. But not everyone has a backyard, figuratively or literally.

⊰⊱

FIGHTS THAT PIT ENVIRONMENTAL PRIORITIES—AND ENVIRONmental organizations—against one another are nothing new for

Patrick Donnelly, the Nevada director of the Center for Biological Diversity (CBD), a national NGO focused on protecting endangered species. We had arranged to meet in late September 2021 at a set of GPS coordinates close to Silver Peak, Nevada. The remote location was just over 11 bumpy miles from Rhyolite Ridge, where Australian company Ioneer planned to build a new open-pit lithium mine.

When I pulled up next to his white truck, I saw a dog lazing in the back seat but couldn't find Donnelly anywhere. The only humans around were two people camping on public land, their life's belongings stuffed into their car. I hadn't noticed the hot spring yet. After a few minutes, a tattooed man with a ponytail, wrap-around sunglasses, and the look of someone who has lived in the desert for a very long time emerged from its steaming waters and said, "Are you Thea?"

After he dried off, Donnelly and I caravanned to Silver Peak. On our way there, we passed the cartoonishly enormous vehicles specific to the large-scale mining industry, with wheels taller than my car. They kicked up so much dust I had to pause and let them pass before I could see well enough to continue. Silver Peak is, at the time of this writing, the only operating lithium mine in the United States. Owned by Albemarle, the same company that operates on the Atacama Salt Flat, Silver Peak is a miniature version of the firm's Chilean mine: brine extraction pumps and an array of evaporation ponds in a desert surrounded by mountains.

The two of us crunched up Rhyolite Ridge in search of a better vantage point. Along the way, we stepped on white sedimentary rocks that were once the floor of an ancient sea and are now more recognizable as a potentially valuable source of lithium and boron. This is where the small but tenacious Tiehm's buckwheat improbably grows. The plant evolved to thrive in lithium- and boron-rich soils in this mountain range. A recent, unseasonal rainfall had graced us with some prime specimens of this tiny wildflower in bloom, a pale yellow globe of petals resting atop a stem in a cluster of delicate leaves. Standing atop the lithium deposit, we had a view of every subpopulation of this endangered flower. If the Ioneer project went forward, everything in our sight would be a mine.

Donnelly's whole career had skidded along the "knife's edge of impacts related to renewable energy."[35] First it was the "solar gold rush" across the Mojave Desert, which is now home to one of the world's largest clusters of solar farms, overlapping with vulnerable habitats of creatures like the endangered desert tortoise.[36] Next was geothermal, which he referred to as "the front lines of extinction." That's because project developers often use hot springs as clues to potential geothermal energy—but these same springs are oases of organic life in the desert, zones of "super biodiversity and endemic species."[37] Donnelly showed me an example later that afternoon. We visited a hot spring that was formerly the site of an Ormat Technologies geothermal facility, now once again lush with marsh grass, a raft of ducks, and several coots—a striking waterfowl species in a tuxedo of white face and black body.

These disputes over the ecological impacts of solar and geothermal "laid the groundwork" for the ensuing battle over lithium. Fifteen years of living in the tense contradiction of renewable energy and environmental harm, all while remaining resolutely committed to fighting climate change, had given Donnelly some perspective. He acknowledged progress. During the solar rush, he said, it took "over a decade" to get the environmental impacts on the table, whereas with lithium, "straight out of the gate we are talking about these impacts." And by the time the CBD started raising alarms about the ecological impacts of Rhyolite Ridge, no other environmental groups opposed their work.

Donnelly, like Hadder, made a point of telling me that he wasn't against all lithium mines. He was intrigued by the potential for less harmful extraction techniques, such as direct lithium extraction, or DLE, which promises lower water use compared with brine evaporation (although just how much lower remains the subject of scientific debate).[38] Amid a lithium boom that he has done more than anyone else to document—his live map collating information from investor forums and state agency websites currently identifies 112 projects in the western states alone—organizations must decide where to focus their scarce resources. For Donnelly, the answer is clear: The threat of species extinction constitutes the organization's "threshold of engagement." In this case, the species happens to be Tiehm's buckwheat.

Donnelly has become enamored by the flower, a passion he has shared through the hashtag #TeamBuckwheat. He nevertheless explained to me that the plant itself is but an indicator of broader ecosystem health—and ecosystem health is essential to biodiversity, which is at a crisis point. Over a million species are at risk of disappearing over the coming decades.[39] Donnelly was emphatic: "Almost every playa in this state is covered in lithium claims," but playas, he said, "are ecosystems." I heard echoes of Chile, where activists, scientists, and regulators alike emphasize the ecological value of deserts and their complex and vulnerable water systems.

Donnelly's description of Rhyolite Ridge as a rich, diverse ecosystem is an implicit response to Ioneer's terra nullius framing of the area. In a textbook case of conjuring an extractive frontier, Ioneer describes Rhyolite Ridge as "relatively remote," in "the most sparsely populated county in Nevada," and "in uninhabited semi-arid desert."[40] Yet, other sections of the firm's promotional materials characterize the site as "easily accessible" from Nevada's major cities and California's ports, just 200 miles from Tesla's Gigafactory, and the potential beneficiary of $2 million in local stimulus funds (despite, apparently, its lack of inhabitants).

Is Rhyolite Ridge an ecosystem worth protecting or a deposit of a "critical mineral" that must be urgently extracted? The US government itself has seemed of two minds on the issue. As a direct result of the CBD's petitioning, lawsuits, and media campaigns, the US Fish and Wildlife Service (USFWS) declared Tiehms buckwheat an endangered species in December 2022, designating 910 acres of critical habitat for the flower—of which 38 percent would be threatened by Ioneer's plans.[41] But just weeks later, the BLM commenced the permitting process for the mine. According to the CBD, the two agencies, both located within the Department of the Interior, "appear to be" operating at "cross purposes."[42]

The plot continued to thicken. In January 2023, the Department of Energy awarded Ioneer a $700 million loan, contingent on the firm's completion of the environmental review process, among other technical and financial conditions.[43] But shortly after the DOE approved the loan, the BLM issued a trespass notice to the firm for transgressing the previously designated zone of critical habitat, thus violating the terms of its exploration permit. It was Donnelly, not agents from the DOE, the BLM, or the USFWS, who discovered the intrusion. He had stumbled on a "drilling staging area with a truck, water tanks, materials and explosive storage" within the boundaries of the protected lands.[44]

In the United States, as in Chile, environmental advocacy complements the often-insufficient capacities of the state. Activists like Donnelly perform a crucial public service amid a chaotic mining boom. More broadly, the seemingly contradictory government decisions on the fate of the Rhyolite Ridge project reveal the state itself to be a contested terrain, populated by bureaucrats, agencies, and politicians working to distinct ends and subject to distinct pressures. For savvy advocates like Donnelly, such fissures constitute potential opportunities for public pressure and accountability—or, at the very least, provide some comfort that somewhere in the depths of the administrative state, there are officials firmly aligned with the goals of biodiversity protection.

Thus far, however, the pro-mining forces have proven stronger than the detractors. In October 2024, the Bureau of Land Management granted final approval to the Rhyolite Ridge mine.[45] In January 2025, just days before Trump would be inaugurated for his second term, the DOE increased Ioneer's loan to nearly $1 billion.[46]

The Center for Biological Diversity stood firm. It also gained allies in its struggle. Within days of the final authorization for the mine, the CBD, joined by the Western Shoshone Defense Project and Great Basin Resource Watch, sued the federal agency for endangering the existence of Tiehm's buckwheat, as well as threatening water resources and land sacred to the Western Shoshone people.[47] The outcome of the case remains to be seen. But the group of plaintiffs, as well as their grievances, is nonetheless noteworthy. What had begun as a fight to save a wildflower had morphed into a broad coalition of Indigenous and environmental activists facing off against a mine financially backed by the US government.

THE LITHIUM FRONTIER IS EXPANDING AND MUTATING. THE NEW geographies of mining invite the possibility of international solidarity, as communities on either side of a starkly unequal world confront similar threats. These communities are increasingly linked to one other, whether in coalitional spaces like Earthworks' "Making Clean Energy Clean, Just & Equitable" or the global network Yes to Life, No to Mining. Beyond such explicit encounters across global divides, we can also detect a more general process of learning and diffusion.

Latin American movements have led the way here. Latin America is a top producer of copper, iron ore, silver, bauxite, and lithium.[48] The region also leads the world in opposition to such projects, with 45 percent of the world's mining-related conflicts.[49] And Latin America is the riskiest part of the globe for these activists, who are more likely to face violent assault or death there than anywhere else on earth.[50] Over and over again, staff members of global NGOs told me that it was in Latin America that an oppositional repertoire of communities saying "No" to extraction—full stop—became a common pattern among mining conflicts.

This pattern of diffusion is itself telling. Researchers have shown that in Latin America, protests against mining tends to cluster in time and space, with communities connected by interpersonal networks linking leaders or by shared membership in trans-local or even transnational networks.⁵¹ Others are simply inspired by stories of resistance shared on social media or through word of mouth.

These connections span borders. On February 1, 2019, a sunny summer afternoon in Santiago, I wandered down a side street, looking for the offices of the Latin American Observatory of Environmental Conflicts (OLCA). The neighborhood's architecture, with its baroque and neoclassical buildings, recalls an earlier era of upper-class urbanity. Today, some of these buildings, like OLCA's graffiti-strewn headquarters, are in disrepair. OLCA, having been established shortly after the transition from Pinochet's dictatorship to a hopeful new democracy, directly supports affected communities with strategic and legal assistance. I had come to understand OLCA's perspective on the growing resistance to lithium projects in Chile and Argentina.⁵²

I did a double take as soon as I was buzzed in through the front door. Standing before me was Cesar Padilla. I had first met the tall and reserved yet steadfast ally of frontline communities across the Americas almost eight years prior, while I was conducting fieldwork in Ecuador. On that day in October 2011, he took to the stage in the town plaza of Victoria del Portete to congratulate members of the town's water association for organizing a vote in their parish that overwhelmingly (93 percent) opposed a gold mine.⁵³ On that windy and joyous afternoon, Padilla's speech invoked a groundswell of democratic resistance against extractivism, framing the day's event as one moment in "the history of peoples and nations that have chosen this path." For a moment, time and space collapsed, with the trajectories of southern Ecuador and northern Chile and my own journey from researching copper, gold, and oil in one South American country to lithium in another, hopscotching alongside Padilla's.

Snapped back to the present, I took a seat in Padilla's office. He told me about the organization's work supporting rural residents opposing lithium mines in Chile and Argentina. He lamented the tactics used to achieve "co-optation"—such as the agreements signed between multinational corporations and community representatives—and the difficulty locals have in obtaining even the most basic information about project impacts. A rare moment of optimism from this hardened activist came when he praised the young people he met in Indigenous communities for their heightened environmental consciousness.[54]

The powerful potential of cross-border organizing was a recurrent theme of my research on the movements and communities contesting lithium in Latin America and beyond. A month after I reconnected with Padilla, I met Ramón Balcázar in a cafe in San Pedro de Atacama. At an early hour when I usually prefer to still be asleep, we meandered through a heady, hours-long conversation surveying the thorny dilemmas posed by green technology's extractive harms. We paused only for sips of *cortado* and bites of *medialunas de manjar de leche*, half-moon-shaped pastries filled with caramel, popular in Argentina and Chile.[55]

"Extractivism," Balcázar stated bluntly, is "colonial."[56] In northern Chile, the state—at least as far as basic welfare provision goes—is relatively absent. Instead, corporations have free reign to "control territories." Governance is effectively privatized. Mining firms directly interact with communities, offering services and infrastructure in exchange for their compliance. The inevitable result, Balcázar argues, is sacrifice zones. Only organized resistance can change the script.

Balcázar, originally from a working-class family on the rural outskirts of Santiago, moved to San Pedro for work as a nature guide in the small city's metastasizing tourist economy. He soon became a fierce defender of the salt flats and desert wetland system of which they are a part. In late 2018, he cofounded the Plurinational Observatory of Andean Salt Flats (*Observatorio Plurinacional de Salares Andinos*, OPSAL), a transnational network of environmentalists, concerned scientists, activist lawyers, and residents of affected Indigenous and *campesino* (peasant) communities across Chile, Bolivia, and Argentina.

Words are important to the group. OPSAL members call the area they seek to protect *la Puna de Atacama* (the Atacama plateau), rather than the "lithium triangle," to emphasize the natural landscape rather than its economically valuable resource. Similarly, the choice to call the organization a "salt flat observatory" rather than an anti-mining group simultaneously nods to the importance of mining to Chile's economy and reminds listeners of the ecosystems at stake.

In the months and years after that early-morning meeting, I witnessed OPSAL flourish into an agile network, organizing multiple day-long seminars that displayed and solidified interconnections between disparate activists and experts. One event, for example, brought together Indigenous leaders like Lesley Muñoz, who saw lithium as the latest existential threat to both her Colla community and the unexploited Maricunga Salt Flat, with scientists like Cristina Dorador, the microbiologist whose deep knowledge of *salar* microbial life had transformed into an equally deep commitment to ensure their protection.

OPSAL takes action both close to home and further afield: screening documentaries about the environmental harms of lithium mining in San Pedro, participating in civil society dialogues about President Boric's plan to nationalize lithium, and intervening in transnational networks linking activists across lithium frontiers and nodes of the EV supply chain. These accomplishments are all the more impressive given the real challenges to organizing across rural peripheries crosscut by dirt roads and underserved by transit and WiFi. On one occasion during my visit to the Atacama, a delegation of Argentinian communities affected by lithium extraction was unable to cross the border to attend an Observatory gathering; snow had rendered the mountainous route impassable.

In effect, OPSAL has attempted to operate at—and connect—the various sites and scales of green capitalism. The organization's approach complicates the romance of "local" community campaigns that successfully resist extractive projects. Communities that are successful are usually, in actuality, not acting alone. Instead, they act trans-locally, in alliance with other such locales, embedded in networks that span countries and world regions, and with legal or technical assistance from sometimes far-flung scientists, lawyers, and NGO advocates.

OPSAL's trajectory also speaks to the enabling condition of having a progressive government in power. When I first met Balcázar, Chile was governed by the right-wing Piñera administration. The "political opportunity structure," as political scientists term it, was extremely constrained. Under such circumstances, social movements often retreat into defensive resistance, consciousness-raising, and base building—until, that is, conditions are ripe for more confrontational mobilization, as occurred with the 2019 uprising. At the time of our original conversation, Balcázar was pessimistic, telling me that he saw "no political path" to nationalizing lithium. And anyway, he added, the socio-environmental record of state-owned copper giant Codelco did not inspire confidence in the ability of national firms to respect ecosystems or Indigenous rights.

Two years later, the political terrain, and Balcázar's sense of possibility, had been transformed. The 2019 uprising had shocked elites, bringing to power a leftist president from outside the political establishment for the first time since 1970, when Salvador Allende was elected, and triggering a constitutional assembly. In the wake of the defeated constitutional referendum, President Boric was moving forward with plans to establish a state-owned lithium company while promising to conserve 30 percent of the Atacama's salt flats. The increased reception for the demands and proposals of environmental movements was undeniable. At the same time, OPSAL has remained vigilant about prioritizing ecosystem health over economic profits and has voiced skepticism about the details of Boric's plan. The group walked a tightrope familiar to activists around the world: seizing moments of opportunity while remaining alert to the threats of co-optation, betrayal, and disappointment.

AS THE LITHIUM FRONTIER EXPANDS AND MUTATES, SO DOES THE geography of protest. The first protests against lithium mining emerged in 2007 in northern Chile, followed by Jujuy, Argentina, in

2010. In what would become a familiar pattern, these protests were sparked by grievances ranging from impacts on desert water systems to the failure to fully enforce Indigenous rights.[57] Portugal would be next, beginning in 2018, when Savannah Resources pushed forward with the Barroso mine.[58] The movement soon spread to major cities like Porto and Lisbon. That same year thousands demonstrated in Cáceres, Spain, to defend a protected nature reserve from lithium mining.[59] Next, in 2019, was Bolivia, with protests in Potosí—the location of one of the Spanish Empire's first and most lucrative silver mines, proposed as the site of a lithium mine developed in partnership between the state-owned mining company and the German firm ACI Systems.[60] Then came Thacker Pass in January of 2021, with its multiple encampments.[61] In Serbia, enormous demonstrations against Rio Tinto's lithium project peaked in December of 2021 and ultimately caused the revocation of the company's permits. And lithium resistance is ongoing. In June 2023, protest erupted again in Jujuy, Argentina, lasting for several months and spreading to the capital, Buenos Aires.[62] In Chile, January 2024 saw the return of militant direct action, with Atacameño community members blocking the access road to SQM's mine. In Serbia, after a court overturned the cancellation of Rio Tinto's permit in July 2024, thousands of activists took to the streets in the capital and towns around the country, with protests continuing to erupt for months thereafter.[63] And in Bolivia, protest reignited in February 2025, both in the capital La Paz and closer to the salt flats in Potosí. The discontent was sparked by recently inked lithium contracts with Chinese and Russian firms, and Indigenous communities' concerns that they had not been consulted prior to either.[64]

Already, the lithium mining boom, particularly the move to onshore lithium production in the United States and Europe, has disrupted the general pattern of resource flows from Global South to North. The phenomenon has forced activists from Nevada to Portugal to take a position on the core claim of US and EU officials: that lithium can be mined more "responsibly" in these jurisdictions than in places like Chile or Argentina—and that building domestic supply chains will help diversify away from China, with positive implications for human rights. Even activists that dispute these claims worry that resisting lithium mining in their own "backyards" will merely reinforce historical patterns of offshoring, exploitation, and unequal exchange.

Is lithium onshoring in the United States and Europe a path to justice that more equitably distributes the environmental harms and economic revenues of extraction? Or is it just a replication of a global pattern of ecological injustice, with the most marginalized communities *within* those Great Powers bearing the brunt?

The Global North frontline activists and NGO staff I spoke with acknowledged the necessity of a more "sustainable" approach to mining, but were skeptical of emerging onshoring consensus. Several criticized the "nationalist" and "xenophobic" anti-China mindset that seems to be driving this policy shift.[65] Organizers split, however, on whether onshoring would actually bring more regulatory oversight and what such oversight might mean for a global anti-extractive strategy. Donnelly, for instance, saw onshoring as a potential route to globally just supply chains: "The blood of Indigenous peoples and migratory birds in Chile is in this [cell] phone [battery] here. We need to deal with it, if that means onshoring our [lithium] production, sure let's do it."[66] But, he quickly added, "that doesn't mean build every single lithium mine." Hadder wondered, "Is our opposition here going to motivate more mining somewhere else where there is less ability to resist it? . . . We don't want it to create pressures somewhere else. . . . It's only acceptable somewhere else if community and environmental issues are addressed."[67]

There is another wrinkle to the notion that building mines in the United States more equitably distributes extractive harm. Even in the Global North, populations do not equally benefit from or pay equal environmental costs for onshoring. Pollution, whether from a mine, a power plant, or a highway, disproportionally affects marginalized groups from Appalachia to Louisiana's "Cancer Alley" to the smoggy port of Los Angeles.[68] The Thacker Pass project—which will impact the Reno-Sparks Indian Colony, the Burns Paiute Tribe, and the Fort McDermitt Paiute-Shoshone Tribe—sits across the valley from landscapes scarred by almost a century of mercury mining, littered with abandoned pits that pose serious health risks.[69] The region of northern Portugal slated for expanded lithium extraction is peppered with abandoned gold and tin/tungsten mines, whose toxic wastes still pose risks to water and soil.[70] Serbia suffers from among the highest levels of air pollution in Europe, a product of coal power plants, petrochemical production, and other extractive activities.[71]

These observations are unsettling—not just because they reveal stark environmental injustices, but because they also upend commonsense notions of the hierarchies of nation-states, world regions, and even that most simplistic set of categories, the binary of Global North and Global South that I have used throughout this book. They are a reminder that peripheries—or frontiers—are fractal. As a top producer of copper and lithium, Chile serves as a resource frontier for all of global capitalism. But you'd never know it sipping wine on a balcony in an affluent sector of Santiago, far away from the dusty mines, disinvested communities, or diminished populations of flamingos. The Atacama is a frontier of a frontier.

It was my conversation with Galina Angarova that helped me see this the most clearly. Angarova was born in "so-called Russia," as she put it.[72] She is Buryat, a member of one of the two largest Indigenous groups in Siberia. She grew up speaking the native language in a community of four hundred people along Lake Baikal. After graduating from the local university, she got a scholarship to study public administration at the University of New Mexico, where she came to understand her own Indigenous identity, in part through encounters with students from Pueblo communities. From 2019 to 2024, she served as executive director of Cultural Survival, an international NGO founded in 1972 that advocates for Indigenous self-determination and rights.[73] And today, she is executive director of the SIRGE Coalition, which stands for "Securing Indigenous Peoples' Rights in the Green Economy."

Cultural Survival was a founding member of SIRGE.[74] The impetus to establish an alliance of Indigenous and environmental groups stemmed out of Cultural Survival's efforts to address the harms stemming from battery supply chains. These efforts commenced in 2020, when the organization first worked with Aborigine Forum, a network of Indigenous leaders and advocates from the Arctic, Siberian, and far eastern regions of the Russian Federation. The campaign pressured Tesla—specifically Elon Musk—to refrain from buying nickel from Nornickel after the company's fuel storage system in Norilsk failed to contain its contents due to corrosion on the bottom of the massive tank. The reservoir released 21,000 tons of diesel into local rivers, which, according to the Forum, constituted the largest oil spill in the Arctic region after the grounding of the Exxon Valdez.[75] Cultural Survival has also successfully pushed the European Union to include Indigenous rights in the due diligence obligations contained in the body's Sustainable Battery Regulation.[76]

Angarova rejects the Global South/North binary, at least when it comes to Indigenous peoples. She explains, "We find some of the most marginalized communities in the Global North." The numbers are stark. Globally, 69 percent of energy transition mineral resources or reserves are located within or in close proximity to the lands of Indigenous peoples and/or peasant communities.[77] Lithium, in particular, stands out, with 85 percent of viable resources or reserves in or near the territory of Indigenous peoples. In line with Angarova's observation, the Global North is no exception to this planetary trend. The vast majority—79 percent—of the United States' known lithium reserves are located within 35 miles of Indigenous reservations.[78]

Extractive frontiers are not simply given by nature but made, by political decisions, economic investments, unequal power relations, and, often, a large dose of violence and conflict. Recall that in the

United States, the 1872 Mining Law, which dates to a period of aggressive westward expansion and Indigenous genocide, remains in force today.[79] Extractive frontiers are history's grooves in the landscape. For corporations and states, these are the paths of least resistance—unless, that is, they become the sites of most resistance.

⊂⊃

HADDER HAD SENT ME A MAP TO HELP ME FIND THE THACKER PASS mine protest camps. Knowing I would have no cell service in the area, the map was a static image that I used for reference as I drove. But I was now lost, and my smartphone's app was no help. I had just begun to despair when I suddenly saw evidence I was in the right place in the form of a handwritten cardboard sign hung underneath an official BLM notice: "No drugs or alcohol. In accordance with cultural customs, the Paiute-Shoshone elders request that people abstain from participating in ceremonies when menstruating."

A smaller dirt road that led farther up the mountain soon took me to the People of Red Mountain's camp. A large white tarp provided a backdrop for banners—"Protect the sacred," "Black Lives Matter," "No More Stolen Sisters"—and LGBTQ and Trans Pride flags. Smaller, painted wood signs reiterated the camp's central demand: "Protect Peehee Mu'huh." Someone had spray painted "Land Back" on the side of a latrine, invoking the name of a decentralized movement demanding that "everything stolen from the original peoples" be reclaimed.[80] Aside from the signs and tents, the camp featured an impeccably organized kitchen tent, with ingredients, utensils, and cookware stacked in labeled tubs. Later that afternoon, the air was suffused with the sweet, woodsy scent of burning cedar as Myron Smart, tribal elder and member of the People of Red Mountain, tended the fire at the camp's physical and spiritual center.

Soon, Daranda Hinkey arrived with her speckled dog. She narrated the landscape for me, sketching a topographical map with sweeping gestures toward the area's dramatic peaks and valleys. Thacker Pass nestles between Nevada's Double H Mountain Range and Montana's mountain ranges, connecting the Quinn River and Kings River valley. We were standing on the rim of the McDermitt caldera, whose periodic volcanic eruptions over the last sixteen million years shaped the landscape and concentrated lithium within the caldera's basin.[81] Below our feet, shards of glossy black obsidian intermingled with the dull white of lithium-laden rocks.

Before I left the lower camp, Smart brought us an offering of that sweet burning cedar; the smoke danced in the crisp mountain air. Hinkey told me that the "smoke connects us to the Milky Way where our ancestors reside."

By the time I arrived at the upper camp, so had some of Hinkey's relatives. I joined them at a picnic table, where her grandmother, Inelda Sam, offered me deer jerky—chewy, musky, and definitely gamy. We snacked as she sifted through a binder of several years' worth of tribal council meeting transcripts, trying to trace the evolution in leadership that had produced the current relationship between extractive companies and the Fort McDermitt Paiute-Shoshone tribe. Since the tribal council was not and still is not obligated to consult the entire tribe on such key decisions, "We don't even know what they [Lithium Americas] have offered the tribe. It's a lump sum in a general fund. We have the right to ask for the minutes. The tribal council is not accountable."

Often, scholars or advocates who invoke "frontline communities" portray them as monoliths, united by shared culture, identity, and direct experiences of environmental harm. The reality is, unsurprisingly, more complicated. Like any group, such communities are riven by divisions, conflicts, and hierarchies—the latter often exacerbated by corporate tactics and promises of economic benefits. Shared interests are achieved through politics, whether by the opaque proceedings of the official tribal council or the public acts of protest of the People of Red Mountain.

The threat of resource extraction can produce surprising coalitions. In the area surrounding Thacker Pass, Indigenous peoples of both Western Shoshone and Paiute descent have historically been at odds with the descendants of white settlers in the ranching and agricultural sector. But the possibility of a fully operational lithium mine at Thacker Pass threatens both their interests, creating a door through which a (not always realized and not always stable) coalition might emerge. Kai Bosworth, writing about a similarly heterogeneous opposition to fossil fuel infrastructure in the Great Plains, calls this phenomenon "pipeline populism."[82]

The plaintiffs in the lawsuit against the Thacker Pass mine included environmental organizations, Indigenous tribes, and one area rancher: Ed Bartell. After departing from the protest encampment, I drove to meet up with Bartell at the entrance to Buffalo Ranch, where he has raised cattle and grown hay for thirteen years after relocating from southern Oregon. Bartell's family has been ranching for generations, but he didn't start out opposing the mine. "When we first heard, we didn't think it was that big a deal," he said. A lithium project nearby struck him as "cool." Then he learned more about how much water it would take to extract lithium from clay. He also looked into the possibility of contamination from the sulfur that would be used to leach out the lithium from the claystone. He became increasingly concerned not only about the water table, but also about the potential ecological impact on the "unique" desert wetlands.

Wetlands in a desert. Standing in the Great Basin, I heard an echo of *la Puna de Atacama*.

Bartell presented his findings to the Bureau of Land Management and helped form the Thacker Pass Concerned Citizens. But most citizens seemed unconcerned. I asked Bartell if he ever expected to stand alongside environmentalists and Indigenous activists in opposing a mine. He said he never thought he would.

Bartell's grazing ground, like Thacker Pass, sits on public land. In his experience, if "you want to do a very minor thing, it's very hard to get permitting." But he noticed that the standards are different for "green" extraction: Thacker Pass is "spun as eco-friendly." Referring to fast-tracking, he said, "Once they put on the green label, it just gets rushed through." Bartell's narrative of the mine's approval misconstrued the facts: The permitting process had not been rushed because the project was "green," but because of the rush to extract "critical minerals" amid intensifying Great Power conflict. But perhaps the specific details do not matter. By 2021, the themes of security and sustainability had fused, becoming almost interchangeable justifications for mining at home.

⊱⊰

AFTER OUR INTERVIEW IN THE VILLAGE CAFÉ, AIDA FERNANDES had insisted that we take a swim in the Covas River (admittedly it did not take much convincing). It was the coolest I'd felt all day. I cautiously dipped my feet in as they alternately touched sandy streambed and mossy rock, before lunging forward and submerging myself into the silky chill of the undulating water. My relief was only accentuated by the nearby grass tinged with pale gold, a vivid reminder of the relentless dry heat of another record-breaking summer.

The final stop on our itinerary was the *miradouro* (lookout point), which afforded a sweeping view of the village from above. We gazed down at a cluster of red roofs and white facades, neat farming plots and narrow roads, all ensconced by green mountains. Some ridges were crowned by wind turbines. For Fernandes, the change in perspective inspired a palpable wistfulness, a future tense nostalgia for a lifeworld not yet lost.[83]

"Do you think Covas is beautiful?" she asked me with unexpected intensity as we stepped away from the overlook. I answered yes, easily and honestly. But the question stuck with me. My mind kept circling back to its latent meaning. Each and every place I'd visited along the expanding lithium frontier, whether the site of an active mine or the location for a proposed project, was deemed worth protecting—in some cases, at all costs—by some group of people, people who valued it as home, as ecosystem, as watershed, as farm, as commons, as the physical anchor to collective memories of violence and courage. In so many of these places, mining wasn't an isolated threat or a discrete harm. It was yet another wound on landscapes parched by global warming, yet another injustice in a community relegated to the margins, yet another false hope for those long promised, and long denied, a share of the riches of our global economy. Put simply, each of these locales I visited felt like the wrong spot for a large-scale, intrusive mine. But this inevitably raised the question: What would be the right place?

Leaving Covas that evening, I grasped for an answer. But before I could find one, I saw the fire. The forest on the outskirts of the municipality of Chaves was ablaze, a terrifying mélange of orange and red that engulfed defenseless trees and sent gray and white smoke plumes billowing up far into the night sky. Suddenly, everything fell in and out of place: the climate crisis, here in the form of the Iberian Peninsula's worst drought in twelve hundred years; the forest we had passed earlier on the way to the river, still recovering from a horrific 2017 fire; the voracious raw materials appetite of the energy transition, now more urgent than ever, continuing its journey through the grooves formed by centuries of power relations. And through it all, the abiding potential, however slim, of upending those relationships. I keep searching for the answer.

CHAPTER 9

Green Futures

Extraction links colonial pasts to unequal presents to ever-more turbulent futures. Along extractive frontiers, we are witnessing unsettling continuities from obdurate fossil capitalism to nascent green capitalism. The climate crisis, born of industrial economies fueled by coal, oil, and gas, is giving way to a still-uncertain energy transition. The promise of zero emissions sits alongside the reality of fossil fuel extraction and combustion, renewable energy deployment, and mining to outfit carbon-free capitalism. In light of these facts, some analysts call our current moment a period of energy addition rather than transition. It is also a period of extractive appendage, as new mines are grafted onto the massive apparatus still wresting fossil fuels from the bowels of the earth.

Extractive appendage implies hybrid frontiers. The rolling hills of North Central Pennsylvania were for two centuries a source of coal. The advent of hydraulic fracking in the early 2000s laid a path for an enormous industry to tap the fossil gas of the Marcellus Shale formation that stretches from Kentucky to New York.[1] The wastewater from fracking, called "produced water," is a toxic environmental hazard. It also turns out to be a liquid lithium mine. Volcanic eruptions released the element at the same time that the Marcellus Shale was deposited 390 million years ago; the water that blasts open the shale to release trapped gas picks up lithium in the process.[2] In the spring of 2024, the news made headlines, with a Department of Energy study estimating that this produced water could supply up to 40 percent of current US demand for lithium.[3]

Recovering lithium from the sludgy stew of fracking waste offers benefits beyond domestic supply security. This region of Pennsylvania is a "brownfield" site: an area already altered by industrial or extractive activity, in this case a long history of coal, oil, and gas extraction. That designation could potentially qualify lithium projects for additional tax credits, since the Inflation Reduction Act provides extra incentives for investments in what the law calls "energy communities." These are localities in the shadow of fossil capital—coal mines, oil and gas wells, pipelines, refineries, and power plants—that have been forced to suffer the consequences of extraction and pollution.[4] With the eventual phasing out of fossil fuels, they also face risks of joblessness and disinvestment. Justice demands that such communities are first in line for projects linked to the energy transition.

Read beyond the flashy headlines and questions emerge. The idea that fracking waste could supply 40 percent of current consumption sounds promising—but as demand for lithium increases, this percentage shrinks. Moreover, potential investors must consider the specific concentration of lithium in a given deposit. The wastewater left behind by fracking wells in rural towns like St. Marys, Pennsylvania, contain just 205 milligrams of lithium per liter. For comparison, the average concentration in the Smackover Formation, a limestone deposit in western Arkansas with abundant lithium-rich brines, is 325 milligrams per liter; the Atacama Salt Flat clocks in at a whopping 1,000 milligrams per liter.[5] Another uncertainty concerns how, exactly, mining companies would recover the valuable element from the sludge. The proposed approach, called direct lithium extraction (DLE), remains in an early stage of commercial development.

Another detail that might give pause is the deep involvement of major oil firms like Exxon and Chevron. On the one hand, it makes sense that the companies producing this toxic waste should pilot the technologies that could convert it into a valuable resource. Any step that encourages fossil fuel companies to pivot away from planet-warming assets and invest instead in the energy transition is preferable to the status quo. But on the other hand, the companies' involvement in supplying the raw materials for the energy transition allows them to greenwash their otherwise oil-soaked operations, while reaping tax credits to boot.[6] The as-yet unknown environmental impacts of recovering lithium from wastewater present another reason for caution. Produced water contains chemicals and radioactive materials, yet the substance is not subject to the Resource Conservation and Recovery Act, which regulates most sources of hazardous waste.[7] Once the lithium has been recovered, the contaminated water it came from will still need to be properly and safely disposed of—not something the industry is famous for.[8]

Still, extracting lithium from the sludgy stew of fracking waste could very well be more environmentally friendly than scarring the earth with new mines. If we're faced with choices like digging a huge open pit in otherwise unspoiled forests, constructing massive pumping and evaporation facilities in arid deserts, or building a mine atop land sacred to Indigenous peoples, filtering out the lithium from fracking wastewater sounds benign in comparison. But as always, assessing the trade-off between the harms of extraction and the urgency of the energy transition ultimately comes down to who reaps the profits, who holds the industry to account, and whether communities have a real seat at the table—or are just a box to tick for investors to gain an additional tax break.

Extraction always implicates power relations that extend far beyond the mine, the company, the community, and the landscape. For that same reason, reducing the harms of mining cannot be achieved by simply governing mining better. To realize that urgent goal, we need to widen our lens and diversify our tool kit.

WHEN I RETURNED TO SANTIAGO AFTER MY FIRST VISIT TO THE Atacama Desert in January 2019, I felt dizzy. It wasn't the bumpy flight or the endless days of fieldwork. It was the vertiginous combination of witnessing an environment of extremes—topography and temperature, aridity and altitude—that simultaneously combined a complex ecosystem, a vast extractive zone, an Indigenous territory, and a cemetery for the victims of a brutal dictatorship.

I wasn't just reeling; I was also torn. Back in the United States, I had become deeply involved in advocating for a rapid transition to renewable energy. Along with my fellow organizers and activists, I had called for this transition to be socially just. A just transition should not only phase out fossil fuels but also transform the unequal social system that carbon energy had helped consolidate in the first place. But here I was, sitting with new knowledge of the harms of green supply chains and with enough honesty to admit that a future of electrified mass transit and publicly owned solar and wind would likewise require batteries produced with lithium from mines like those despoiling the Atacama. I had to ask myself an uncomfortable question: If climate action requires more extraction, do the ends justify the means? The question implied an existential trade-off—a dilemma with no exit.

I tend to be suspicious of zero-sum formulations. They often presume false choices or unmovable constraints. They limit the imagination and forestall strategy and creativity. Dissatisfied with the assumptions of my own question, I began to explore. There was no denying that mining is ecologically destructive, often irreparably so. Ditto for the notorious record of human rights abuses, lax regulation, and corporate corruption associated with extractive operations. But none of this knowledge could negate the reality that a climate-friendly energy system required a material substrate of manufacturing and mining. Even if the end goal was a low-impact, circular economy, with recycled minerals replacing new mining, the climate time frame demanded new technologies and infrastructures in the here and now, well before enough recycled feedstock could possibly be available.

Once I accepted that I couldn't dismiss these tensions outright, I started to think anew about the ominous predictions foretelling several hundred new mines in the next decade alone. Most of these forecasts have been issued by powerful institutions with little incentive to challenge the critical minerals consensus. That doesn't mean their findings on what it would take to service green supply chains were wrong, but it does mean that they baked certain kinds of assumptions into their models: assumptions that it would be easier to dig innumerable new mines than to nudge Americans to move around differently; that the only way forward is to change as little as possible; that our economies must simply produce what's most profitable, rather than what's most urgent, useful, or just.

With different assumptions, perhaps forecasting could serve instead as an exercise in world-building: a potent tool to imagine radically different green futures.

※

UPON MY RETURN FROM THE ATACAMA, I BEGAN THINKING ABOUT the definitions of some seemingly basic words: *transportation*, for one; *need*, for another. I wondered if the mining requirements might be lower, depending on the prevailing mode of transportation, or if there was a way to conceptualize social need as something distinct from the stream of inputs demanded by downstream industries. I pondered whether a reimagined transportation sector in which many more Americans rode buses or bikes would require the same massive volumes of minerals as one in which every household owned their own electric vehicle. I speculated about the per person material footprint under distinct mixes of electrified mobility.

Surely, I thought, some other researcher had already tested these hypotheses. I turned to databases of academic articles and browsed the reports of climate think tanks. To my surprise, no such studies existed. Instead, and without exception, all the extant models assumed that the only way to eliminate emissions from transportation is to replace individual gas-powered vehicles with individual electric vehicles. The best possible future, "net-zero emissions" (per the International Energy Agency), envisioned a world full of cars powered by batteries. Successful climate action meant a Tesla or a BYD in every garage.

Three years after I had first hypothesized that different transportation choices might require less mining, I stopped waiting for someone else to produce the data to put my hunch to the test. By that point, I had begun working with a climate think tank. I reached out to environmental engineers, transit wonks, and battery experts and asked if we could build a model from scratch. We were guided by an approach called "industrial ecology," which studies industrial systems in terms of their material and energy flows. In this case, we were looking for the amount of lithium required to meet the needs of fully electric mobility. We pitted a scenario in which all traditional cars had been replaced with electric ones against a scenario in which more Americans rode to work, school, or shopping centers in clean energy buses or got around by bikes or by walking. In other words, and in sharp contrast to prevailing models, instead of comparing a zero-emissions world with one in which we continued to rely on fossil fuels, we compared multiple zero-emissions worlds with one another.

We didn't stop there. Having set our imaginations free to roam, we tinkered with additional features of the worlds we were building. We imagined denser cities and suburbs, with less sprawl enabling less car use; cars with a range of battery sizes (American EV batteries are twice as large as the global median); high rates of mineral recycling and recovery. The futures we mapped out ultimately ranged from an electrified status quo to a fundamental shift in how Americans live and move. We did try to temper our dreaming with a healthy dose of realism. We only tested changes in the cities and suburbs, understanding the obstacles to rapidly building out mass transit in rural America. Even in our most transformative vision, the energy transition would still require tens of millions of EVs.[9]

I expected these different green scenarios to entail distinct material footprints, measured in the total volume of lithium mining. But the results shocked me. The best-case scenario—smaller batteries, more recycling, denser cities and towns, and more mass transit use, walking, and cycling—requires 66 percent less lithium than the worst-case scenario (batteries get even bigger, suburbs stay sprawled, recycling is nonexistent).[10] That percentage difference was based on a cumulative assessment across all the years we modeled (2023–2050). If instead we just look at 2050, the final year, the spread was more dramatic: the difference in lithium demand between the best- and worst-case scenarios was *92 percent*.[11] That's in large part because recycling takes time to have an impact on reducing mining, with recycled feedstock increasing as the batteries from EVs purchased in the 2020s, '30s, and '40s reach the end of their life and become available for material recovery.

These findings put the supposedly zero-sum trade-off between climate action and protecting landscapes and communities from extraction in a new light. The futures we conjured showed that it is, in fact, possible to achieve climate targets without the alarming amount of mining predicted by all other forecasts. And there's more: Increasing mass transit use and housing density will get us to zero emissions much faster than swapping every traditional car for an electric vehicle. To put it bluntly, a path to zero emissions that relies on electrifying individual cars is not only the most resource-intensive route to zero emissions, but also the slowest route to that urgent goal. We fully recognize that the political and even cultural obstacles to realizing our most ambitious scenario are formidable. But the prevailing approach not only requires much more extraction than socially necessary. It also runs afoul of climate science.

The implications of this modeling exercise completely changed the way I viewed mining. It suddenly dawned on me that extraction is not a problem that can be addressed solely at the sites of mining alone. It is absolutely vital to govern extractive frontiers better, improving environmental regulations and enforcing Indigenous rights. But some of our most potent tools to reduce the harms of mining reside elsewhere, all the way at the other end of far-flung supply chains. These tools take the form of the policy choices, investment decisions, and built environments that shape how we cut emissions from polluting sectors like transportation. The responsibility for protecting the Atacama's watersheds does not rest only with Chilean bureaucrats, nor should Atacameño communities have to shoulder the burden of standing up to multinational mining firms on their own. We in the United States are also implicated in the supply chains that start in Chile's northern reaches. Achieving a globally just energy transition requires understanding supply chains in reverse, starting from what we produce and consume and working backward to their material inputs, and further still, to the relentless scramble for new extractive frontiers.

The task of achieving a just energy transition is daunting. But this holistic view also opens up possibilities for action, revealing multiple and dispersed levers for reducing mining's harms. Policies that promote alternatives to car use, reduce sprawl, encourage more compact batteries, and require recycling would all reduce the scale of mining needed for carbon-free transportation.

Confronting emissions as a holistic problem, rather than a purely technical question about the fastest way to electrify an ever-growing fleet of personal automobiles, entails a leap of political faith. New models and forecasts like the ones my colleagues and I built at our think tank, the Climate and Community Institute, can help us tell galvanizing stories about the future we want. If we can see and feel that alternate future, desire and describe it, then we can commit to creating the foundations for it in the here and now. Forecasts chart a path from our present to the world we want to build. But seeing something and building it aren't the same. Better research or data can only carry us so far; concrete, bold, even risky actions are the stuff of real change. What practical steps can we take today to call forth a different tomorrow?

We can start by demanding supply chains organized around justice for everyone they touch, rather than profits for just a few. Just as any workplace is simultaneously a site of exploitation and locus of worker power, and any mine is at once a setting for extraction and a potential scene of community resistance, the supply chains of green technologies are both a means of domination—of people and of nature—and fertile ground for making the world anew.

Supply chains are currently organized for profit, but they can nonetheless become arenas for grassroots organizing and unexpected alliances. Lithium battery supply chains don't just link mines to factories to consumers, or upstream to downstream corporations. They also connect Indigenous land defenders and urban transit users, workers manufacturing e-bikes and battery recycling advocates, bus drivers and avid cyclists, and climate activists and promoters of dense, walkable cities and towns. These communities, workers, and advocates are already bound together by the global operations of green capitalism—and in many cases, are already organizing locally. What would it take for them to join hands and fight for globally just supply chains, together?

Today, a coalition like this may feel impossible. Electrifying the status quo to stave off the scariest warming scenarios already seems hard enough. Electrifying while *also* changing engrained habits, like car dependency and suburban sprawl, seems far-fetched, if not utopian. But fear of radical change is misplaced: Radical, turbulent, accelerating, and yes, frightening, change is already baked into the carbon in the atmosphere and in the reign of sclerotic elites, predatory corporations, and moribund institutions.

There is no escaping the harsh reality of mounting instability—

political, economic, ecological. This turmoil touches everything, including the material underbelly of the energy transition. This is the paradox of extraction: It is at once the most enduring feature of the world order and among the most prone to disruptive conflict, whether between Global North and South, between geopolitical rivals, or between local communities and huge corporations. Such contests are asymmetric, yet over the past century have provided openings to challenge the entrenched power relations of our global economy.

Extractive frontiers are so sedimented that they may feel like second nature, but it is precisely from these frontiers that we must begin again, from the underground on up.

ACKNOWLEDGMENTS

This book owes its existence to serendipity and collectivity. On the long and winding path from conception to execution, chance encounters led to unexpected questions and findings. And a growing community of colleagues, comrades, and collaborators supported and challenged me in equal measure.

My interest in the nexus of resource extraction and energy transition stems from a fortuitous conversation with Chris Erway at a party in Providence in late 2017. Knowing I researched mining, he asked my thoughts on lithium, the next frontier of extraction. I didn't have any yet, but immediately wanted to learn more. By the summer of 2018, I was making plans to spend several months in Chile.

The research that commenced this book began in earnest the following January. Less than a week after landing in Santiago, I was lucky enough to hitch rides to the Atacama Salt Flat and the village of Toconao with Professors Godofredo Pereira and Jon Goodbun, who were visiting the area with a group of students from the Royal College of Art. I would like to thank Godofredo in particular for teaching me so much about the political ecology of the region and for his excellent analysis of the morbid connections between the histories of extraction and political violence. I also owe tremendous gratitude to Ramón Balcázar, whom I met on that first trip to the Atacama. Our hours-long interview was just the beginning of what became a long friendship and ongoing collaboration. Ramón is at once generous and rigorous; he invited me into meetings of the *Observatorio Plurinacional de Salares Andinos*, allowing me to witness the cross-border network of salt flat defenders come into being and treating me as a *compañera* who could be trusted but also argued with when necessary. There is no greater mark of solidarity than that.

Martín Arboleda, Lucas Cifuentes, and Pedro Glatz Brahm: You helped me navigate the complexity of Chilean politics at a moment of upheaval and possibility. I also want to thank Martín for the insights of his essential book *Planetary Mine*, which taught me to see mining as a sprawling set of infrastructures, logistics, finances, and politics—and reinforced my belief in the transformative power of anti-extractive politics in Latin America. Romina Pistacchio and Andres Mitnik: Thank you for making Santiago feel like home, for your endless hospitality, late-night adventures, and always sharp analysis of Chilean society. Cristina Dorador, you singlehandedly facilitated my visit to the constitutional assembly. And from your groundbreaking research, I learned to see the beauty and ecological complexity of salt flats, desert wetlands, and brine.

During those months in Chile, I simultaneously conducted fieldwork and drafted my portion of a coauthored book, *A Planet to Win: Why We Need a Green New Deal*. I am deeply thankful to my coauthors Kate Aronoff, Alyssa Battistoni, and Daniel Aldana Cohen for their encouragement as I offered my first analysis of the global supply chains of the energy transition, and again to Ramón, for his feedback on the manuscript.

My decision to range far afield from Latin America—the region that, due to family history and dramatic political transformations, has always captivated and inspired me—was thanks to another coincidence. Rolande Kulke, Manuela Karp, and Nessim Achouche, of the

Rosa Luxemburg Foundation, invited me to speak at a conference, "European Industrial Policy: A Tool for a Green New Deal," at the European Parliament. While in Brussels, I learned for the first time about the relevance of industrial policy to renewable energy—and listened to European party leaders, social movement activists, and labor union organizers detail their concerns about green capitalism. I also took the opportunity to interview officials at the European Commission and other EU institutions. I realized then and there that this would not only be a book about Chile, as central as that place would always be to my perspective on the extractive frontiers of green capitalism. Instead, I would for the first time conduct fieldwork outside of South America, making plans to visit Nevada, Spain, and Portugal.

My trip to the Iberian Peninsula would have been impossible without the guidance of Catarina Loureiro Alves Scarott and Joams Evans Pim—and my visit to Covas do Barroso owes everything to the generosity of Aida Alves Fernandes. In Nevada, my conversations with John Hadder were revelatory, as was my trip to Rhyolite Ridge with Patrick Donnelly. Just as Ramón and Cristina had done for the Atacama, John and Patrick helped me see deserts for what they are: not blank canvases for colonization or extraction, but hardy, vibrant ecosystems and socio-natural landscapes deserving admiration and care. I learned this lesson from Daranda Hinkey, too, as she invited me into both her home and the sacred space of the Peehee Mu'huh protest encampment, sharing intergenerational knowledge along with her own trenchant analyses of the harms of mining and Indigenous resistance.

The primary methodological challenge of this book involved simultaneously staying abreast of breaking news about lithium, batteries, electric vehicles, and the energy transition writ large, placing these events in the ever-evolving contexts of a pandemic, geopolitical tension, climate crisis, and economic rivalry, while also attending to the longer histories revealed or upended in the process. I subscribed to the business press and industry outlets. I read chronicles of sixteenth-century colonialism, early twentieth-century imperialism, economic planning during World War II, and Cold War nuclear supply chains. I grappled with the origins of OPEC, the canon of dependency theory, and 1970s energy politics. I delved into studies of anti-extractive protest and USGS mineral surveys spanning decades. I also consulted historians.

Here, I want to thank Tim Barker in particular, who not only fielded queries but helped me think through challenges of interpretation. And there was a lot to interpret. The resonances across time and space were uncanny. Lithium is the "new oil" and coordination between lithium-rich states the new OPEC; the escalation between the United States and China is the New Cold War; deviations from neoliberal orthodoxy mark the return to mid-century industrial policy. The analogies are inevitably imprecise. But they are nonetheless revealing. I learned to see ruptures as moments when people looked to history as a repository of ideas to bring back to life, yet under conditions unimaginable to their original authors.

As I shifted from fieldwork to drafting, the Climate and Community Institute was not only a crucial source of support, but a space where I could draw out the implications of my research for climate policy and movement strategy with collaborators, and we could collectively grapple with both stark dilemmas and political openings. Here I want to thank Daniel Aldana Cohen in particular: Fellow schemer, sounding board, dear friend, constant interlocutor—I could not have embarked on this intellectual and political journey without you. I also want to thank Patrick Bigger, James Blair, Johanna Bozuwa, Batul Hassan, Emmett Hopkins, Kira McDonald, Alissa Kendall, Kristi Dayemo, Matthew Haugen, Meg Slattery, and Rithika Ramamurthy.

Translating empirical research and academic knowledge into a compelling story is no small feat. And insofar as I came anywhere close to achieving it, I didn't do so alone. I want to first thank Bathsheba Demuth for thoughtfully recommending me to Alane Mason, my intrepid editor at Norton. Alane pushed me to my limits and beyond, helping me understand how landscape, character, and prose can anchor complex ideas and render them not only accessible but interesting and even moving to nonexperts. In this same vein, I am tremendously grateful to Audra Wolfe. I was extremely lucky to find a developmental editor who not only has a rare gift for language, the ability to see how part and whole connect, and a preternatural ability to detect a bad metaphor, a scientific error, or a dangling narrative thread, but also truly understood the political commitments that drive my work. I relied on the brilliant coaching of Teri Chettiar, who taught me lessons that go well beyond the pages of my manuscript: how to handle uncertainty, get comfortable with risk and experimentation, and see my book as one piece of a broader project. And I want of course to thank Don Fehr, a wise and veteran literary agent who took a chance on me, seeing the general audience potential in my work, and who painstakingly taught me how to write a trade book proposal.

For all these reasons, I was not the sole author of this book. I was also not the sole researcher. I am tremendously grateful to Matthew Haugen for vital secondary research, fact-checking, and bibliographic labor, and to Lucas Cifuentes for additional fact-checking, as well as for his help interpreting regulatory disputes over lithium in Chile. I also want to thank Jing-Jing Shen and Jack Walker for research assistance during my time at Harvard's Radcliffe Institute (and to Jack for continuing to work with me for a year thereafter). And I again want to thank the Radcliffe Institute, along with the Carnegie Corporation, Providence College, and the Climate and Community Institute for providing essential support for research and writing, and Dalila Alves at PC's grant office for helping me secure these funding sources.

Many people read drafts of chapters and provided generative feedback. Thank you to Tim Barker, Alyssa Battistoni, James Blair, Nora Caplan-Bricker, Daniel Aldana Cohen, Daniel Denvir, Jessica Green, Alissa Kendall, Adam Leeds, Lida Maxwell, Timmons Roberts, Meg Slattery, Quinn Slobodian, Thomas Stackpole, Jake Werner, and a crew of scholars at the Yale Agrarian Studies Workshop. I want to thank Alyssa and Adam again for their lovely company during writing retreats. I presented this work countless times, but I want to note in particular the Radcliffe Institute, University of Chicago's Comparative Politics Workshop, New York University's Climate Change Doctoral Group, Princeton University's Climate Futures Workshop, Ohio State University's "Worlds in Contention" conference, Utrecht University's "Tackling Climate Change and Inequality Together" conference, Cornell University's political science seminar series, and the International Studies Association (2023) as forums that helped me share, develop, and refine my ideas. I also want to thank two anonymous reviewers at Global Environmental Politics as well as managing editor Susan Altman for their comments on my 2023 article "The Security-Sustainability Nexus," the arguments of which formed the basis of chapter 6, in rewritten and updated form.

A tight-knit crew of lovely friends in Providence supported me when I needed it most. Sarah Thomas: Thank you for the long walks, yoga accountability, lady dinners, uncontrollable laughter, and all manner of life and work advice. Tom and Nora: Your hospitality, emotional support, editorial insight, and political acuity constantly inspire me. Nina: My life in Providence is so much richer for our cooking, our conversations, and, of course our wonderful dogs' adorable friendship.

I am forever indebted to Adam Leeds, who has been by my side from my first years in our Ph.D. programs through my dissertation, first monograph, and this book. Your patience for my anxieties and indecisions is endless, as is your loving care during some of the most challenging moments of the past few years. And you especially went above and beyond in the final months of crafting this book, with brilliant edits and restructuring help. I couldn't have done it without you.

My one and only and favorite momma, Joyce Ilson: your authentic curiosity about all my interests, your ability to remember every single one of my friends' names, your patient listening during our evening phone calls, and above all, your infinite well of unconditional love. You taught me what love is, just as you taught me the power of friendship, the joy of learning, and the importance of an ethical orientation in every moment of our lives.

Dearest Daniel Denvir, where do I begin? We have been partners for over two decades. You are not just the love of my life; my very sense of self is bound up with yours. I am in constant awe of your boundless energy, your political principles, and your expansive desire to understand everything and anything. You are the most other-oriented person I know, dedicating your life to political education and community organizing. And you are game for anything: For this book, you moved with me to Chile twice and accompanied me to Spain and Portugal. I can't wait to see what adventures our next twenty years will bring.

And finally, my father, Maro Riofrancos, was born February 17, 1944, in Buenos Aires, Argentina, and died on December 9, 2023, in New York City, his home since he immigrated to America in 1956. His life traced the arc of world history: He lived on a houseboat on the Seine in early-1960s Paris, joined leftist study groups at City College, attended a Malcolm X rally, was immersed in the theater world, and published the radical magazines *Streets* and *Chalk Circle*. He read me Proust when I was just a child; he likewise shared his passion for Brecht and Adorno, Calder mobiles, and found objects. Above all, he instilled in me Karl Marx's favorite maxim, *Nihil humani a me alienum puto* (nothing human is alien to me), and for that I am forever grateful.

NOTES

PROLOGUE: MINING WATER IN A DESERT

1. Global reserves are a subset of known deposits that are technically and economically feasible to extract. USGS, "Lithium," *Mineral Commodity Summaries*, January 2025, 111.
2. USGS, "Lithium," 111.
3. Manuel Mendez, Manuel Prieto, and Milton Godoy, "Production of Subterranean Resources in the Atacama Desert: 19th and Early 20th Century Mining/Water Extraction in The Taltal District, Northern Chile," *Political Geography* 81 (2020); Diego Salazar et al., "Cronología y organización económica de las poblaciones arcaicas de la costa de Taltal," *Estudios atacameños* 50 (2015): 7–46.
4. Jerónimo de Vivar, *Crónica y Relación Copiosa y Verdadera de Los Reinos de Chile* (Santiago: Fondo Histórico y Bibliográfico José Toribio Medina, 1966), chap. 4.
5. Raúl Molina Otárola, "El Despoblado de Atacama: Diversidad ambiental, evidencias historicas y etnograficas de su poblamiento," Actas del XVII Congreso Nacional de Arqueología Chilena, Tomo 2, Valdivia (2006): 1415–27.
6. Mendez, Prieto, and Godoy, "Production of Subterranean Resources in the Atacama Desert," 4–6.
7. Otárola, "Despoblado De Atacama," 4.
8. Mendez, Prieto, and Godoy, "Production of Subterranean Resources in the Atacama Desert," 6.
9. LeeAnn Munk et al., "Lithium Brines: A Global Perspective," in *Rare Earth and Critical Elements in Ore Deposits*, ed Philip L. Verplanck and Murray W.

Hitzman (Society of Economic Geologists, 2016), 345–46; Brendan J. Moran et al., "Relic Groundwater and Prolonged Drought Confound Interpretations of Water Sustainability and Lithium Extraction in Arid Lands," *Earth's Future* 10, no. 7 (2022): 2–3.
10. Munk et al., "Lithium Brines," 346.
11. Beatriz Bustos-Gallardo, Gavin Bridge, and Manuel Prieto, "Harvesting Lithium: Water, Brine and the Industrial Dynamics of Production in the Salar de Atacama," *Geoforum* 119 (2021): 180–82.
12. María L. Vera et al., "Environmental Impact of Direct Lithium Extraction from Brines," *Nature Reviews Earth & Environment* 4, no. 3 (2023): 149–65.
13. Felipe Smith (commercial VP Iodine & Lithium APAC, SQM), "A View from the Majors," panel at Lithium Supply & Markets Conference (virtual), October 26, 2020.
14. Ándres Ángel, "From Boom to Burden: Perpetual Impacts and Mining," Heinrich Böll Foundation, December 2024.
15. Bustos-Gallardo et al., "Harvesting Lithium," 185; Victoria Flexer, Celso Fernando Baspineiro, and Claudia Inés Galli, "Lithium Recovery from Brines: A Vital Raw Material for Green Energies with a Potential Environmental Impact in Its Mining And Processing," *Science of the Total Environment* 639 (2018): 1193.
16. Bustos-Gallardo et al., "Harvesting Lithium," 185; Flexer et al., "Lithium Recovery from Brines," 1195; John Houston et al., "The Evaluation of Brine Prospects and the Requirement for Modifications to Filing Standards," *Economic Geology* 106, no. 7 (2011): 1231.
17. Moran et al., "Relic Groundwater," 6.
18. Moran et al., "Relic Groundwater," 17.
19. Gonzalo Gajardo and Stella Redón, "Andean Hypersaline Lakes in the Atacama Desert, Northern Chile: Between Lithium Exploitation and Unique Biodiversity Conservation," *Conservation Science and Practice* 1, no. 9 (2019): e94.
20. Cristóbal Bonelli and Cristina Dorador, "Endangered Salares: Micro-Disasters in Northern Chile," *Tapuya: Latin American Science, Technology and Society* 4, no. 1 (2021): 9.
21. Gonzalo M. Gajardo and John A. Beardmore, "The Brine Shrimp *Artemia*: Adapted to Critical Life Conditions," *Frontiers in Physiology* 3 (2012): 185.
22. Patricia Marconi, personal communication with author, October 12, 2022; Frau Diego at al., "Controlling Factors in Planktonic Communities over a Salinity Gradient in High-Altitude Lakes," *Annales de Limnologie—International Journal of Limnology* 51, no. 3 (2015): 261–72.
23. Patricia Marconi, F. Arengo, and A. Clark, "The Arid Andean Plateau Waterscapes and the Lithium Triangle: Flamingos as Flagships for Conservation of High-Altitude Wetlands under Pressure from Mining Development," *Wetlands Ecology and Management* 30, no. 4 (2022): 827–52.
24. Jorge S. Gutiérrez et al., "Climate Change and Lithium Mining Influence Fla-

mingo Abundance in the Lithium Triangle," *Proceedings of the Royal Society B* 289, no. 1970 (2022): 6–10; Nathan Senner, interview with author, October 21, 2022.
25. Gil Eshel et al., "Plant Ecological Genomics at the Limits of Life in the Atacama Desert," *Proceedings of the National Academy of Sciences* 118, no. 46 (2021): e2101177118.
26. Eshel et al., "Plant Ecological Genomics."
27. "Chile's Observatories: The World's Eyes to the Universe," Marca Chile, October 11, 2022.
28. Gajardo and Redón, "Andean Hypersaline Lakes in the Atacama Desert, Northern Chile."
29. Bonelli and Dorador, "Endangered Salares," 21–23; Flexer et al., "Lithium Recovery from Brines," 1196; Carolina F. Cubillos et al., "Microbial Communities from the World's Largest Lithium Reserve, Salar de Atacama, Chile: Life at High LiCl Concentrations," *Journal of Geophysical Research: Biogeosciences* 123, no. 12 (2018): 3677–78.
30. Cubillos et al., "Microbial Communities," 3675.
31. Cubillos et al., "Microbial Communities," 3675–77; Cristina Dorador, personal communication with author, November 24, 2022.
32. Flexer et al., "Lithium Recovery from Brines," 1195; Bustos-Gallardo et al., "Harvesting Lithium," 185.

CHAPTER 1: EARTHLY ENTANGLEMENTS

1. IEA, "Global Critical Minerals Outlook 2024," IEA, May 2024, 127.
2. IEA, "Global Critical Minerals Outlook 2024," 110.
3. Susan Moreira, Timothy Laing, and Adriana Unzueta Saavedra, "Cost-Competitive, Low-Carbon Aluminum Is Key to the Energy Transition," *Sustainable Energy for All*, World Bank Blogs, March 13, 2023.
4. Benchmark Mineral Intelligence, "More Than 300 New Mines Required to Meet Battery Demand by 2035," *Benchmark Source*, September 6, 2022; Cameron Perks, personal communication with author, October 26, 2022.
5. Kirsten Hund et al., "Minerals for Climate Action: The Mineral Intensity of the Clean Energy Transition," World Bank 2020, 40.
6. Camille Grosjean et al., "Assessment of World Lithium Resources and Consequences of Their Geographic Distribution on the Expected Development of the Electric Vehicle Industry," *Renewable and Sustainable Energy Reviews* 16, no. 3 (2012): 1735–44; W. Berry Lyons and Kathleen A. Welch, "Lithium in Waters of a Polar Desert," *Geochimica et Cosmochimica Acta* 61, no. 20 (1997): 4309–19.
7. IEA, "Global Critical Minerals Outlook 2024," 133.
8. Allan Pederson and Mamta Jaswal, "Five Options to Address the Looming Lithium Surplus," Wood Mackenzie, September 23, 2024.
9. Camila Hodgson, "Cornish Miner Hoping to Capitalize on Global Race for Lithium," *Financial Times*, October 27, 2024.
10. IEA, "Global Critical Minerals Outlook 2024," 208.

11. Jamie Smyth and Amanda Chu, "US Approves Lithium Project in Push to Break China's Grip on EV Minerals," *Financial Times*, October 24, 2024, 3.
12. Anthea Roberts, Henrique Choer Moraes, and Victor Ferguson, "Toward a Geoeconomic Order in International Trade and Investment," *Journal of International Economic Law* 22, no. 4 (2019): 655–76.
13. Andy Home, "Canada Slams the Door on China in Critical Minerals Race," Reuters, November 7, 2022.
14. For the pessimistic view, see Simon Michaux, "Assessment of the Extra Capacity Required of Alternative Energy Electrical Power Systems to Completely Replace Fossil Fuels," Sustainable Minerals Institute, University of Queensland, August 18, 2022, recorded presentation, 1:12:37. For the optimistic view, see Seaver Wang et al., "Future Demand for Electricity Generation Materials Under Different Climate Mitigation Scenarios," *Joule* 7, no. 2 (2023): 309–32.
15. Ted Nordhaus, "An Ecomodernist Manifesto," The Breakthrough Institute, April 15, 2015.
16. Genevieve Guenther, "We Need to Talk About the Carbon Footprints of the Rich," *Noema*, April 19, 2022.
17. David Deming, "M. King Hubbert and the Rise and Fall of Peak Oil Theory," *AAPG Bulletin* 107, no. 6 (2023): 851–61.
18. IEA, "The US Shale Revolution Has Reshaped the Energy Landscape at Home and Abroad, According to Latest IEA Policy Review," IEA, September 13, 2019; "What Countries Are the Top Producers and Consumers of Oil?," FAQs, US Energy Information Administration, accessed July 11, 2023; "Natural Gas Production by Country," Worldometer, accessed July 11, 2023; "U.S. Field Production of Crude Oil," Petroleum & Other Liquids, US Energy Information Administration, accessed July 11, 2023; "U.S. Natural Gas Marketed Production," Natural Gas, US Energy Information Administration, accessed July 11, 2023.
19. Jason W. Moore, "'Amsterdam Is Standing on Norway' Part I: The Alchemy of Capital, Empire and Nature in the Diaspora of Silver, 1545–1648," *Journal of Agrarian Change* 10, no. 1 (2010): 34–36.
20. Alyssa Battistoni, *Free Gifts: Capitalism and the Politics of Nature* (Princeton University Press, 2025).
21. Joseph McQuade, "Earth Day: Colonialism's Role in the Overexploitation of Natural Resources," *The Conversation*, April 18, 2019.
22. See Jake Sullivan, "Remarks by National Security Advisor Jake Sullivan on Renewing American Economic Leadership at the Brookings Institution," The White House, April 27, 2023; Gavin Bade, "Joe Biden Wants a 'New Economic World Order.' It's Never Looked More Disordered," *Politico*, May 25, 2023.
23. "Unleashing American Energy," The White House, January 20, 2025.
24. Moore, "'Amsterdam Is Standing on Norway,'" 35.
25. Randolph R. Resor, "Rubber in Brazil: Dominance and Collapse, 1876–1945," *Business History Review* 51, no. 3 (1977): 341–66.
26. David Harvey, *The Condition of Postmodernity: An Enquiry into the Origins of Cultural Change* (Wiley-Blackwell, 1991), 125–40.

27. Greg Grandin, *Fordlandia: The Rise and Fall of Henry Ford's Forgotten Jungle City* (Metropolitan Books, 2010).
28. Deborah Cowen, *The Deadly Life of Logistics: Mapping Violence in Global Trade* (University of Minnesota Press, 2014), 23–52.
29. Tim Barker, personal communication with author, July 13, 2023.
30. "Rhyolite Ridge Project," Mining Data Online, accessed July 8, 2024.
31. Jael Holzman, "Lithium Miner Rips Its Own Research in ESA Fight," *E&E News*, November 17, 2021.
32. Emerson Marcus, "When Nevada Was Golden: Battles Pitted Bosses and Labor in Goldfield," *Reno Gazette Journal*, March 1, 2014.
33. Jason and Rae Miller, "The (Mostly) Abandoned Town of Goldfield, Nevada, Is Spine-Chilling," HWY.CO, May 23, 2022.
34. "The Devastating Fire of July 6, 1923," The Goldfield Historical Society, accessed July 9, 2024.
35. Emily Grubert and Sara Hastings-Simon, "Designing the Mid-Transition: A Review of Medium-Term Challenges for Coordinated Decarbonization in the United States," *Wiley Interdisciplinary Reviews: Climate Change* 13, no. 3 (2022): e768.

CHAPTER 2: PERIPHERIES AND POWER

1. Simon L. Lewis and Mark A. Maslin, *The Human Planet: How We Created the Anthropocene* (Yale University Press, 2018), 193.
2. Christian Dorninger et al., "Global Patterns of Ecologically Unequal Exchange: Implications for Sustainability in the 21st Century,' *Ecological Economics* 179 (2021): 106824.
3. United Nations Environment Programme, "Global Resources Outlook 2024: Bend the Trend–Pathways to a Liveable Planet as Resource Use Spikes," International Resource Panel, March 1, 2024.
4. United Nations Environment Programme, "Global Resources Outlook 2024," 30.
5. Dorninger et al., "Global Patterns," 5. I take "exploiter and exploited" from Immanuel Wallerstein, "The Rise and Future Demise of the World Capitalist System: Concepts for Comparative Analysis," *Comparative Studies in Society and History* 16, no. 4 (September 1974): 405. For Latin America's raw materials export to China, see Juan Infante-Amate, Alexander Urrego-Mesa, Pablo Pinero, and Enric Tello, "The Open Veins of Latin America: Long-Term Physical Trade Flows (1900–2016)," *Global Environmental Change* 76 (2022): 7.
6. Jason Hickel, Dylan Sullivan, and Huzaifa Zoomkawala, "Plunder in the Post-Colonial Era: Quantifying Drain from the Global South Through Unequal Exchange, 1960–2018," *New Political Economy* 26, no. 6 (2021): 1030–47; Dorninger et al., "Global Patterns."
7. Takuma Watari and Ryosuke Yokoi, "International Inequality in In-Use Metal Stocks: What It Portends for the Future," *Resources Policy* 70 (2021): 101968.

8. Michael L. Ross, "Does Oil Hinder Democracy?," *World Politics* 53, no. 3 (2001): 325–61.
9. Thea Riofrancos, "The Security–Sustainability Nexus: Lithium Onshoring in the Global North," *Global Environmental Politics* 23, no. 1 (2023): 23.
10. Erich W. Zimmermann, *World Resources and Industries* (Harper, 1951); Thomas R. De Gregori, "Resources Are Not; They Become: An Institutional Theory," *Journal of Economic Issues* 21, no. 3 (1987): 1241–63.
11. Matthew T. Huber, "The Social Production of Resources: A Marxist approach," in *The Routledge Handbook of Critical Resource Geography*, ed. Matthew Himley, Elizabeth Havice, and Gabriela Valdivia (Routledge, 2021), 167–76.
12. Karen Bakker and Gavin Bridge, "Regulating Resource Use," *The SAGE Handbook of Political Geography*, ed. Kevin R. Cox, Murray Low, and Jennifer Robinson (SAGE Publications, 2008), 219–34.
13. James O'Connor, "Capitalism, Nature, Socialism a Theoretical Introduction," *Capitalism Nature Socialism* 1 (1988): 11–38; Alyssa Battistoni, "State, Capitalism, Nature: State Theory for the Capitalocene," in *Marxism and the Capitalist State: Towards a New Debate*, ed. Rob Hunter, Rafael Khachaturian, and Eva Nanopoulos (Palgrave MacMillan, 2023), 31–51.
14. Eduardo Gudynas, "Natural Resource Nationalisms and the Compensatory State in Progressive South America," in *The Political Economy of Natural Resources and Development*, ed. Paul A. Haslam and Pablo Heidrich (Routledge, 2016), 103–17.
15. This was later reversed, but then YPF was again renationalized. See Richard Huizar, "Why Was Yacimientos Petrolíferos Fiscales (YPF), Argentina's National Oil Company, Privatized?," *Extractive Industries and Society* 6, no. 3 (2019): 863–72; Elana Shever, *Resources for Reform: Oil and Neoliberalism in Argentina* (Stanford University Press, 2020): 1–74.
16. "Bolivia: Nationalization Day," *Time*, November 10, 1952.
17. Ruben Berrios, Andrae Marak, and Scott Morgenstern, "Explaining Hydrocarbon Nationalization in Latin America: Economics and Political Ideology," *Review of International Political Economy* 18, no. 5 (2011): 673–97; Antulio Rosales, "Resource Nationalism: Historical Contributions from Latin America," in *Handbook of Economic Nationalism*, ed. Andreas Pickel (Edward Elgar Publishing, 2022), 155.
18. Important exceptions were Cuba, Suriname, and French Guiana; the former two did achieve sovereignty while the latter remains an overseas department of France.
19. Ruben Berrios, Andrae Marak, and Scott Morgenstern, "Explaining Hydrocarbon Nationalization in Latin America: Economics and Political Ideology," *Review of International Political Economy* 18, no. 5 (2011): 676. See also Rosales, "Resource Nationalism."
20. Steven Levitsky and Kenneth M. Roberts, "Latin America's 'Left Turn,'" in *The Resurgence of the Latin American Left*, ed. Steven Levitsky and Kenneth M. Roberts (Johns Hopkins University Press, 2011), 1–30.

21. Margarito Fajardo, *The World That Latin America Created: The United Nations Economic Commission for Latin America in the Development Era* (Harvard University Press, 2021)
22. Fajardo, *The World That Latin America Created*, 161; Fernando Henrique Cardoso and Enzo Faletto, *Dependency and Development in Latin America* (University of California Press, 1979).
23. Giuliano Garavini, "Completing Decolonization: The 1973 'Oil Shock' and the Struggle for Economic Rights," *International History Review* 33, no. 3 (September 2011): 473–87; Nils Gilman, "The New International Economic Order: A Reintroduction," *Humanity: An International Journal of Human Rights, Humanitarianism, and Development* 6, no. 1 (2015): 1–16; Adom Getachew, *Worldmaking After Empire: The Rise and Fall of Self-Determination* (Princeton University Press, 2019).
24. Giuliano Garavini, *The Rise and Fall of OPEC in the Twentieth Century* (Oxford University Press, 2019), 39.
25. Garavini, "Completing Decolonization," 479.
26. For a list of original OPEC countries, see "Member Countries," Organization of the Petroleum Exporting Countries.
27. Gilman, "The New International Economic Order," 1–3.
28. Garavini, *The Rise and Fall of OPEC*.
29. Garavini, *The Rise and Fall of OPEC*; Matthew T. Huber, *Lifeblood: Oil, Freedom, and the Forces of Capital* (University of Minnesota Press, 2013).
30. Garavini, *The Rise and Fall of OPEC*.
31. Giuliano Garavini, "Thatcher's North Sea: The Return of Cheap Oil and the 'Neo-liberalisation' of European Energy," *Contemporary European History* 33, no. 1 (2024): 37–52; Daniel Yergin, "Energy Security in the 1990s," *Foreign Affairs* 67 (1988): 110.
32. Carlo E. Sica and Matthew Huber, "'We Can't Be Dependent on Anybody': The Rhetoric of 'Energy Independence' and the Legitimation of Fracking in Pennsylvania," *Extractive Industries and Society* 4, no. 2 (2017): 338.
33. Richard Nixon, "Address to the Nation About Policies to Deal with the Energy Shortages," online by Gerhard Peters and John T. Woolley, The American Presidency Project, accessed July 6, 2024.
34. "SPR Origins," Office of Cybersecurity, Energy Security, and Emergency Response, US Department of Energy, accessed July 6, 2024.
35. Jimmy Carter, "Crisis of Confidence," *American Experience*, PBS, accessed July 6, 2024.
36. Megan Black, *The Global Interior: Mineral Frontiers and American Power* (Harvard University Press, 2018), 68–83.
37. "Strategic and Critical Materials Stock Piling Act of 1939," GovTrack, accessed July 6, 2024; Black, *The Global Interior*, 68–83; National Research Council, Division on Earth and Life Studies, Board on Earth Sciences, Committee on Earth Resources, and Committee on Critical Mineral Impacts of the US Economy, *Minerals, Critical Minerals, and the US Economy* (National Academies Press, 2008), 29–30.

38. Harry S. Truman, "Letter to William S. Paley on the Creation of the President's Materials Policy Commission," online by Gerhard Peters and John T. Woolley, The American Presidency Project, accessed July 6, 2024; Congressional Budget Office, *Strategic and Critical Nonfuel Minerals: Problems and Policy Alternatives*, The Congress of the United States Congressional Budget Office, August 1983, 9.
39. Manuel Regueiro and Antonio Alonso-Jimenez, "Minerals in the future of Europe," *Mineral Economics* 34, no. 2 (2021): 211.
40. John R. McNeill and Peter Engelke, *The Great Acceleration: An Environmental History of the Anthropocene since 1945* (Harvard University Press, 2016).
41. Huber, *Lifeblood*, 101; "U.S. Field Production of Crude Oil," U.S. Energy Information Administration.

CHAPTER 3: LITHIUM FRONTIERS

1. Charles J. Murray, "Who Really Invented the Rechargeable Lithium-Ion Battery?," *IEEE Spectrum*, July 30, 2023.
2. James Turner, *Charged: A History of Batteries and Lessons for a Clean Energy Future* (University of Washington Press, 2022), 95–130.
3. Turner, *Charged*, 98; Murray, "Who Really Invented."
4. "How Lithium-Ion Batteries Work," Energy Saver, US Department of Energy, accessed June 24, 2024.
5. Caroline White-Nockleby, "Grid-Scale Batteries and the Politics of Storage," *Social Studies of Science* 52, no. 5 (2022): 689–709.
6. Turner, *Charged*, 99–100
7. Turner, *Charged*, 101, Murray, "Who Really Invented."
8. Charles J. Murray, "The Untold Story of the Lithium-Ion Battery's Roots in Boston," *The Boston Globe*, July 22, 2022.
9. Charles J. Murray, *Long Hard Road: The Lithium-Ion Battery and the Electric Car* (Purdue University Press, 2022), 93–106.
10. Rho Motion, "Over 17 million EVs sold in 2024—Record Year," press release, January 14, 2025, and personal communication with Rho Motion Press, March 14, 2025.
11. Johnny Wood, "More Electric Cars Are Now Sold Every Week Than in the Whole of 2012," Forum Agenda, World Economic Forum, February 18, 2022, accessed June 6, 2024.
12. IEA, "Global EV Outlook 2024," IEA, April 2024, 11.
13. Rho Motion, "Over 17 million EVs sold in 2024—Record Year."
14. Neil Thomas, "The Rise, Fall, and Restoration of the Kingdom of Bicycles," MacroPolo, October 24, 2018.
15. Lukasz Bednarski, *Lithium: The Global Race for Battery Dominance and the New Energy Revolution* (Hurst Publishers, 2021).
16. Agnes Chang and Keith Bradsher, "How China Became the World's Largest Car Exporter," *New York Times*, November 9, 2024.

17. Bednarski, *Lithium*, 15–17.
18. Zeyi Yang, "How Did China Come to Dominate the World of Electric Cars?," *MIT Technology Review*, February 21, 2023.
19. Bednarski, *Lithium*, 18–23.
20. Bednarski, *Lithium*, 23–29.
21. Henry Sanderson, "China's Electric Vehicle Battery King," *Time*, September 29, 2023.
22. For the battery manufacturing statistic, see IEA, "Status of Battery Supply and Demand," *Batteries and Secure Energy Transitions*, IEA, April 2024.
23. Quinn Slobodian, *Crack-Up Capitalism: Market Radicals and the Dream of a World Without Democracy* (Metropolitan Books, 2023), 2.
24. Slobodian, *Crack-Up Capitalism*, 29.
25. Bednarski, *Lithium*, 31–37.
26. Judd C. Kinzley, *Natural Resources and the New Frontier: Constructing Modern China's Borderlands* (University of Chicago Press, 2019), 139–48.
27. Matthew Wills, "A Messy Divorce: The Sino-Soviet Split," *JSTOR Daily*, January 17, 2024.
28. "$2 Billion Xinjiang Lithium Investments to Double Region's Supply" *Benchmark Mineral Intelligence*, May 31, 2023.
29. Office of the United Nations High Commissioner for Human Rights, "OHCHR Assessment of human rights concerns in the Xinjiang Uyghur Autonomous Region, People's Republic of China," August 2022.
30. Bednarski, *Lithium*, 35–36.
31. Judd Kinzley, personal communications with the author, August 24, 2023, and June 24, 2024. A Chinese state-owned newspaper directly states that Koktokay lithium fed into the Soviet nuclear program: Liu Xin and Fan Lingzhi, "Exhibition Shows Vital Role Koktokay Played in Building Country," *Global Times*, July 17, 2019, accessed on June 24, 2024. However, the USSR also boasted large lithium deposits.
32. Kinzley, *Natural Resources*, 173.
33. Alessio Miatto et al., "The Rise and Fall of American Lithium," *Resources, Conservation and Recycling* 162 (2020): 2; Rakesh Krishnamoorthy Iyer and Jarod C. Kelly, "Lithium Production in North America: A Review," Argonne National Laboratory, October 1, 2023.
34. Jack Ryan, "Expansion Pushed in Lithium Output," *New York Times*, December 12, 1954, F1, F10.
35. Patrik Andersson, "Chinese Assessments of 'Critical' and 'Strategic' Raw Materials: Concepts, Categories, Policies, And Implications," *Extractive Industries and Society* 7, no. 1 (2020): 127–37.
36. For the role of these battery makers, see Julian Busch, "BYD Invests $4.2 Billion in Lithium Projects in Jiangxi Province," MPR China Certification GmbH, June 15, 2023; "China's CATL Says Unit Wins Jiangxi Lithium Mining Rights for $135 Mln," Reuters, April 20, 2022; Lei Kang, "Gotion High-Tech Secures New Lithium Mining Right in Jiangxi," *CnEVPost*, December 5, 2022.

37. IEA, "Global Critical Minerals Outlook 2024," IEA, May 2024, 129.
38. Samir Bhattacharya, "China, Africa, and the Geopolitics of Lithium," Observer Research Foundation, November 9, 2023.
39. For the Zimbabwe statistic, see Nosmot Gbadamosi, "Zimbabwe's 'White Gold'," *Foreign Policy*, August 16, 2023; for the Argentinian statistic, see Global China Unit, "Tensions Grow as China Ramps Up Global Mining for Green Tech," BBC News, April 29, 2024.
40. Bednarski, *Lithium*, 41.
41. Natasha Frost, "Australia Tries to Break Its Dependence on China for Lithium Mining," *New York Times*, May 23, 2023; Jacqueline Holman, "IGO, Tianqi Successfully Produce First Lithium Hydroxide at Australia's Kwinana Refinery," S&P Global, August 23, 2021.
42. Rohan Somwanshi, "Australia Set to Boost Lithium Refining Capacity, to Surpass Spodumene Output," S&P Global, October 3, 2023.
43. Joseph Morton, "What Are the Top 5 Largest Lithium Companies in the World?," *Mugglehead Magazine*, September 15, 2023.
44. Lee Ying Shan, "Mining Giant Rio Tinto to Acquire Arcadium Lithium in $6.7 Billion Dollar Deal," CNBC, October 9, 2024.
45. "Arcadium Lithium Announces Completion of Merger of Equals Between Allkem and Livent," PR Newswire, January 4, 2024.
46. Benoît Morenne and Collin Eaton, "Exxon Joins Hunt for Lithium in Bet on EV Boom," *Wall Street Journal*, May 21, 2023.
47. John O'Dell, "Making the EV Transition: Understanding Kilowatts," *Forbes Wheels*, last updated May 6, 2022.
48. Martin Placek, "Worldwide Battery Capacity in Electric Vehicles 2025," Statista, March 22, 2021; "Light-Duty Electric Vehicle Sales Model," EV Volumes, EV Data Center, 2022.
49. Micah S. Ziegler, Juhyun Song, and Jessika E. Trancik, "Determinants of Lithium-Ion Battery Technology Cost Decline," *Energy & Environmental Science* 14, no. 12 (2021): 6074–98.
50. Prices are volume-weighted averages and given in 2023 dollars. See "Lithium-Ion Battery Pack Prices Hit Record Low of $139/kWh," BloombergNEF, November 26, 2023.
51. Hannah Ritchie, "The Price Of Batteries Has Declined by 97% in the Last Three Decades," Our World in Data, June 4, 2021, which draws on Ziegler et al., "Determinants."
52. For a helpful explanation, see "Energy Density: The Basics," QuantumScape, May 4, 2023.
53. Ziegler et al., "Determinants," 6090, 6092.
54. Mazzucato, Mariana, "The Entrepreneurial State," *Soundings* 49, no. 49 (2011): 131–42.
55. Ziegler et al., "Determinants," 6089.
56. John Helveston and Jonas Nahm, "China's Key Role in Scaling Low-Carbon

Energy Technologies," *Science* 366, no. 6467 (2019): 795; Scott Kennedy, "Made in China 2025," Center for Strategic & International Studies, June 1, 2015; Jameson Dow, "ICE Car Values Plummet in China and It Is the Canary in the Coal Mine," *Electrek*, April 1, 2023.

57. Ziegler et al., "Determinants," 6087.
58. Priscilla Barrera, "Will Lithium Hydroxide Really Overtake Lithium Carbonate?," *Investing News Network*, June 27, 2019; Madhumitha Jaganmohan, "Average Lithium Carbonate Price from 2010 to 2023," Statista, April 25, 2024; Lukas Boer et al., "Soaring Metal Prices May Delay Energy Transition," IMF Blog, November 10, 2021.
59. Govind Bhutada, "Breaking Down the Cost of an EV Battery," *Visual Capitalist*, February 22, 2022. For the contribution from 1995 through 2015, see Ziegler et al., "Determinants," 6087.
60. "Manchin Supports Inflation Reduction Act of 2022," Senator Joe Manchin of West Virginia, July 27, 2022.
61. IEA, "Trends in Electric Light-Duty Vehicles," Global EV Outlook 2022, IEA, May 2022.
62. David Stanway, "China Faces Heatwave Havoc on Power, Crops and Livestock," Reuters, August 24, 2022.
63. "Lithium-Ion Battery Pack Prices Rise for First Time to an Average of $151/kWh," BloombergNEF, December 6, 2022; IEA, "Global EV Outlook 2023," IEA, April 2023, 62.
64. Stanley Reed and Ivan Penn, "Offshore Wind Runs into Rising Costs and Delays," *New York Times*, August 7, 2023; Micah Toll, "Electric Bicycle Prices Are Rising, and It's Not Only Because the Tariff Exceptions Expired," *Eletrek*, March 7, 2021.
65. Isabella M. Weber and Evan Wasner, "Sellers' Inflation, Profits and Conflict: Why Can Large Firms Hike Prices in an Emergency?," *Review of Keynesian Economics* 11, no. 2 (2023): 183–213.
66. BloombergNEF, "Lithium-Ion Battery Pack Prices See Largest Drop Since 2017, Falling to $115 per Kilowatt-Hour: BloombergNEF," BloombergNEF, December 10, 2024.
67. Tom Randall, "Long-Range EVs Now Cost Less Than the Average New Car in the US," Bloomberg, June 7, 2024.
68. Simon M. Jowitt, Gavin M. Mudd, and John F. H. Thompson, "Future Availability of Non-Renewable Metal Resources and the Influence of Environmental, Social, and Governance Conflicts on Metal Production," *Communications Earth & Environment* 1, no. 1 (2020): 13.
69. Dennis P. Cox and Donald A. Singer, "Mineral Deposit Models," USGS, 1986.
70. US Bureau of Mines and the US Geological Survey, "Principles of a Resource/Reserve Classification for Minerals," USGS 1980, 1.
71. USGS, *Suggestions to Authors of the Reports of the United States Geological Survey* (U.S. Government Printing Office, 1991).

72. USBM and USGS, "Principles of a Resource," 1–5.
73. Brett Christophers, *Rentier Capitalism: Who Owns the Economy, and Who Pays for It?* (Verso Books, 2020), 100–101.
74. "EJ Atlas," Global Atlas of Environmental Justice, accessed July 6, 2024; Liz Kimbrough, "Ecuador Court Upholds 'Rights of Nature,' Blocks Intag Valley Copper Mine," *Mongabay*, March 31, 2023.
75. Jowitt et al., "Future Availability."
76. Daniel M. Franks et al., "Conflict Translates Environmental and Social Risk into Business Costs," *Proceedings of the National Academy of Sciences* 111, no. 21 (2014): 7576–81.
77. Franks et al., "Conflict," 7578.
78. Przemyslaw Kowalski and Clarisse Legendre, "Raw Materials Critical for the Green Transition: Production, International Trade and Export Restrictions," *OECD Trade Policy Papers*, No. 269, OECD Publishing, 37.
79. Anna Ilyina et al., "Industrial Policy Is Back but the Bar to Get it Right Is High," IMF Blog, April 12, 2024.
80. Kowalski and Legendre, "Raw Materials," 51.
81. Kowalski and Legendre, "Raw Materials," 36.
82. Otto Svendsen, "Seizing Greenland Is Worse Than a Bad Deal," Center for Strategic and International Studies, January 21, 2025; Nadine Yousif "Trudeau Says Trump Threat to Annex Canada 'Is a Real Thing'," BBC, February 7, 2025.
83. "Global Mining Exploration Trends 2020," Market Intelligence, S&P Global, 2020.
84. S&P Global, "World Exploration Trends 2024," Market Intelligence, S&P Global, March 2024, 3, 9; Richard Schodde, personal communication with author, May 30, 2023.
85. Richard Schodde, "Long Term Trends in Global Exploration—Are We Finding Enough Metal?," 11th Fennoscandian Exploration and Mining Conference, October 31, 2017, 11.
86. Schodde, "Long Term Trends"; Richard Schodde, "Exploration and Discovery of Base and Precious Metal Deposits in the Pacific Rim over the Last 50 Years," Mineral Systems of the Pacific Rim (PACRIM) Congress, April 3, 2019.
87. United Nations Environment Programme, "Global Resources Outlook 2024: Bend the Trend—Pathways to a Liveable Planet as Resource Use Spikes," International Resource Panel, 28.
88. Liang Tang and Tim T. Werner, "Global Mining Footprint Mapped from High-Resolution Satellite Imagery," *Communications Earth & Environment* 4, no. 1 (2023): 134.
89. Stefan Giljum et al., "A Pantropical Assessment of Deforestation Caused by Industrial Mining," *Proceedings of the National Academy of Sciences* 119, no. 38 (2022): e2118273119.

90. Tang and Werner, "Global Mining Footprint Mapped from High-Resolution Satellite Imagery," 8.
91. S&P, "World Exploration Trends 2024," 3.
92. James Attwood, "Battery Boom Keeps Lithium Recession-Proof for Top Miner SQM," Bloomberg, August 18, 2022.
93. IEA, "Global Critical Minerals Outlook 2024," 36.
94. IEA, "Global Critical Minerals Outlook 2024," 47–48, 61–62, 134; see also Harry Dempsey, "World's Biggest Lithium Producer Urges State Help to Compete with China," *Financial Times*, August 4, 2024.
95. S&P, "World Exploration Trends 2024," 10.
96. Alex Lubben, "Inside the 'White Gold' Rush to Mine American Lithium and Make Millions," *Vice News*, May 15, 2023; Steve Emerman, interview with author, June 29, 2022.
97. Eric Onstad, Siyi Liu, and Mai Nguyen, "Lithium Prices Bounce After Big Plunge, but Surpluses Loom," Reuters, May 2, 2023; IRENA, "Geopolitics of the Energy Transition: Critical Materials," International Renewable Energy Agency, July 2023; IEA, "Global Critical Minerals Outlook 2024," 133–34.
98. Annie Lee and Mark Burton, "Lithium's Next Big Risk Is Grand Supply Plans Falling Short," Bloomberg, January 15, 2023.
99. Isabella Weber, "Could Strategic Price Controls Help Fight Inflation?," *The Guardian*, December 29, 2021; IEA, "Global Critical Minerals Outlook 2024," 232–42; Thea Riofrancos et al., "Achieving Zero Emissions with More Mobility and Less Mining," Climate and Community Institute, 2023.
100. Laleh Khalili, *Sinews of War and Trade: Shipping and Capitalism in the Arabian Peninsula* (Verso Books, 2021).
101. Transport & Environment, "From Dirty Oil to Clean Batteries," 2021, 40. For the additional information that these numbers refer only to refined metals (not surrounding ore), I am grateful to personal communications with Lucien Mathieu, cars director for Transport & Environment, August 25, 2023.
102. MiningWatch Canada, "Pour que Québec ait meilleure mine!," Presentation at University of Quebec, April 22, 2021, 13. For similar figures see IEA, "The Role of Critical Minerals in Clean Energy Transitions," IEA, May 2021, 8 (NB: IEA figure does not include aluminum, a key EV input).
103. Martin Placek, "Worldwide Battery Capacity in Electric Vehicles 2025," Statista, March 22, 2021; "Light-Duty Electric Vehicle Sales Model," EV Volumes, EV Data Center, 2022.
104. Nedal T. Nassar et al., "Rock-to-Metal Ratios of the Rare Earth Elements," *Journal of Cleaner Production* 405 (2023): 136958.
105. Summary from SOMO 2023 based on Nassar et al., "Rock-to-Metal" (retrieve original Table S6).
106. USGS, "Lithium," *Mineral Commodity Summaries*, January 2025, 111.
107. Ugo Lapointe, personal communication, June 12, 2023. See also Ugo Lapointe,

"Pour une transition post-extractiviste juste et equitable: quelles possibilités?'," séminaire Conflits socio-écologiques, extractivisme et transition énergétique: apprentissages, luttes et perspectives. Cycle de séminaires Résistaction du Centre de recherche en éducation relative à l'environnement, Université du Québec à Montréal, April 22, 2021. Tesla did not respond to requests for comment on these estimates.

108. Irving Fisher, "What Is Capital?," *The Economic Journal* 6, no. 24 (1896): 514.
109. Kingsmill Bond, "Mineral Constraints for Transition Overstated by IEA," Carbon Tracker, May 10, 2021.
110. IEA, "The Role of Critical Minerals in Clean Energy Transitions," 6
111. For these figures, see Statista Research Department, "Average Weight of Metal Content in U.S. and Canadian-Built Light Vehicles Between 2007 and 2017, by Type," Statista, January 5, 2023.
112. Bond, "Mineral Constraints."
113. Transport & Environment, "From Dirty Oil to Clean Batteries."
114. Hannah Ritchie, "Electric Cars Are Better for the Climate Than Petrol or Diesel," *Sustainability by Numbers*, January 26, 2023.
115. Ryosuke Yokoi, Takuma Watari, and Masaharu Motoshita, "Future Greenhouse Gas Emissions from Metal Production: Gaps and Opportunities Towards Climate Goals," *Energy & Environmental Science* 15, no. 1 (2022): 146–57.
116. Unless otherwise noted, this paragraph draws on Ritchie, "Electric Cars."
117. Along with Ritchie, "Electric Cars," see Paul Lienert, "When Do Electric Vehicles Become Cleaner Than Gasoline Cars?", Reuters, July 7, 2021.
118. See Jonatan J. Gómez Vilchez, Roberto Pasqualino, and Yeray Hernandez, "The New Electric SUV Market Under Battery Supply Constraints: Might They Increase CO_2 Emissions?," *Journal of Cleaner Production* 383 (2023): 135294.
119. Thea Riofrancos, "Electric Vehicles Alone Won't Take Us to a Decarbonized Future," The Hill, February 17, 2023.
120. IEA, "Global EV Outlook 2024," 104.
121. Liesbet Gregoir and Karel van Acker, "Metals for Clean Energy: Pathways to Solving Europe's Raw Materials Challenge," KU Leuven, 2022, 20.
122. PwC, "Mine 2023: 20th edition, The Era of Reinvention," PwC, June 8, 2023, title and p. 3.
123. "Transition Minerals Tracker: 2025 Global Analysis," Business & Human Rights Resource Centre, accessed May 8, 2025.

CHAPTER 4: LITHIUM FOR CHILE

1. On UNCTAD's history, see Margarita Fajardo, *The World That Latin America Created: The United Nations Economic Commission for Latin America in the Development Era* (Harvard University Press, 2022), 71, 178–81.
2. Ken Qiu Sun, "Overwriting the Memory of a Modern Ruin in Chile: From UNCTAD III to GAM," *ARENA Journal of Architectural Research* 6 (2021); David

Maulén, "An Exceptional Trajectory Civic Integration and Collective Design in the UNCTAD III Building," *ARQ* 92 (2016): 68–79.
3. Salvador Allende, "Día de la Dignidad Nacional. Discurso del camarada Allende pronunciado ante la juventud chilena, en el edificio de la UNCTAD," in *Textos de Salvador Allende 1972* (Biblioteca Clodomiro Almeyda (Partido Socialista de Chile, 2016) 510.
4. Allende, "Día de la Dignidad Nacional," 510–12.
5. US Senate, "Covert Action in Chile, 1963–1973: Staff Report of the Select Committee to Study Governmental Operations with Respect to Intelligence Activities" (Government Printing Office, 1975), 32.
6. US Senate, "Covert Action in Chile," 33.
7. Joseph Novitski, "Chile Nullifies Payments for Seized Copper Mines," *New York Times*, September 29, 1971.
8. US Senate, "Covert Action in Chile," 30–31, 35.
9. Qiu Sun, "Overwriting the Memory."
10. Jonathan Kandell, "Chile to Return Seized Companies to Their Owners," *New York Times*, October 20, 1973.
11. Jewellord T. Nem Singh, "Governing the Extractive Sector: The Politics of Globalisation and Copper Policy in Chile," *Journal of Critical Globalisation Studies* 3 (2010): 71.
12. Nem Singh, "Governing the Extractive Sector."
13. Godofredo Pereira, "Geoforensics: Underground Violence in the Atacama Desert," in *Forensis: The Architecture of Public Truth*, ed. Forensic Architecture (Sternberg Press, 2014), 593.
14. Karen L. Remmer, "Political Demobilization in Chile 1973–1978," *Comparative Politics* 12, no. 3 (April 1980): 278, 280–82.
15. Zapata S. Francisco, "The Chilean Labor Movement Under Salvador Allende: 1970–1973," *Latin American Perspectives* 3, no. 1 (1976): 89–92.
16. Thomas Miller Klubock, "Copper Workers, Organized Labor, and Popular Protest Under Military Rule in Chile, 1973–1986," *International Labor and Working-Class History*, no. 52 (Fall 1997): 106–33.
17. Klubock, "Copper Workers, Organized Labor, and Popular Protest," 106, 117–22.
18. Klubock, "Copper Workers, Organized Labor, and Popular Protest," 106.
19. Ami Lebdioui, "Chile's Export Diversification Since 1960: A Free Market Miracle or Mirage?," *Development and Change* 50, no. 6 (2019): 1624–63.
20. Nem Singh, "Governing the Extractive Sector," 72, 86–87; "Anuario de Estadísticas del Cobre y Otros Minerales," La Comisión Chilena del Cobre, 2024, 15, https://www.cochilco.cl/web/anuario-de-estadisticas-del-cobre-y-otros-minerales/. I am grateful to Cristián Flores Fernandez at Humboldt University for assistance navigating this data (Flores Fernandez, personal communication with author, April 26, 2024).
21. Nem Singh, "Governing the Extractive Sector," 70.
22. This was due to a 1958 law, which was only reversed in 2019. See David Sher-

wood, "Chilean Lawmakers Abolish Law Requiring Codelco to Finance Military," Reuters, July 24, 2019.
23. Chile, Ministerio de Minería, "Modifica la Ley Organica de la Comision Chilena de Energia Nuclear y dicta normas sobre Contratos de Operacion," Decreto Ley 1557, adopted September 16, 1976, Article 1 and Article 37(b).
24. Alden P. Armagnac, "What Is the H-bomb?," *Popular Science*, April 1950, 145.
25. Chile, Ministerio de Minería, "Deja sujeta a las Normas Generales del Código de Minería la Constitución de Pertenencia Minera sobre Carbonato de Calcio, Fosfato, y Sales Potásicas, reserva de Litio en favor del Estado e interpreta y modifica las Leyes que se señalan," Decreto No. 2886, adopted October 22, 1979, Preamble clauses 1–2 and Article 1, 6; Chile, Ministerio de Minería, "Codígo de la Minería," Ley 18248, adopted September 26, 1983, Article 7.
26. "New Lithium Frontier in Chile," *Foote Prints* 47, no. 1 (1984): 3; SRK Consulting, "SEC Technical Report Summary: Pre-Feasibility Study, Salar de Atacama Región II, Chile," January 28, 2022. Neither source specifies this specific date of Rudolph's discovery, perhaps because of the elapse between discovery and technical laboratory analysis of the brine.
27. "New Lithium Frontier in Chile," 4.
28. "New Lithium Frontier in Chile," 4.
29. "New Lithium Frontier in Chile," 4–5.
30. Federico Nacif, "Dominio minero y reserva de litio en Chile. Una indagación histórica para el debate constituyente," *Realidad Económica*, no. 346 (February/March 2022): 21–23.
31. The company that eventually became SQM got its start in 1968 as a sodium nitrate mining company jointly owned by CORFO, the state development agency, and a US firm. The process of privatization occurred between 1983 and 1989. Edmundo Polanco Valenzuela, "Historia de SOQUIMICH, una revisión," Servicio Nacional de Geología y Minería, 2015.
32. SQM first bought out the shares belonging to two private firms, then those held by CORFO (which predated the 1979 ban), making it the sole proprietor of the lucrative lithium asset by 1995. Fernando Aguirre, "The Rise of Brine: Exploration and Development Challenges in the Lithium Triangle—Argentina, Bolivia, and Chile," in *Special Institute on International Mining and Oil & Gas Law, Development, and Investment* (Rocky Mountain Mineral Law Foundation, 2017), 9; Arlene Ebensperger, Philip Maxwell, and Christian Moscoso, "The Lithium Industry: Its Recent Evolution and Future Prospects," *Resources Policy* 30, no. 3 (2005): 229; Rafael Poveda Bonilla, *Políticas Públicas para la Innovación y la Agregación de Valor del Litio en Chile*, 34 (CEPAL, 2021).
33. Eleanor R. E. O'Higgins, "Corruption, Underdevelopment, and Extractive Resource Industries: Addressing the Vicious Cycle," *Business Ethics Quarterly* 16, no. 2 (2006): 240–41.
34. Felipe Mujica, interview with author, February 12, 2019.
35. Naomi Klein, *The Shock Doctrine: The Rise of Disaster Capitalism* (Henry Holt, 2007), 89–159.

36. Brett Clark and John Bellamy Foster, "Ecological Imperialism and the Global Metabolic Rift: Unequal Exchange and the Guano/Nitrates Trade," *International Journal of Comparative Sociology* 50, nos. 3–4 (2009): 324–28.
37. Paul Marr, "Ghosts of the Atacama: The Abandonment of Nitrate Mining in the Tarapaca Region of Chile," *Middle States Geographer* 40 (2007): 22.
38. For this concept, see James C. Scott, *Seeing Like a State: How Certain Schemes to Improve the Human Condition Have Failed* (Yale University Press, 1998).
39. James Petras and Steve Vieux, "The Chilean 'Economic Miracle': An Empirical Critique," *Critical Sociology* 17, no. 2 (1990): 64–67.
40. Amir Lebdioui, "Chile's Export Diversification Since 1960," 1624–63.
41. Dave Sherwood, "Exclusive: Chile Nuclear Watchdog Weighs Probe into Fraud over Lithium Exports—Documents," Reuters, January 19, 2019.
42. Sherwood, "Chile Nuclear Watchdog."
43. Official at La Comisión Chilena de Energía Nuclear, personal communication with Lucas Cifuentes, research assistant to author, January 27, 2025.
44. Patricio Aguilera, interview with author, February 20, 2019.
45. Comisión Nacional del Litio, *Informe Final*, Ministerio de Minería de Chile, January 2015, 1, 31–36.
46. Dave Sherwood and Ernest Scheyder, "Exclusive: Albemarle Pushes Chile to Reverse Lithium Quota Decision—Filings," Reuters, December 5, 2018. In May of 2024, the Chilean government offered Albemarle the option to triple its quota, pending "its ability to use sustainable technology such as direct lithium extraction, consult local indigenous communities, and obtain environmental permits." ("Chile Gives Albemarle Option to Boost Lithium Quota By 240,000 Metric Tons," Reuters, May 15, 2024.)
47. Dave Sherwood, "EXCLUSIVE Chile Threatens Legal Action to Get Albemarle to Disclose Lithium Reserves," Reuters, January 7, 2021.
48. Dave Sherwood, "Chile Strikes Deal with Lithium Miner Albemarle in Contract Dispute," Reuters, January 24, 2019; Oliver Hailes, "Lithium in International Law: Trade, Investment, and the Pursuit Of Supply Chain Justice," *Journal of International Economic Law* 25, no. 1 (2022): 158.
49. "Corfo y Albemarle ponen fin a arbitraje con acuerdo que permite un desarrollo más sostenible de la producción de litio en el Salar de Atacama," CORFO, May 15, 2024 (https://www.corfo.cl/sites/cpp/sala_de_prensa/nacional/15_05_2024_corfo_albemarle).
50. Regarding the links to the Pinochet dictatorship and family nepotism, when Pinochet privatized SQM, it was handed over to his son-in-law, Julio Ponce Lerou, whose investor group acquired it for a price well below market value. In addition, in 1983, the same year the SQM privatization process was initiated, Ponce Lerou was named the director of the state agency overseeing all such privatizations. See Timothy L. O'Brien and Larry Rohter, "The Pinochet Money Trail," *New York Times*, December 12, 2004, and Benedict Mander, "Chile: Potash, a Billionaire and a Scandal," *Financial Times*, September 17, 2013. Regarding the illegal trading, see "Chile Regulator Issues More Fines

in SQM Trading Scandal," *Reuters*, October 30, 2014; "Chile's SQM Fires CEO Tied to Campaign Finance Scandal," *Reuters*, March 17, 2015; and Henry Sanderson, "Lithium: Chile's buried treasure," *Financial Times*, July 7, 2016.

51. "Chile's SQM Paying $30 Mln To Resolve U.S. Corruption Cases," *Reuters*, January 13, 2017; Benjamin Witte-Lebhar, "Chilean President Bogged Down by Concurrent Corruption Cases," *NotiSur*, April 24, 2015; Benjamin Witte-Lebhar, "Corruption Scandals Fade as Chile Prepares for Leadership Change," *NotiSur*, February 16, 2018, accessed June 28, 2022.

52. Nicolás Sepúlveda, "La intervención de SQM que cambió la Ley de Medioambiente," *CIPER*, May 24, 2018.

53. Witte-Lebhar, "Corruption Scandals Fade."

54. "Chile's SQM Paying"; Benjamin Witte-Lebhar, "Corruption Scandals Fade."

55. On the environmental violations, see chapter 3 and Michelle Carrere, "Chile Renews Contract with Lithium Company Criticized for Damaging Wetland," *Mongabay*, December 26, 2018. For the tax fraud allegations, see "Chile's Tax Office Files Lawsuit Against SQM," BNAmericas, March 23, 2015. On the allegations that SQM registered mining and water rights that belonged to CORFO, see Alberto Arellano, "SQM-CORFO: Las jugadas maestras que consolidaron el poder de Ponce Lerou," *CIPER*, June 13, 2018, and "Declaración Pública Corfo—SQM no llegan a acuerdo por Salar de Atacama," *CORFO*, October 16, 2017. For the violations of labor law, see "Trabajadores de SQM denuncian prácticas antisindicales y exportaciones no autorizadas por parte de la empresa," *Camera de diputadas y diputados*, August 2, 2016, and for the penalty imposed by the labor ministry, see "Empresas y/o empleadores condenados por prácticas antisindicales," Dirección del Trabajo, 2016.

56. US Securities and Exchange Commission, "Chemical and Mining Company of Chile, Inc.," January 2018.

57. Alberto Arellano, "Litio: cómo SQM le sacó los dientes al control de la Comisión de Energía Nuclear," *CIPER*, June 25, 2018.

58. Miguel Silva, "'Por qué es necesario defender el Litio' por Miguel Soto, dirigente sindical Constramet," *Revista de Frente*, January 6, 2022, accessed June 28, 2022.

59. Rodrigo Fuentes, "Movimiento Litio para Chile se manifiesta contra acuerdo Corfo-SQM," *Radio Universidad de Chile*, January 29, 2018.

60. Cronica Digital, "Comuneros Bloquearon el Ingreso a San Pedro de Atacama en Protesta Por Acuerdo Entre Corfo y Sqm," *Cronica Digital*, January 31, 2018; Jonathan Flores, "Comunidades atacameñas bloquean ruta internacional en rechazo al acuerdo entre Corfo y SQM," *BioBioChile*, January 30, 2018.

61. "Daniel Núñez y rechazo de la Cámara a acuerdo Corfo-SQM: 'Se da una señal contra la corrupción'," *Nuevo Mundo*, January 25, 2018; Romina Jara Oliva, "Diputados aprueban proyecto que pide al gobierno expropriar SQM que el litio sea explotado por el Estado," *Diario Financiero*, October 4, 2018.

62. Alberto Arellano, "SQM-CORFO: las jugadas maestras que consolidaron el poder de Ponce Lerou," *CIPER,* June 13, 2018.
63. "Chile Free Trade Agreement," Office of the United States Trade Representative, accessed May 16, 2024; "U.S.-Chile FTA Investor-State Arbitrations," U.S Department of State, accessed May 16, 2024.
64. "Technical Report Summary: Operation Report, Salar de Atacama," SQM, April 2022, 258; "SQM Annual Report 2023," SQM, accessed May 16, 2024, 59.
65. Raymond Vernon, *Sovereignty at Bay: The Multinational Spread of U.S. Enterprises* (Basic Books, 1971).
66. Patricio Aguilera, interview with author, February 20, 2019.
67. Eduardo Bitran, interview with author, June 19, 2019. Bitran's statement is, to date, true. See Michel Jorratt, *"Renta económica, régimen tributario y transparencia fiscal de la minería del litio en la Argentina, Bolivia (Estado Plurinacional de) y Chile,"* Comisión Económica para América Latina y el Caribe (CEPAL), 2022, 16.
68. "Eduardo Bitran defiende acuerdo con SQM," *El Mostrador.*
69. Eduardo Bitran, interview with author, June 19, 2019.
70. "Eduardo Bitran defiende acuerdo con SQM y pregunta a parlamentarios que lo cuestionaron: ¿qué podrían haber hecho que fuera mejor para el país?," *El Mostrador,* January 26, 2018.
71. Marcelo Valdebenito, interview with author, June 25, 2019; Marcelo Valdebenito and Ignacio Mehech, interview with author, May 4, 2022.
72. Pablo Altimiras (vice president of lithium and iodine business, SQM), panel at Lithium Supply & Markets Conference, June 10, 2019.
73. Ellen Lenny-Pessagno (Chile country manager, Albemarle Corporation), "Sustainable Lithium Production," panel at Lithium Supply & Markets Conference (Santiago, Chile), June 11, 2019.
74. Felipe Smith, (commercial VP Iodine & Lithium APAC, SQM), "A View from the Majors," panel at Lithium Supply & Markets Conference (virtual), October 26, 2020.
75. "Sustainable Lithium," SQM, accessed November 9, 2022, https://www.sustainablelithium.com/portfolio/home/.
76. Lenny-Pessagno, "Sustainable Lithium Production."
77. Calcium hydroxide and sodium carbonate are not very toxic as far as chemicals go. However, it is also unclear if these are the only chemicals used, given the proprietary nature of the process. María L. Vera et al., "Environmental Impact of Direct Lithium Extraction from Brines," *Nature Reviews Earth & Environment* 4, no. 3 (2023): 149–65; Victoria Flexer, Celso Fernando Baspineiro, and Claudia Inés Galli, "Lithium Recovery from Brines: A Vital Raw Material for Green Energies with a Potential Environmental Impact in Its Mining And Processing," *Science of the Total Environment* 639 (2018): 1193.
78. Mojtaba Ejeian et al., "Is Lithium Brine Water?," *Desalination* 518 (2021): 115169.

79. "Sustainable Lithium—Who?," SQM, accessed November 9, 2022, https://www.sustainablelithium.com/#WHO.
80. Deborah M. Finch et al., "Conservation and Restoration of Sagebrush Ecosystems and Sage-Grouse: An Assessment of USDA Forest Service Science," United States Department of Agriculture, Forest Service, Rocky Mountain Research Station, 2016; see also US Bureau of Land Management and US Fish and Wildlife Service, "Thacker Pass Lithium Mine Project: Final Environmental Impact Statement," US Bureau of Land Management, December 4, 2020, Appendix R-138.
81. Beatriz Bustos-Gallardo, Gavin Bridge, and Manuel Prieto, "Harvesting Lithium: Water, Brine and the Industrial Dynamics of Production in the Salar de Atacama," *Geoforum* 119 (2021): 185; Bárbara Jerez, Ingrid Garcés, and Robinson Torres, "Lithium Extractivism and Water Injustices in the Salar de Atacama, Chile: The Colonial Shadow of Green Electromobility," *Political Geography* 87 (2021): 6; Manuel Prieto et al., "The (Not-So-Free) Chilean Water Model. The Case of the Antofagasta Region, Atacama Desert, Chile," *Extractive Industries and Society* 11 (2022): 5.
82. Prieto et al., "The (Not-So-Free) Chilean Water Model."
83. Sally Babidge et al., "'That's the Problem with That Lake; It Changes Sides': Mapping Extraction and Ecological Exhaustion in the Atacama," *Journal of Political Ecology* 26, no. 1 (2019): 746.
84. Brendan J. Moran et al., "Relic Groundwater and Prolonged Drought Confound Interpretations of Water Sustainability and Lithium Extraction in Arid Lands," *Earth's Future* 10, no. 7 (2022): 10.
85. See Amanda Maxwell and James J. A. Blair, "Lithium Mining Must Not Dry Up the Atacama Desert," NRDC, May 12, 2022; Chile Sustentable.net, "Cada tonelada de litio requiere la evaporación de 2 mil litros de agua," OCMAL, May 29, 2019.
86. Michelle Carrere, "Chile Renews Contract with Lithium Company Criticized for Damaging Wetland," *Mongabay*, December 26, 2018.
87. James J. A. Blair et al., "Exhausted: How We Can Stop Lithium Mining from Depleting Water Resources, Draining Wetlands, and Harming Communities in South America," National Resource Defense Council (2022), 18; Jerez et al., "Lithium Extractivism," 8.
88. Ministero de Obras Públicas, "Resolución 13 Declara Como Zona De Prohibición Para Nuevas Explotaciones De Aguas Subterráneas En El Sector Hidrogeológico De Aprovechamiento Común Denominado C2 De La Cuenca Del Salar De Atacama, Región De Antofagasta," Biblioteca del Congreso Nacional de Chile, August 16, 2018.
89. "Tras Sobrextracción de Salmuera: SMA Abre Procedimiento Sancionatorio Contra Minera Albemarle," Superintendencia del medioambiente, March 11, 2022. The sanctioning procedure was still ongoing as of November 2024. In the meantime, in May 2024, Albemarle asked the Environmental Assessment Service (SEA) to reassess the permits of both Albemarle and SQM on the ground

that Albemarle had found variations in the water table that it claimed were attributable to overextractions of brine by SQM and that, Albemarle claimed, were causing Albemarle to have to activate its early warning plan. In October 2024, SQM filed a response denying those claims and urging the SEA not to grant Albemarle's request. See https://litoralpress.cl/sitio/Prensa_Texto?LPKey=SHERUG2HYXXRLHDEPIOND2AI7OKC5C6R753JUIN64CE6WQDRTDHA; and https://www.redimin.cl/disputa-litio-sqm-y-albemarle-enfrentan-controversia-ambiental-en-atacama/.

90. Fabian Cambero, "Chilean State Sues BHP, Antofagasta Mines over Atacama Water Use," Reuters, April 8, 2022.
91. "Tribunal Ambiental aprueba conciliación en la demanda por daño ambiental contra de Minera Escondida, Albemarle y Zaldívar," *Revista Nueva Minería y Energía*, December 18, 2024.
92. Evaristus Oshionebo, "Corporations and Nations: Power Imbalance in the Extractive Sector," *American Journal of Economics and Sociology* 77, no. 2 (2018): 419–46.
93. Carolina Diaz, interview with author, April 2, 2019.
94. Dave Sherwood, "Exclusive: Lithium Giants Albemarle and SQM Battle over Access to Atacama Water Study," Reuters, November 17, 2022.
95. National Lithium Commission, *Lithium: A Source of Energy, an Opportunity for Chile* (Final Report) (Santiago: Ministry of Mining, 2014), 32–33.
96. Ramón Balcázar, personal communication with author, December 7, 2022.
97. Monica Musalem Jara, interview with author, February 19, 2019.
98. El Mostrador, "Atacameños se enfrentan con Soquimich por contaminación y uso de aguas," *El Mostrador*, February 18, 2007.
99. "ICMM Toronto Declaration," ICMM, May 15, 2022; Felix Malte Dorn and Hans Gundermann, "Mining Companies, Indigenous Communities, and the State: The Political Ecology of Lithium in Chile (Salar de Atacama) and Argentina (Salar de Olaroz-Cauchari)," *Journal of Political Ecology* 29, no. 1 (2022): 351–52; Lorca et al., "Mining Indigenous Territories: Consensus, Tensions and Ambivalences in the Salar de Atacama," *Extractive Industries and Society* 9 (2022): 7.
100. Dorn and Gundermann, "Mining Companies, Indigenous Communities, and the State," 352.
101. "SQM's Salar de Atacama Operation Becomes the World's First Lithium Mining Operation to Achieve IRMA 75," SQM, September 6, 2023; "Chilean Lithium Miner SQM Says Relations with Indigenous Communities Are Improving," Reuters, January 17, 2021.
102. Heledd Jenkins, "Corporate Social Responsibility and the Mining Industry: Conflicts and Constructs," *Corporate Social Responsibility and Environmental Management* 11, no. 1 (2004): 23–34.
103. "Our Approach," ICMM, accessed July 12, 2024.
104. "ICMM Toronto Declaration," ICMM.
105. For Albemarle's funding of a new community center, see "Communities in Chile," https://www.albemarle.com/cl/en/sustainability/chile-operations/social/

communities-chileac, accessed January 13, 2025. For SQM's vineyard project, see "Vino Ayllu," https://sqmlitio.cl/program-litio/vino-ayllu/, accessed January 13, 2025.

106. Dorn and Gundermann, "Mining Companies, Indigenous Communities, and the State," 353; James J. A. Blair et al., "The 'Afterlives' of Green Extractivism: Lithium Mining and Exhausted Ecologies in the Atacama Desert," *The Afterlives of Extraction: Alternatives and Sustainable Futures* (Brill, 2023), 267–69.

107. Blair et al., "The 'Afterlives' of Green Extractivism," 267–69.

108. "Chilean Lithium Miner SQM."

109. Francisco Mundaca, interview with author, March 13, 2019.

110. Sally Babidge, "Seeing Water: Slow Resistance and the Material Enigma of Extractive Effects on Society and ecology," *HAU: Journal of Ethnographic Theory* 11, no. 2 (2021): 407.

111. This figure includes those working as contractors in lithium installations. See Sally Babidge, "Consultation's Overburden: Indigenous Participation in the Extractives Industry in the Salar de Atacama, Chile," *Transformations* 33 (2020): 56; Fernanda Kalazich, "Memory as Archaeology: An Experience of Public Archaeology in the Atacama Desert," *Public Archaeology* 14, no. 1 (2015): 47.

112. Sergio Cubillos, "Charla: Extractivismo y territorio Indígena," March 12, 2019 (San Pedro de Atacama, Chile).

113. Babidge et al., "'That's the Problem with That Lake'," 747–49.

114. Sergio Cubillos, interview with author, March 13, 2019, San Pedro.

115. Sergio Cubillos, interview with author, March 13, 2019.

116. Babidge, "Consultation's Overburden," 53–54; Dorn and Gundermann, "Mining Companies, Indigenous Communities, and the State," 348–49; Nikolaj Houmann Mortensen, "Much of the World's Lithium Is Being Extracted from Indigenous Peoples' Territories Against Their Will," *Danwatch*, December 1, 2019.

117. Achille Mbembe, "On Private Indirect Government," in *On the Postcolony* (University of California Press, 2001).

118. Beatriz Bustos-Gallardo and Hernán Blanco, "Patta Hoiri and Likanantay People: Rescuing the Knowledge Of The Land," Document presented at Bridging Scales and Epistemologies: Linking Local Knowledge and Global Science in Multi-Scale Assessments conference, Alexandria, Egypt, March 2004; Elizabeth Torrico-Ávila, "The Struggle to Revive the Kunza Language by the Likan Antai Community of San Pedro de Atacama-Chile," Document presented at the 8th Annual Conference of Latin American and Caribbean Social Sciencies, November 2018.

119. Anita Carrasco, "A Biography of Water in Atacama, Chile: Two Indigenous Community Responses to the Extractive Encroachments of Mining," *Journal of Latin American and Caribbean Anthropology* 21, no. 1 (2016): 130–50; Anita Carrasco Moraga, "A Sacred Mountain and the Art of 'Impression Management'," *Mountain Research and Development* 30, no. 4 (2010): 391–97.

CHAPTER 5: THE RETURN OF RESOURCE NATIONALISM

1. Joe Lowry, Emily Hersch, and Eduardo Bitran, "E29: Man on a Mission—Part Two," *Global Lithium Podcast*, December 17, 2018.
2. Rebecca Ann Hughes, "A Powerful Energy Cocktail: Chile Is Taking the Latin Lead in the Race for Renewables," Euronews, December 21, 2023.
3. Ricardo Cuevas, Joaquín Lazo, and Rodrigo Verdejo, "Disputa por los fondos del litio: las zonas grises de la millonaria licitación del Instituto de Tecnologías Limpias," CIPER, February 9, 2021.
4. "Instituto de Tecnologías Limpias: el revelador informe que aprobó la Cámara de Diputados," *Fundación Terram*, April 5, 2022; R. Olmos and A. Rivera, "Corte Suprema anula adjudicación de ITL de Corfo a consorcio extranjero," *Diario Financiero*, July 22, 2022; "Víctor Pérez de ASDIT 'El ITL es un sueño que impactará en todo el mundo,'" *Universidad de Antofagasta*, May, 16, 2023.
5. Dave Sherwood, "How Lithium-Rich Chile Botched a Plan to Attract Battery Makers" Reuters, July 17, 2019; "Controversy over Chile's Lithium Tender Process," IndustriALL Global Union, January 21, 2022; "Chilean Court of Appeals Suspends Lithium Bidding Process," teleSUR, January 14, 2022; Reuters, "Chile Open to All Paths to Lithium Mining, Minister Says," *Mining.com*, June 2, 2022.
6. "CORFO selects BYD to Boost Lithium Added Value," InvestChile Blog, April 24, 2023; James Attwood and Leonardo Lara, "China's BYD Takes Next Steps on $290 Million Lithium Project in Chile," Bloomberg, July 3, 2023.
7. Lionel Lim, "EV Giant BYD Is Getting Serious about a Mexico Plant, as Chinese EV Makers Hope the Country Can Be a Path into the U.S.," *Fortune*, February 14, 2023.
8. "China's Tsingshan Plans $233 Million Lithium-Related Investment in Chile—Chile's President," Reuters, October 16, 2023.
9. "CORFO selects BYD"; "Lithium: Chilean President Announces US$233 Million Chinese Investment in Mejillones," InvestChile Blog, October 16, 2023.
10. Glenn Dyer, "BYD Delays Lithium Cathode Project in Chile," *Sharecafe*, May 15, 2024. Thus far, the Tsingshan plant is still slated for May 2025; see Valeria Ibarra, "Tsingshan avanza en su fábrica de baterías de litio en Mejillones por US$ 233 millones," *Diario Financiero*, May 16, 2024; https://www.mining.com/web/byd-says-fate-of-lithium-project-is-in-hands-of-chile-government/.
11. James J. A. Blair et al., "The 'Afterlives' of Green Extractivism: Lithium Mining and Exhausted Ecologies in the Atacama Desert," *The Afterlives of Extraction: Alternatives and Sustainable Futures* (Brill, 2023), 274.
12. John Bartlett, "Chile Students' Mass Fare-Dodging Expands into City-Wide Protest," *The Guardian*, October 18, 2019.
13. Fabian Cambero, "Chile Election Favorite Talks Up State Lithium Firm, Slams 'Error' of Privatization," Reuters, December 1, 2021.
14. Cambero, "Chile Election Favorite."
15. Gabriel Boric, "Presidente de la República, Gabriel Boric Font, presenta

Estrategia Nacional del Litio," Presidencia de la República de Chile, April 20, 2023.
16. Boric, "Estrategia Nacional del Litio."
17. Liz Kimbrough, "Ecuador Court Upholds 'Rights of Nature,' Blocks Intag Valley Copper Mine," *Mongabay*, March 31, 2023.
18. Rose J. Spalding, *Breaking Ground: From Extraction Booms to Mining Bans in Latin America* (Oxford University Press, 2023); Paul Cisneros, "A Comparative Study of the Introduction of Restrictions to Large-Scale Mining in Four Latin American Countries," *Review of Policy Research* 37, no. 5 (2020): 687–712; Mariana Walter and Joan Martinez-Alier, "How to Be Heard When Nobody Wants to Listen: Community Action Against Mining in Argentina," *Canadian Journal of Development Studies/Revue canadienne d'études du développement* 30, nos. 1–2 (2010): 281–301; Sandra Cuffe, "Guatemalans Strongly Reject Mining Project in Local Referendum," *Mongabay*, September 23, 2022. NB: Under pressure from President Nayib Bukele, lawmakers recently overturned El Salvador's mining ban, despite public support for the prohibition. See Maxwell Radwin, "El Salvador Reverses Landmark Mining Ban, Setting up Clash with Activists," *Mongabay*, January 13, 2025.
19. Boric, "Estrategia Nacional del Litio."
20. Boric, "Estrategia Nacional del Litio."
21. Evo Morales Ayma, Presidente Constitucional de la Republica, Bolivia, Decreto Supremo N° 29496, adopted April 1, 2008.
22. Martín Obaya, "The Evolution of Resource Nationalism: The Case of Bolivian Lithium," *Extractive Industries and Society* 8, no. 3 (2021): 100932.
23. David Agren, "Mexico Nationalises Lithium in Populist President's Push to Extend State Control," *Financial Times*, April 20, 2022.
24. Andrés Manuel López Obrador, Presidente de los Estados Unidos Mexicanos, "Decreto por el que se reforman y adicionan diversas disposiciones de la Ley Minera," adopted April 20, 2022.
25. Andrés Manuel López Obrador, Presidente de los Estados Unidos Mexicanos, "Decreto por el que se crea el organismo público descentralizado denominado Litio para México," adopted August 23, 2022.
26. Cecilia Jamasmie, "South America Looks at Creating 'Lithium OPEC'," *Mining.com*, March 6, 2023; Elias Ferrer, "Is This the Dawn of a 'Lithium OPEC'?," *Forbes*, August 8, 2023.
27. Isabeau van Halm, "Zimbabwe Joins the Wave of Resource Nationalism," *Mining Technology*, January 19, 2023; Nosmot Gbadamosi, "Zimbabwe's 'White Gold'," *Foreign Policy*, August 16, 2023.
28. Jonah Allen et al., "Mineral Wealth and Electrification: A Producer-Country Perspective," Jain Family Institute, November 21, 2024. For Tanzania, see Temitope Oke, "Lithium Refinery Surge in Africa as Export Bans Bite," *News Central – Africa*, September 5, 2024.
29. Angela Tritto, "How Indonesia Used Chinese Industrial Investments to Turn Nickel into the New Gold," Carnegie Endowment for International Peace,

April 11, 2023. For a helpful time line of the process, see "Prohibition of the Export of Nickel Ore," IEA, last updated December 12, 2023. For battery plant investments, see Erwida Maulia, "Hyundai and LG Start Building $1.1Bn EV Battery Plant in Indonesia," *Nikkei Asia*, September 15, 2021; "Indonesia Says Tesla Plans to Invest in Battery Material Facility," Reuters, August 14, 2023.

30. Jimena Blanco and Jess Middleton, "Protectionism Spiking as Critical Minerals Race Intensifies," *Verisk Maplecroft*, December 12, 2024.
31. Eva Vergara and Daniel Politi, "Chile's Plan for State Control in Lithium Dismays Business," *Associated Press*, April 21, 2023; Adam Williams, "Mexican Mining Industry Under Threat from Sweeping New Regulations," *Financial Times*, June 5, 2023; Clara Denina and Wendell Roelf, "Africa Gears up to Keep More of the Profits from Lithium Boom," Reuters, February 9, 2023.
32. Gonzalo Gutierrez, interview with author, April 27, 2022.
33. "'Una política de fomento al extractivismo': las críticas por los avances de la Estrategia Nacional del Litio," Diario UChile, Radio UChile, March 3, 2024,
34. "Consejo de Pueblos Atacameños rechazó Estrategia Nacional del Litio," Diario UChile, May 4, 2023.
35. This pattern is discussed in more depth in chapter 8.
36. The ILO adopted the "Indigenous and Tribal Peoples Convention," No. 169, in 1989; this was the first international agreement recognizing Indigenous peoples' rights to prior consultation. See International Labour Organization, "Indigenous and Tribal Peoples Convention, 1989," C169, adopted June 27, 1989.
37. For discussion of the limitations on consultations in Chile, resulting in both infrequent and superficial application, see Alexandra Tomaselli, "Processes and Failures of Prior Consultations with Indigenous Peoples in Chile," in *The Prior Consultation of Indigenous Peoples in Latin America*, ed. Claire Wright and Alexandra Tomaselli (Taylor & Francis, 2019), 121–22.
38. Antoine Maillet and Francisco Martínez, "La instalación de las demandas ambientales en el inicio de la Convención Constitucional," *Colectivo de Estudios Político-Ambientales* (2021), 17; Antoine Maillet and Francisco Martínez, "El despliegue para la arremetida ambiental en la Convención," *Colectivo de Estudios Político-Ambientales* (2021): 3.
39. Flora Genoux, "In the Midst of Chile's Megadrought, Anger Turns Toward Avocados," *Le Monde*, October 20, 2022; "Meet Six People Fighting Water Scarcity Across the Globe," Blomberg News, October 26, 2021.
40. Genoux, "Anger Turns Toward Avocados"; Bloomberg News, "Meet Six People Fighting Water Scarcity"; "Quienes Somos," MODATIMA, accessed July 15, 2024 (Vilches listed as a member in Maillet and Martínez, "La instalación de las demandas ambientales"). For more on MODATIMA, see Robinson Torres-Salinas and Amaya Alvez Marin, "Water Commons as a Socioenvironmental Project for the 21st Century in Chile," *Water Policy* 25, no. 2 (2023): 117–18.
41. Escenarios Hídricos 2030, "Radiografía del Agua: Brecha y Riesgo Hídrico en Chile," Fundación Chile, June 2018. On desalination, see "Anuario de

Estadísticas del Cobre y Otros Minerales 2001–2020," COCHILCO, 2021, 74; Scott D. Odell and Anthony Bebbington, "Mine Ownership and Community Relations: Comparing Hydrosocial Dynamics of Public and Private Companies in Chile," *Resources Policy* 81 (2023): 103380.

42. "Escondida Water Supply," Bechtel, accessed July 15, 2024.
43. James Attwood, "Chile Copper Mines Dodge Radical Changes as Convention Vote Ends," Bloomberg, last updated May 16, 2022.
44. Cecilia Jamasmie, "Chile a Step Closer to Nationalizing Copper and Lithium," *Mining.com*, March 7, 2022.
45. Jonathan Gilbert and Daniela Sirtori, "Lithium Nationalism Is Taking Root in Region with Most Resources," Bloomberg, June 29, 2021.
46. Ignacio Mehech and Marcelo Valdebenito, interview with author, April 26, 2022.
47. Reuters, "Chile Open to All Paths to Lithium Mining, Minister Says," *Mining Weekly*, June 3, 2022.
48. Pedro Glatz Brahm, interview with author, April 28, 2022.
49. Consejo de Pueblos Atacameños (@CP_Atacamenos), "Si no nos quieren oír, es tiempo de hablar más fuerte. El Acuerdo #Codelco #SQM repite la historia de los acuerdos inconsultos, el pueblo Atacameño hace llamado urgente a," X, January 8, 2024.
50. James Attwood, "Chile's SQM Reaches Lithium Mining Accord with Codelco," Bloomberg, last updated December 28, 2023.
51. "Comunidades Indígenas Atacameñas, Codelco y SQM acuerdan constituir Mesa de diálogo en el marco de la Estrategia Nacional del Litio," Codelco, December 15, 2023.
52. "Protest at Chile's Lithium Salt Flats Snarls Roads to SQM, Albemarle," Reuters, January 10, 2024; "Protest Ends at Chile's Lithium Salt Flats with Promise of Boric Visit," Reuters, January 13, 2024.
53. María del Mar Parra, "Comunidades andinas piden mostrar a Boric 2 lugares dañados por minería en Salar de Atacama," *El Desconcierto*, January 16, 2024.
54. Carlos Ulloa Fuentes, "Atacameño Communities Maintain Protest Camps in the Atacama Salt Flat and Raise Awareness About the Environmental Impacts of Lithium Mining," Observatorio Plurinacional de Salares Andinos, January 29, 2024.
55. Mauricio Becerra, "Litio: Comunidades lickanantay vuelven a tomarse acceso a planta de SQM," *El Ciudadano*, January 1, 2023.
56. CARM, "Chile abre 26 salares de litio a explotación privada en nueva estrategia nacional," Pachamama Radio, March 27, 2023.
57. Barinia Montoya, "Expertos critican ausencia de criterios científicos en red de salares protegidos anunciados por el gobierno de Chile," *Mongabay*, April 11, 2024.
58. Montoya, "Expertos critican ausencia." See also this declaration: "Declaración Organizaciones socioambientales alertan: Gobierno ecológico planea explotar cerca del 50% de la superficie de los salares del país," Google Forms, accessed July 15, 2024, https://docs.google.com/forms/d/e/1FAIpQLSdUQRYGF9pTqqRfEDPD81bWHfCBPTDBfQxFKtiHWyUOQ3zE6w/viewform.

CHAPTER 6: GREEN DOMINANCE

1. Peter Handley, interview with author, December 11, 2019.
2. J. W. Mason, "The Economy During Wartime," *Dissent* 64, no. 4 (2017): 140–44. For the importance of raw materials from across the Western Hemisphere, see José L. Bolívar Fresneda, *The Caribbean Front in World War II: The Untold Story of U-Boats, Spies, and Economic Warfare* (Markus Wiener Publishers, 2021); María Emilia Paz, *Strategy, Security, and Spies: Mexico and the US as Allies in World War II* (Penn State University Press, 1997); Erasmo Gamboa, *Mexican Labor & World War II: Braceros in the Pacific Northwest, 1942–1947* (University of Washington Press, 2000); Frank D. McCann, "Brazil and World War II: The forgotten ally. What did you do in the war, Zé Carioca?," *Estudios interdisciplinarios de America Latina y el Caribe* 6, no. 2 (1995): 35–70; Seth Garfield, "The Amazon's Greatest Generation? A Forgotten History of World War II," *Americas Quarterly* 11, no. 1 (2017): 16; Alfred E. Eckes, *The United States and the Global Struggle for Minerals* (University of Texas Press, 1979), 89–120.
3. G. Richards Gwinn, "Minor Nonmetals," in *Minerals Yearbook 1942*, ed. C. E. Needham (United States Government Printing Office, 1943), 1530; Jack Ryan, "Expansion Pushed in Lithium Output," *New York Times*, December 12, F1, F10.
4. Alden P. Armagnac, "What is the H-bomb?," *Popular Science*, April 1950, 145.
5. Alice L. Buck, "A History of the Atomic Energy Commission," US Department of Energy, 1983, 2.
6. Buck, "A History of the Atomic Energy Commission."
7. Fabio Bulfone, "The Political Economy of Industrial Policy in the European Union," MPIfG Discussion Paper 20/12, Max Planck Institute for the Study of Societies, 5–8; Paul Cohen, "Lessons from the Nationalization Nation: State-Owned Enterprises in France," *Dissent*, Winter 2010; Barbara Ward, "Europe Debates Nationalization," *Foreign Affairs*, October 1, 1946; David Parker, "Privatization in the European Union: A Critical Assessment of Its Development, Rationale and Consequences," *Economic and Industrial Democracy* 20, no. 1 (1999): 16.
8. Parker, "Privatization in the European Union," 10–12.
9. Gregory Hooks, "The Rise of the Pentagon and U.S. State Building: The Defense Program as Industrial Policy," *American Journal of Sociology* 96, no. 2 (September 1990): 358–404.
10. John D. Graham, Keith B. Belton, and Suri Xia, "How China Beat the US in Electric Vehicle Manufacturing," *Issues in Science and Technology* 37, no. 2 (2021): 72–79.
11. Shiqi Ou et al., "The Dual-Credit Policy: Quantifying the Policy Impact on Plug-In Electric Vehicle Sales and Industry Profits in China," *Energy Policy* 121 (2018): 597–610.
12. Melissa Eddy, "European Union to Ban Gas-Powered Cars by 2035," *New York Times*, February 14, 2023. On the subsequent exemption for synthetic fuels, see Stephen Edelstein, "EU Adds e-Fuels Loophole to 2035 ICE Ban, EV Charging Guidelines," *Green Car Reports*, March 30, 2023.

13. John Helveston and Jonas Nahm, "China's Key Role in Scaling Low-Carbon Energy Technologies," *Science* 366, no. 6467 (2019): 794–96.
14. Steve LeVine, "A Looming New Supply Shortage Threatens the EV Industry's Hopes for the 2020s," *The Information*, October 3, 2021; Neil Winton, "Lithium Shortage May Stall Electric Car Revolution and Embed China's Lead: Report," *Forbes*, last updated November 15, 2021; Marian Willuhn, "How Long Will the Lithium Supply Last?," *pv magazine*, September 15, 2020.
15. Jeniece Pettitt, "How the U.S. Fell Behind in Lithium, the 'White Gold' of Electric Vehicles," CNBC, last updated January 17, 2022; "China Dominates the Lithium-Ion Battery Supply Chain, but Europe Is on the Rise," BloombergNEF, September 16, 2020.
16. European Commission, "Tackling the Challenges in Commodity Markets and on Raw Material," COM(2011) 25, March 2, 2011; National Research Council, *Minerals, Critical Minerals, and the U.S. Economy* (National Academies Press, 2008), ix–x, 57–61, 76–77; Slavko V. Šolar, Luca Demicheli, and Patrick Wall, "Raw Materials Initiative: A Contribution to the European Minerals Policy Framework," in *Non-Renewable Resource Issues: Geoscientific and Societal Challenges*, ed. Richard Sinding-Larsen and Friedrich-W. Wellmer (Springer, 2012), 22.
17. European Commission, "Tackling the Challenges"; National Research Council, *Minerals*, ix–x, 57–61, 76–77; Šolar et al., "Raw Materials Initiative," 22.
18. US Geological Survey, "Rare Earths," *Mineral Commodity Summaries 2023*, January 2023. For surveying efforts, see e.g., "Earth Mapping Resources Initiative," US Geological Survey, accessed July 18, 2024.
19. Stephen B. Castor, "Rare Earth Deposits of North America," *Resource Geology* 58, no. 4 (2008): 337–47.
20. US Geological Survey, "Rare Earths."
21. Michael Standaert, "China Wrestles with the Toxic Aftermath of Rare Earth Mining," *Yale Environment 360*, July 2, 2019; Alice Su, "The Hidden Costs of China's Rare-Earth Trade," *Los Angeles Times*, July 29, 2019.
22. Julie Michelle Klinger, *Rare Earth Frontiers: From Terrestrial Subsoils to Lunar Landscapes* (Cornell University Press, 2018), 128–43.
23. Klinger, *Rare Earth Frontiers*, 143–46.
24. US Department of Energy, "Critical Materials Strategy," 2010, 6; Klinger, *Rare Earth Frontiers*, 113–14; Tobin Hansen, "Securing U.S. Access to Rare Earth Elements," *Defense360*, 2020, 4; National Research Council, *Minerals*, 22–23, 40–41, 128–36.
25. US Department of Energy, "Critical Materials Strategy," 99.
26. U.S. Department of the Interior, "Final List of Critical Minerals 2018," 83 FR 23295, Federal Register, May 18, 2018.
27. Trump's 2018 executive order designating new minerals for inclusion in the category was paired with a directive to expedite their permitting, and the list of critical minerals that get tax breaks in the IRA is the same as the 2022 USGS list with some more specificity around purity.

28. Executive Office of the President, United States of America, "Addressing the Threat to the Domestic Supply Chain from Reliance on Critical Minerals from Foreign Adversaries and Supporting the Domestic Mining and Processing Industries," E.O. 13953, adopted September 30, 2020.
29. Albemarle Corporation, "Albemarle Selected by U.S. Department of Energy for Lithium Research Projects," PRNewswire, September 2, 2020.
30. "Murkowski, Manchin, Colleagues Introduce Bipartisan Legislation to Strengthen America's Mineral Security," Senate Committee on Energy & Natural Resources, May 3, 2019.
31. Francis Fannon, panel at EV Fest 2020 (online), May 28, 2020.
32. "U.S. Department of Energy Announces New Vehicle Technologies Funding and Future Partnerships with Battery Industry," Office of Energy Efficiency & Renewable Energy, US Department of Energy, June 14, 2021.
33. US Congress, "Defense Production Act of 1950, As Amended," 50 USC § 4501 et seq., last amended August 13, 2018, Sec. 101.
34. Brett Hansard, "New Argonne Study Puts Charge into Drive for Sustainable Lithium Production," Argonne National Laboratory press release, July 13, 2021; Jarod C. Kelly, "Energy, Greenhouse Gas, and Water Life Cycle Analysis of Lithium Carbonate and Lithium Hydroxide Monohydrate from Brine and Ore Resources and Their Use in Lithium Ion Battery Cathodes and Lithium Ion Batteries," *Resources, Conservation and Recycling* 174 (2021): 105762; Beth Burmahl, "Bridging the Lithium Battery Supply Chain Gap—A New Alliance in the US," Argonne National Laboratory, October 27, 2021; "DOE Announces $209 Million for Electric Vehicles Battery Research," US Department of Energy, October 27, 2021; US Congress, "Defense Production Act," Section 302. See also Ana Swanson, "Biden Invokes Cold War Statute to Boost Critical Mineral Supply," *New York Times*, March 31, 2022; Joseph R. Biden, Jr., President, US, "Memorandum on Presidential Determination Pursuant to Section 303 of the Defense Production Act of 1950, As Amended," Presidential Determination No. 2022-11, March 31, 2022.
35. Emma Dumain and Jael Holzman, "Biden's Boost for Mineral Mining Splits Hill Climate Hawks," *E&E News*, March 31, 2022.
36. US House of Representatives, "Infrastructure Investment and Jobs Act," H.R.3684, adopted November 15, 2021.
37. See US House of Representatives, "Infrastructure Investment and Jobs Act," Secs. 40201, 40204, 40206, 40207, 40208, 40210.
38. US House of Representatives, "Inflation Reduction Act of 2022," H.R.5376, adopted August 16, 2022, Sec. 13502; "Accounting for Inflation Reduction Act Energy Incentives," PwC, last updated August 10, 2023.
39. Ana Swanson, "Congress Is Giving Billions to the Chip Industry. Strings Are Attached," *New York Times*, August 3, 2022.
40. "FACT SHEET: President Biden Takes Action to Protect American Workers and Businesses from China's Unfair Trade Practices," The White House, May 14, 2023.

41. Brendan Murray, "Why Biden Is Escalating Trump's China Tariffs," Bloomberg, July 12, 2024.
42. Brad Setser, "EMERGENCY POD: Setser on Biden's Electric Curtain," interview by Jordan Schneider, *ChinaTalk*, May 15, 2024, audio, 1:18.
43. "Unleashing American Energy," The White House, January 20, 2025; Ernest Scheyder and Jarrett Renshaw, "Exclusive: Trump Seeks Minerals Refining on Pentagon Bases to Boost US Output, Sources Say," Reuters, March 10, 2025.
44. European Commission, "Critical Raw Materials: Ensuring Secure and Sustainable Supply Chains for EU's Green and Digital Future," press release, March 16, 2023. See also, Ben Judah, Shahin Vallée, and Tim Sahay, "Escaping the Permanent Suez: Navigating the Geopolitics of European Decarbonization," Atlantic Council, January 2024, 12–15. NB: At the time of writing, and in response to the US withdrawal of military aid to Ukraine, Germany's parliament has voted to loosen these fiscal rules, and the EU Commission is considering similar proposals at the regional level. See Anne-Sylvaine Chassany, "Germany's Parliament Approves Friedrich Merz's €1tn Spending Plan," *Financial Times*, March 18, 2025.
45. See Bentley B. Allan and Jonas Nahm, "Strategies of Green Industrial Policy: How States Position Firms in Global Supply Chains," *American Political Science Review* (2024): 1–15; Lisa O'Carroll, "EU announces €4bn State Aid to Back Battery and Green Tech Factories," *The Guardian*, January 8, 2024.
46. See the terms of the EU's "Stability and Growth Pact" here: "Glossary: Stability and Growth Pact (SGP)," Statistics Explained, Eurostar, accessed May 23, 2024.
47. Christian Scheinert, "EU's Response to the US Inflation Reduction Act (IRA)," European Parliament Think Tank, June 2, 2023.
48. For the phrase "bottomless mimosas," referring to uncapped tax credits, see Ted Fertik, Daniela Gabor, and Tim Sahay, "Defining Bidenomics," interview by Daniel Denvir, *Phenomenal World*, September 2, 2023.
49. Analysts at Roskill, interviews with author, February 23, March 4, and March 11, 2021.
50. European Commission et al., "Clean Energy Technology Observatory: Batteries for Energy Storage in the European Union—2022 Status Report on Technology Development, Trends, Value Chains and Markets," Publications Office of the European Union, 2022, 4.
51. See Bentley B. Allan and Jonas Nahm, "Strategies of Green Industrial Policy: How States Position Firms in Global Supply Chains," *American Political Science Review* (2024): 1–15; "Zero Carbon Lithium," European Investment Bank, February 22, 2024.
52. These investments occur via the fund EIT InnoEnergy. See Ben Kilbey, "Infinity Lithium Secures EU-Backing for Spanish Project," S&P Global, June 18, 2020; Alexander Richter, "Vulcan Secures Agreement on Help Launching Geothermal Lithium Project," ThinkGeoEnergy, May 27, 2020; "The Business Investment Platform Closes Agreement to Support Savannah Resouces," EIT

InnoEnergy, May 28, 2020; *Mining.com* editor, "Snapshot: Key Lithium Mining Projects Around The World," *Mining.com*, January 22, 2021. For the new fund, see "EIT InnoEnergy and Demeter Launch EUR 500 Million European Battery Raw Materials Fund," European Institute of Innovation & Technology, January 22, 2024.

53. "KfW Establishes Raw Materials Fund" KfW, October 2, 2024; Aleksandra Kozaczyńska, "A New Tool in Germany's Raw Materials Policy," Centre for Eastern Sudies, October 11, 2024.
54. Maroš Šefčovič, "Speech by Vice-President Šefčovič at the Press Conference Following the 5th High-Level Meeting of the European Battery Alliance," European Commission, March 12, 2021.
55. See Council of the EU, "Strategic Autonomy: Council Gives Its Final Approval on the Critical Raw Minerals Act," press release, March 18, 2024, for the announcement of adoption of the act; for the main components of the act, see European Commission, "Critical Raw Materials."
56. European Commission, "Green Deal: EU Agrees New Law on More Sustainable and Circular Batteries to Support EU's Energy Transition and Competitive Industry," press release, December 9, 2022.
57. European Commission, "Proposal for a Regulation of the European Parliament and of the Council Concerning Batteries and Waste Batteries, Repealing Directive 2006/66/EC and Amending Regulation (EU) No 2019/1020," December 10, 2020.
58. European Commission, "Green Deal: Sustainable Batteries for a Circular and Climate Neutral Economy," press release, December 10, 2020. For strategic autonomy, see Mario Damen, "EU Strategic Autonomy 2013–2023: From Concept to Capacity," European Parliament Think Tank, July 8, 2022; Kjeld van Wieringen and Marcos Fernández Álvarez, "Securing the EU's Supply of Critical Raw Materials," European Parliament Think Tank, July 7, 2022.
59. Handley, interview with author.
60. Joanna Szychowska, interview with author, December 10, 2019.
61. Scooter Doll, "CATL's Battery Plant in Germany, Its First Outside of China, Receives Production Approval for 8 GWh Per Year," *Elektrek*, April 6, 2022; AMS, "CATL's German Plant Starts Battery Cell Production," *AMS*, January 4, 2023.
62. "CATL Announces Its Second European Battery Plant in Hungary," CATL, August 12, 2022.
63. "CATL in Germany," CATL, accessed April 3, 2025.
64. Doll, "CATL's Battery Plant."
65. Seth Lightcap, "Thacker Pass: The Crossroads of Lithium, Wild Snow and Sacred Land," *Tahoe Quarterly*, December 6, 2021.
66. "Thacker Pass Lithium Mine in Humboldt County, NV," Great Basin Resource Watch, accessed July 18, 2024.
67. *Mining.com* staff writer, "Lithium Americas' Thacker Pass Closer to Production," *Mining.com*, December 4, 2020.

68. EVANNEX, "Nevada's 'Lithium Valley' Could Provide Domestic Supply For Tesla Batteries," *InsideEVs*, May 1, 2020.
69. In October 2023, Lithium Americas formally split into Lithium Argentina and Lithium Americas. "LAAC Separation," Lithium Americas, October 3, 2023.
70. Megan Janetsky et al., "Native Groups Sit on a Treasure Trove of Lithium. Now Mines Threaten Their Water, Culture and Wealth" Associated Press, March 13, 2024.
71. Patrick Donnelly, "Western U.S. Lithium," Google map, accessed June 26, 2023.
72. US Government Accountability Office, "Mining on Federal Lands: More Than 800 Operations Authorized to Mine and Total Mineral Production Is Unknown," US Government Accountability Office, 2020.
73. See chapter 7 for further discussion of this law, as well as activist demands to reform it.
74. "1872 Mining Law," Earthworks, accessed July 18, 2024.
75. Jael Holzman, "Mining Companies Strike Gold with New Climate Law," *E&E News*, August 18, 2022.
76. For specific loan details, see Lithium Americas, "Lithium Americas Receives Conditional Commitment for $2.26 Billion ATVM Loan from the U.S. DOE for Construction of Thacker Pass," press release, March 14, 2024. For DOE's general approach to direct loans, see "LPO's Loans and Loan Guarantees: Overview and Characteristics of Its Financing Options," Loans Program Office, US Department of Energy, March 14, 2024.
77. Ines Ferré, "Crashing Lithium Prices Turn the Industry from 'Euphoria' to 'Despair.' What's Next?," *Yahoo Finance*, last updated February 20, 2024.
78. Bradley Crowell, interview with author, October 14, 2021.
79. Mining accounts for 3 percent of the state's share of GDP and 1 percent of employment. For total state income, see US Bureau of Economic Analysis, "Gross Domestic Product: All Industry Total in Nevada," FRED, Federal Reserve Bank of St. Louis, accessed July 22, 2024. For mining contribution, see US Bureau of Economic Analysis, "Gross Domestic Product: Natural Resources and Mining (11, 21) in Nevada," FRED, Federal Reserve Bank of St. Louis, accessed July 22, 2024. For employment statistics, see "Economy at a Glance: Nevada," US Bureau of Labor Statistics, accessed July 22, 2024.
80. Mike Visher, interview with author, December 1, 2021.
81. Visher, interview with author.

CHAPTER 7: GREEN MINING

1. Javier Martinez de Olcoz Cerdan, panel at Lithium Supply & Markets Conference, Santiago, Chile, June 11, 2019.
2. In the words of Ken Hoffman, of Mckinsey & Company, during the same session. Ken Hoffman, panel at Lithium Supply & Markets Conference, Santiago, Chile, June 11, 2019.

3. Spot market prices, with CYN converted to USD, obtained from "Lithium," Trading Economics, accessed May 27, 2024.
4. Ahmed Mehdi, "Lithium Price Volatility: Where Next for the Market?," Oxford Institute for Energy Studies, February 2024.
5. Mehdi, "Lithium Price Volatility," 5–6.
6. Aleksandra Natalia Wojewska et al., "The Criticality of Lithium and the Finance-Sustainability Nexus: Supply-Demand Perceptions, State Policies, Production Networks, and Financial Actors," *Extractive Industries and Society* 17 (March 2024): 5–7.
7. For more on commodities exchanges, as well as contrasting views on whether such financial instruments smooth or exacerbate commodity price volatility, see Javier Blas and Jack Farchy, *The World for Sale: Money, Power, and the Traders Who Barter the Earth's Resources* (Oxford University Press, 2021); Rupert Russell, *Price Wars: How the Commodity Markets Made Our Chaotic World* (Weidenfeld & Nicholson, 2022).
8. Yvonne Yue Li, "Lithium Trading Hits Record on CME as Funds Seize Budding Market," Bloomberg, April 2, 2024.
9. Yue Li, "Lithium Trading Hits Record."
10. "Executive Panel," panel at Lithium Supply & Markets Conference, Santiago, Chile, June 11, 2019.
11. Frik Els, "And the Winner for Most Volatile Commodity This Decade Goes to . . . Lithium," *Mining.com*, January 12, 2023.
12. IEA, "Global Critical Minerals Outlook 2024," IEA, 2024.
13. "Chile's SQM Profits Jump More Than Ten-Fold on Lithium Price Surge," Reuters, November 16, 2022; Zhang Yushuo, "Tianqi, Other Chinese Lithium Miners Say 2022 Profits Shot Up on Higher Prices," Yicai Global, January 20, 2023; "Albemarle Sees Quarterly Earnings Above Estimates on Tight Lithium Supply," Reuters, January 23, 2023.
14. Ernest Scheyder, "Albemarle Calls for High Lithium Prices to Fuel EV Industry Growth," Reuters, January 24, 2023. In addition, see slides 32 and 39 of the slide deck shown at the meeting: "2023 Strategic Update," Albemarle, January 23, 2023.
15. For Albemarle margins, see Scheyder, "Albemarle Calls for High Lithium Prices." For industry average, see M. Garside, "Net Profit Margin of the Top Mining Companies Worldwide from 2002 to 2023, with a Forecast for 2024," Statista, July 4, 2024.
16. Mehdi, "Lithium Price Volatility," 2.
17. Marija Maisch, "New Sodium-Ion Developments from CATL, BYD, Huawei," *PV Magazine*, November 28, 2024.
18. "BriefCASE: Sodium-Ion Batteries to Unseat Lithium? Na, but They'll Be Worth Their Salt," S&P Global Mobility, March 20, 2024.
19. Maisch, "New Sodium-Ion Developments from CATL, BYD, Huawei."
20. Sarah Raza, "Lithium-Ion Batteries Have Ruled for Decades. Now They Have a Challenger," *Washington Post*, November 3, 2024.

21. Maisch, "New Sodium-Ion Developments from CATL, BYD, Huawei."
22. General Motors Co., "GM and Lithium Americas to Develop U.S.-Sourced Lithium Production Through $650 Million Equity Investment and Supply Agreement," press release, January 31, 2023.
23. Lithium Americas, "Unlocking Thacker Pass," press release, October 16, 2024.
24. Harry Dempsey and Peter Campbell, "Carmakers Switch to Direct Deals with Miners to Power Electric Vehicles," *Financial Times*, November 14, 2022.
25. See "Sustainability Now a Critical Metric for Lithium Supply Agreements," Benchmark Source, January 26, 2024.
26. Wojewska et al., "The Criticality of Lithium and the Finance-Sustainability Nexus," 10.
27. Stefano Ponte, "Green Capital Accumulation: Business and Sustainability Management in a World Of Global Value Chains," *New Political Economy* 25, no. 1 (2020): 72–73.
28. "Fact-finding Expedition to the Lithium Desert of Chile," Volkswagen Newsroom, March 10, 2020; Ford Motor Company, "Ford Motor Company Is First American Automaker to Join Initiative Promoting Responsible Mining," press release, February 15, 2021.
29. BMW Group, "BMW Group Commissions Study on Sustainable Lithium Extraction," press release, December 16, 2020.
30. Ben Kilbey, "VW Aims to Increase Battery Supply Chain Transparency," S&P Global, September 11, 2020; "Transform the Future," BMW of North America, accessed July 19, 2024; Daimler North America, "Mercedes-Benz Will in Future Only Source Battery Cells with Cobalt & Lithium from Certified Mining Sites, While Significantly Reducing Cobalt," press release, November 12, 2020.
31. Volkswagen Newsroom, "Fact-Finding Expedition."
32. For these biographical details, see Franziska Killiches's LinkedIn account, https://www.linkedin.com/in/franziska-killiches-60343210b/, accessed January 22, 2024.
33. Volkswagen Newsroom, "Fact-Finding Expedition."
34. Volkswagen Newsroom, "Fact-Finding Expedition."
35. Volkswagen Newsroom, "Fact-Finding Expedition."
36. Franziska Killiches, "Ich versuche, Licht ins Dunkel zu bringen," interview by Nina Treml, *Der Bund*, September 25, 2021.
37. "Responsible Raw Materials Report 2023," Volkswagen, May 2024, 7.
38. "Responsible Raw Materials Report 2023," Volkswagen, 25.
39. Killiches, "Ich versuche, Licht ins Dunkel zu bringen."
40. Killiches, "Ich versuche, Licht ins Dunkel zu bringen."
41. Volkswagen Newsroom, "Fact-Finding Expedition."
42. "Responsible Raw Materials Report 2023," 15–18.
43. "Lithium Extraction Company Vulcan Adds VW to Customer Line-Up," Reuters, December 8, 2021.
44. "Lithium Extraction with a Carbon-Free Footprint," EIT InnoEnergy, accessed January 13, 2025.

45. Monica Raymunt, "VW Warns Soaring EU Energy Costs Render Battery Plants Unviable," Bloomberg, November 28, 2022.
46. Volkswagen Newsroom, "Fact-Finding Expedition."
47. Sebastian Schaffer, "Volkswagen Group, BASF, Daimler AG and Fairphone Start Partnership for Sustainable Lithium Mining in Chile," Volkswagen, June 8, 2021.
48. Franziska Killiches's LinkedIn account, https://www.linkedin.com/in/franziska-killiches-60343210b/, accessed January 22, 2024.
49. For Killiches's discussion of the Responsible Lithium Partnership, see "Cross-Sector Collaboration is Key for Effective Due Diligence," CSR Europe, June 24, 2021. See also Schaffer, "Volkswagen Group, BASF, Daimler AG and Fairphone Start Partnership for Sustainable Lithium Mining in Chile." For Fairphone, see "Our Impact," Fairphone, https://www.fairphone.com/en/impact/, accessed January 13, 2025.
50. GIZ staff, interview with author, August 26, 2021.
51. GIZ staff, interview with author, April 26, 2022.
52. See "RCS Global Group," RCS Global Group, accessed January 13, 2025, and "About RCS Global Group," RCS Global Group, accessed January 13, 2025, respectively, for quotes.
53. "Global Witness," Global Witness, accessed July 20, 2024. For Mitchell's résumé, see "Harrison Mitchell," LinkedIn, accessed July 20, 2024.
54. Harrison Mitchell, "Responsible Sourcing of Lithium," panel at Lithium Supply & Markets Conference (virtual), October 28, 2020.
55. Amnesty International, "Amnesty Challenges Industry Leaders to Clean Up Their Batteries," press release, March 21, 2019; "'This is What We Die For': Human Rights Abuses in the Democratic Republic of the Congo Power the Global Trade in Cobalt," Amnesty International, January 2016. Amnesty first announced its five-year challenge at the Nordic Electric Vehicle Summit in Oslo. Afrewatch is an NGO based in Lubumbash, DRC.
56. The organization's "Powering Change" report was released the following February; see "Powering Change: Principles for Businesses and Governments in the Battery Supply Chain," Amnesty International, 2022.
57. For examples of positive portrayals of IRMA, from academics and journalists, respectively, see Gavin M. Mudd, "Sustainable/Responsible Mining and Ethical Issues Related to the Sustainable Development Goals," *Geoethics: Status and Future Perspectives* (Geological Society of London, 2021), and Ernest Scheyder, "How Tiffany & Co. Helped Make Mining More Sustainable," *Time*, January 18, 2024. For NGOs, see, for example, this chapter's discussion of Earthworks' role in IRMA's creation, as well as "The Initiative for Responsible Mining Assurance," Earthworks, accessed January 14, 2025, and "Can Mining Certification Benefit Communities, Workers and the Environment?," Earthworks, July 6, 2018.
58. Aimee Boulanger, interview with author, March 22, 2021.
59. Boulanger, interview with author, March 22, 2021.

60. See United Nations Security Council Resolution 1173, adopted June 12, 1998; *A Rough Trade*, Global Witness, December 1, 1998.
61. Scheyder, "How Tiffany & Co. Helped Make Mining More Sustainable."
62. "BMW Group Joins the Initiative for Responsible Mining Assurance," IRMA, January 10, 2020, and "IRMA Welcomes New Board Members," IRMA, June 7, 2024.
63. "Members / Partners," IRMA, accessed January 28, 2025.
64. "Salar de Atacama (SQM) Commences Assessment," IRMA, January 12, 2022 (NB: The name of the map has since been changed to "Engagement Map").
65. SQM, "SQM Joins the IRMA Initiative to Deepen Its Sustainability Commitments," press release, February 23, 2021.
66. Albemarle Corporation, "Albemarle Strengthens Sustainability Commitment with Initiative for Responsible Mining Assurance (IRMA) Alliance," press release, October 26, 2020.
67. Such a market has been proposed for nickel, although at the time of this writing it has not yet come to fruition. See Eddie Spence, "LME Says Market Isn't Large Enough for Green Nickel Futures," Bloomberg, March 5, 2024.
68. This paragraph draws on Aimee Boulanger, personal communication with author, March 3, 2023.
69. See "Membership—What It Is," Members/Partners, IRMA, accessed May 30, 2024.
70. "Membership—What It Is."
71. IRMA, *SQM Salar de Atacama Audit Packet*, September 2023, 5 (Stage 2 Audit is the on-site visit).
72. IRMA, *SQM Salar de Atacama Audit Packet*, 12.
73. IRMA, *SQM Salar de Atacama Audit Packet*, 12.
74. IRMA, *SQM Salar de Atacama Audit Packet*, 111–14.
75. Aimee Boulanger, interview with author, March 22, 2021.
76. Boulanger, interview with author.
77. Aimee Boulanger, personal communication with author, March 3, 2023.
78. For the concept of social engineering, see Judith Verweijen and Alexander Dunlap, "The Evolving Techniques of the Social Engineering of Extraction: Introducing Political (Re) Actions 'From Above' in Large-Scale Mining and Energy Projects," *Political Geography* 88 (2021): 102342. For the argument that protest drives improved governance outcomes, see Scheidel et al., "Ecological Distribution Conflicts as Forces for Sustainability: An Overview and Conceptual Framework," *Sustainability Science* 13 (2018): 585–98.
79. For an in-depth discussion of these various forms of private authority, see Jessica F. Green, *Rethinking Private Authority: Agents and Entrepreneurs in Global Environmental Governance* (Princeton University Press, 2013).
80. "CERA Project: A Universal Standard for Ethics, Sustainability and Environmental Impact," EIT RawMaterials, January 13, 2020; "CERA Blockchain Certification Program to Track Raw Material Sustainability Credentials," *International Mining*, October 30, 2019.
81. Chelsea Hodgkins, personal communication with author, January 25, 2025.

82. Chelsea Hodgkins, "The Consolidated Mining Standard Initiative: The Mining Industry's Latest Attempt to Self-Regulate and Greenwash, an Inherent Conflict of Interest with Public Good," Public Citizen, September 17, 2024.

CHAPTER 8: RESISTING GREEN EXTRACTIVISM

1. "Barroso Agro-Sylvo-Pastral System, Portugal," Food and Agricultural Organization of the United Nations, accessed July 28, 2024.
2. Aida Fernandes, interview with author, July 15, 2022.
3. "Greenalia: Lamas de Feás Wind Farm," REVE, April 19, 2022.
4. Martín Arboleda. *Planetary Mine: Territories of Extraction Under Late Capitalism* (Verso Books, 2020).
5. "Land and Environmental Defenders," Global Witness, accessed July 28, 2024.
6. "Missing Voices," Global Witness, September 10, 2024.
7. Thea Riofrancos, *Resource Radicals: From Petro-Nationalism to Post-Extractivism in Ecuador* (Duke University Press, 2020), 29–76.
8. Mirja Schoderer and Marlen Ott, "Contested Water- and Miningscapes—Explaining the High Intensity of Water and Mining Conflicts in a Meta-Study," *World Development* 154 (2022): 7.
9. EJAtlas, Category: Mineral Ores and Building Materials Extraction, accessed July 30, 2024. I applied the filters "mineral ores and building materials extraction" and "groundwater pollution or depletion" or "mineral ores and building materials extraction" and "surface water pollution/ decreasing water quality." Out of 786 mining related conflicts, 680 involve concerns about surface water pollution, and 602 involve concerns about groundwater depletion or pollution.
10. Schoderer and Ott, "Contested Water- and Miningscapes," 10.
11. Mirja Schoderer, Jampel Dell'Angelo, and Dave Huitema, "Water Policy and Mining: Mainstreaming in International Guidelines and Certification Schemes," *Environmental Science & Policy* 111 (2020): 44.
12. Max Wilbert, Michon Eben, and Bethany Sam, "Why Is Thacker Pass / Peehee Mu'Huh So Important?," Reno-Sparks Indian Colony, accessed July 28, 2024.
13. John Hadder, interview with author, September 27, 2021.
14. See this survey: Jairo Yunis and Elmira Aliakbari, "Annual Survey of Mining Companies, 2021," Fraser Institute, April 12, 2022.
15. Steven H. Emerman, interview with author, June 29, 2022.
16. Jan Morrill et al., "Safety First: Guidelines for Responsible Mine Tailings Management," Earthworks, MiningWatch Canada, and London Mining Network, May 2022, 6.
17. Steven H. Emerman, "Prediction of Seepage from the Clay Tailings Filter Stack (CTFS) at the Lithium Nevada Thacker Pass Mine, Northern Nevada," prepared for Great Basin Resource Watch, last updated April 21, 2022.
18. Great Basin Resource Watch, "Great Basin Resource Watch Appeal Hearing to NV Commission on Faulty Lithium Mine Permit," press release, June 24, 2022.

19. Lithium Nevada did not argue that Emerman was not an expert and it did not challenge Emerman's findings. Indeed, in another brief that Lithium Nevada submitted on appeal, Lithium Nevada arguably agreed with Emerman's claims about the filtered tailings stack. (Email communication from Steven Emerman, December 19, 2024). The argument, and the Commission's order to strike the report from the record, was solely one of procedure over substance.
20. Latoya Hill, Samantha Artiga, and Nambi Ndugga, "COVID-19 Cases, Deaths, and Vaccinations by Race/Ethnicity as of Winter 2022," KFF, March 7, 2023; German Lopez and Ashley Wu, "Covid's Toll on Native Americans," *New York Times*, September 8, 2022.
21. Sascha Brodsky, "Why Indigenous Tribes Struggle to Get Fast Internet, and How It's Improving," *Lifewire*, October 28, 2022.
22. Schoderer and Ott, "Contested Water- and Miningscapes," 7.
23. See Wilbert, Eben, and Sam, "Why Is Thacker Pass / Peehee Mu'Huh So Important?" For more detail, see the Reno-Sparks Indian Colony legal filing: Julie Cavanaugh-Bill, William Falk, and Terry J. Lodge, Document 141, Case 3:21-cv-00080-MMD-CLB, US District Court of Nevada, filed November 29, 2021, 9–10, 26.
24. Cavanaugh-Bill, Falk, and Lodge, Document 141, 10.
25. Daranda Hinkey, interview with author, September 29, 2021. See also Evan Malmgren, "The Battle for Thacker Pass," *The Nation*, September 23, 2021.
26. Hinkey, interview with author; People of Red Mountain, "Save Our Hunter-Gatherer Ways from an Open Pit Lithium Mine Help Us Protect Peehee Mu'huh," Change.org, accessed July 28, 2024.
27. Hinkey, interview with author.
28. The protesters were Max Wilbert, coauthor of *Bright Green Lies*, a critique of the climate movement, and Will Falk, a lawyer who subsequently represented the People of Red Mountain in court. The Indigenous group severed ties with both Wilbert and Falk after learning of their transphobic stance, which, as Hinkey told me, directly conflicts with the inclusion of Two Spirit people. Daranda Hinkey, interview with author, October 1, 2021. See also Jael Holzman, "How a Fight Over Transgender Rights Derailed Environmentalists in Nevada," *Politico*, February 6, 2022.
29. Hinkey, interview with author, October 1, 2021.
30. People of Red Mountain, "People of Red Mountain Statement of Opposition to Lithium Nevada Corp's Proposed Thacker Pass Open Pit Lithium Mine," *Sierra Nevada Ally*, May 20, 2021; Ngaire McDiarmid, "Digging Delayed at Thacker Pass as Protestors Hit Reno," *Mining Journal*, June 14, 2021.
31. Under pressure from the People of Red Mountain, the council subsequently revoked the 2019 agreement with Lithium Americas. But the tribal council later entered a "community benefits agreement" with the company. For the revocation of the 2019 agreement, see "Press Release: Fort McDermitt Paiute-Shoshone Tribe Cancels Agreement with Lithium Mine, Promising Lawsuit," *Protect Thacker Pass*, April 5, 2021; Brian Bahouth, "Fort McDermitt

Paiute and Shoshone Tribal Members Protest Thacker Pass Lithium Mine," interview with Daranda Hinkey, *Sierra Nevada Ally*, April 8, 2021, audio, 13:51. For the subsequent community benefits agreement, see "Community Engagement at Thacker Pass," *Lithium Americas*, 2022, https://web.archive.org/web/20230925172608/https://www.lithiumamericas.com/_resources/thacker-pass/Community-Engagement-at-Thacker-Pass.pdf, accessed January 13, 2025.

32. Riofrancos, *Resource Radicals*, 138–63; Tulia G. Falleti and Thea N. Riofrancos, "Endogenous Participation: Strengthening Prior Consultation in Extractive Economies," *World Politics* 70, no. 1 (2018): 86–121.
33. International Labor Organization, "Ratifications of C169 - Indigenous and Tribal Peoples Convention, 1989 (No. 169)," accessed July 30, 2024.
34. Thea N. Riofrancos, "Scaling Democracy: Participation and Resource Extraction in Latin America," *Perspectives on Politics* 15, no. 3 (2017): 678–96.
35. Patrick Donnelly, interview with author, August 4, 2021.
36. For more on solar development in the Mojave Desert, see Oliver Wainwright, "How Solar Farms Took Over the California Desert: 'An Oasis Has Become a Dead Sea,'" *The Guardian*, May 21, 2023; "Solar Energy in the Mojave," The Nature Conservancy, accessed May 30, 2024.
37. Patrick Donnelly, interview with author, September 24, 2021.
38. María Vera et al., "Environmental Impact of Direct Lithium Extraction from Brines," *Nature Reviews Earth & Environment* 4, no. 3 (2023): 149–65.
39. Center for Biological Diversity, "1 Million Species Are Counting on Us to Get This Right," *Pop X*, no. 102, May 18, 2019.
40. "Overview," Ioneer, accessed October 2021.
41. Center for Biological Diversity, "Tiehm's Buckwheat Protected as Endangered Species," press release, December 14, 2022.
42. Center for Biological Diversity, "BLM Starts Permitting for Nevada Lithium Mine That Threatens Rare Wildflower," press release, December 19, 2022.
43. Jigar Shah, "LPO Announces Conditional Commitment to Ioneer Rhyolite Ridge to Advance Domestic Production of Lithium and Boron, Boost U.S. Battery Supply Chain," US Department of Energy Loan Programs Office, January 13, 2022.
44. Scott Sonner, "Lithium Miner Cited for Violating Endangered Flower Habitat," Associated Press, January 19, 2023.
45. Ernest Scheyder, "Biden Administration Approves Ioneer's Nevada Lithium Mine," Reuters, October 25, 2024.
46. Ernest Scheyder, "Biden Boosts Loan for Ioneer's Nevada Lithium Mine to Nearly $1 Billion," Reuters, January 17, 2025.
47. "Lawsuit Aims to Protect Rare Flower, Cultural Sites from Nevada Lithium Mine," Center for Biological Diversity, October 31, 2024.
48. Henry Veltmeyer, "Extractive Capital, the State and the Resistance in Latin America," *Sociology and Anthropology* 4, no. 8 (2016): 775–76; Alejandra Bernal et al., "Latin America's Opportunity in Critical Minerals for the Clean Energy

Transition," IEA, April 7, 2023; Anke Schaffartzik et al., "The Global Metabolic Transition: Regional Patterns and Trends of Global Material Flows, 1950–2010," *Global Environmental Change* 26 (2014): 93.
49. EJAtlas, Mineral Ores and Building Materials Extraction, accessed July 28, 2024.
50. "Land and Environmental Defenders: Annual Report Archive," Global Witness, accessed July 28, 2024; "Missing Voices," Global Witness, September 10, 2024.
51. Bryce W. Reeder, Moises Arce, and Adrian Siefkas, "Environmental Justice Organizations and the Diffusion of Conflicts over Mining in Latin America," *World Development* 154 (2022): 105883.
52. César Padilla, "Q&A: Mining-Issues Activist Tries to Build Community Clout," interview by Barbara Fraser, *EcoAméricas*, January 2006.
53. Riofrancos, "Scaling Democracy."
54. César Padilla, interview with author, February 1, 2019.
55. Thea Riofrancos, "What Green Costs," *Logic*, no. 9, December 7, 2019.
56. Ramón Balcázar, interview with author, March 12, 2019.
57. Bárbara Jerez, Ingrid Garcés, and Robinson Torres, "Lithium Extractivism and Water Injustices in the Salar de Atacama, Chile: The Colonial Shadow of Green Electromobility," *Political Geography* 87 (2021): 102382; Lucas I. González and Richard Snyder, "Modes of Extraction in Latin America's Lithium Triangle: Explaining Negotiated, Unnegotiated, and Aborted Mining Projects," *Latin American Politics and Society* 65, no. 1 (2023): 47–73.
58. Catarina Scarrott, interview with author, May 31, 2022; Aida Fernandes, interview with author, July 25, 2022.
59. Emily Macintosh, "Thousands Take to Streets to Protest Spanish Mining Boom," META, February 13, 2018.
60. Martin Obaya, "The Evolution of Resource Nationalism: The Case of Bolivian Lithium," *Extractive Industries and Society* 8, no. 3 (2021): 100932; Jonas Köppel, "Defending Lithium: On the Streets with Protestors in Potosi," Lithium Worlds.
61. Max Wilbert, interview with author, October 1, 2021. See also Brian Bahouth, "Thacker Pass Lithium Mine Approval Draws Around-the-Clock-Protest," *Sierra Nevada Ally*, January 19, 2021.
62. Ynske Boersma, "Trouble in the Triangle," *Earth Island Journal*, Spring 2024.
63. "Thousands Across Serbia Protest Lithium Mine Restart," Euractiv, July 29, 2024; Sofia Ferreira Santos, "Thousands Protest Against Lithium Mining in Serbia," BBC News, August 10, 2024; Aleksandar Vasovic, "Serbian Protestors Rally to Oppose Rio Tinto's Lithium Mine Project," Reuters, October 16, 2024.
64. "Bolivians Protest Deals Allowing Foreign Firms to Exploit Lithium," *Democracy Now*, February 14, 2025; "Nor López: El tiempo del litio se acabó para el gobierno," *Fundación Solon*, February 20, 2025.
65. Staff at 11th Hour Project, interview with author, June 24, 2021; staff at Business and Human Rights Resource Center, interview with author, August 18,

2021; staff at Greenpeace, interview with author, February 4, 2021; staff at Earthjustice, interview with author, July 2, 2021.
66. Donnelly, interview with author, August 4, 2021.
67. John Hadder, interview with author, September 27, 2021.
68. Paul Mohai, David Pellow, and J. Timmons Roberts, "Environmental Justice," *Annual Review of Environment and Resources* 34, no. 1 (2009): 405–30; "Environmental Racism in Louisiana's 'Cancer Alley', Must End, Say UN Human Rights Experts," UN News, March 2, 2021; Pablo Unzueta, "In the Shadows of Industry: LA County's Port Communities," CalMatters, February 1, 2022.
69. Johnnye Lewis, Joseph Hoover, and Debra MacKenzie, "Mining and Environmental Health Disparities in Native American Communities," *Current Environmental Health Reports* 4 (2017): 130–41.
70. Maria R. Costa et al., "*In vitro* Toxicity of Arsenic Rich Waters from an Abandoned Gold Mine in Northeast Portugal," *Environmental Research* 202 (2021): 111683; P. J. C. Favas et al., "Chapter 17: Acid Mine Drainages from Abandoned Mines: Hydrochemistry, Environmental Impact, Resource Recovery, and Prevention of Pollution," in *Environmental Materials and Waste*, ed. M. N. V. Prasad and Kaimin Shih (Academic Press, 2016), 413–62.
71. Daniel Boffey, "Rio Tinto's Past Casts a Shadow over Serbia's Hopes of a Lithium Revolution," *The Guardian*, November 19, 2021.
72. Galina Angarova, interview with author, May 17, 2022.
73. "About Us," Cultural Survival, accessed July 28, 2024.
74. "The Coalition," SIRGE Coalition, accessed January 28, 2025; Galina Angarova, "It's Not a Goodbye but a 'See You Later,'" Cultural Survival, February 19, 2024.
75. Indigenous Russia, "The Appeal to IP Leaders on the #AnswerUsElonMusk Public Campaign," September 9, 2020; Yuliya Fedorinova, "Huge Spill Stains Arctic and Climate Change Could Be the Cause," Bloomberg, June 4, 2020.
76. Galina Angarova, interview with author, May 17, 2022; Cultural Survival, "Advocating for the Inclusion of Indigenous Peoples' Rights in European Due Diligence Laws," April 4, 2022; European Union, "Regulation (EU) 2024/1781 of the European Parliament and of the Council of 13 June 2024 Establishing a Framework For the Setting of Ecodesign Requirements for Sustainable Products, Amending Directive (EU) 2020/1828 and Regulation (EU) 2023/1542 and Repealing Directive 2009/125/ECText with EEA Relevance," L 1781, adopted June 28, 2024.
77. John R. Owen et al., "Energy Transition Minerals and Their Intersection with Land-Connected Peoples." *Nature Sustainability* 6, no. 2 (2023): 204.
78. See Samuel Block, "Mining Energy-Transition Metals: National Aims, Local Conflicts," MSCI, June 3, 2021.
79. Akilah Jenga Kinnison, "Indigenous Consent: Rethinking U.S. Consultation Policies in Light of the UN Declaration on the Rights of Indigenous Peoples," *Arizona Law Review* 53 (2011): 1306–7.
80. "LANDBACK Manifesto," LANDBACK, NDN Collective, accessed July 28, 2024.

81. Michelle Werdann, "How Lithium-Rich Ores Are Made," *Nevada Today*, December 23, 2022.
82. Kai Bosworth, *Pipeline Populism: Grassroots Environmentalism in the Twenty-First Century* (University of Minnesota Press, 2022).
83. Thea N. Riofrancos, "Proleptic Protest: Local Resistance to New Extractive Projects in Ecuador," Working Paper no. 415, University of Notre Dame, December 2016.

CHAPTER 9: GREEN FUTURES

1. "Fossil gas" is a more accurate term than the industry-preferred "natural gas." Rebecca Leber, "The End of Natural Gas Has to Start with Its Name," *Vox*, February 10, 2022.
2. Justin Mackey et al., "Estimates of Lithium Mass Yields from Produced Water Sourced from the Devonian-aged Marcellus Shale," *Scientific Reports* 14, no. 1 (2024): 8813.
3. Hannah Northey, "Marcellus Shale Could Supply 40% of US Lithium—Study," *E&E News*, May 8, 2024.
4. "What Are Energy Communities and How Can They Benefit from the IRA?," Evergreen Action, accessed June 27, 2024.
5. Northey, "Marcellus Shale"; Mikaila Adams, "ExxonMobil Drills First Lithium Well in Arkansas' Smackover Formation," *Oil & Gas Journal*, November 14, 2023; Jafar Al-Jawad, Jonathan Ford, Evi Petavratzi, and Andrew Hughes, "Understanding the Spatial Variation in Lithium Concentration of High Andean Salars Using Diagnostic Factors," *Science of the Total Environment* 906 (2024): 167647.
6. Hannah Northey, "How Big Oil's Wastewater Could Fuel the EV Revolution," *E&E News*, September 12, 2023.
7. Northey, "How Big Oil's Wastewater."
8. Stacey Burling, "Awash in Toxic Wastewater from Fracking for Natural Gas, Pennsylvania Faces a Disposal Reckoning," *Inside Climate News*, April 16, 2023.
9. Riofrancos et al., "Achieving Zero Emissions with More Mobility and Less Mining," Climate and Community Institute, 2023, 46.
10. Riofrancos et al., "Achieving Zero Emissions," 14.
11. Riofrancos et al., "Achieving Zero Emissions" (Executive Summary).

INDEX

Page numbers in *italics* refer to photos.
Page numbers after 223 refer to endnotes.

Aborigine Forum, 199
ACI Systems, 196
"Addressing the Threat to the Domestic Supply Chain from Reliance on Critical Minerals from Foreign Adversaries" (Executive Order 13953), 24, 133, 141
Advanced Battery Project (Exxon), 47
"advanced manufacturing," 136
aerospace industry, 129
Afrewatch, 162–63
Africa, 33, 34, 37, 39, 40, 108–9, 164; *See also specific countries*
agriculture, 10, 26, 33, 37, 39, 58, 91, 94, 97, 113, 174, 177, 178, 202
Aguilera, Patricio, 83, 85–88
air pollution, 29, 51, 198
Alaska, 43
Albemarle, 9, 54–55, 77–79, 82–85, 88, 89, 92, 94–98, 106, 115, 116, 133, 150, 152, 153, 165, 166, 187, 242–43
Algeria, 40
Allende, Salvador, 73–76, 79, 81, 105–7, 110, 114, 195
Allkem, 55

ALMA (Atacama Large Millimeter/submillimeter Array), 12
aluminum, 16, 17, 34, 68, 69
Amakaik, 93
Amargosa Range, 29
Amazon River and Basin, 7, 26, 176
American Mineral Act, 134
American national identity, 71
Amnesty International, 162–63, 165, 257
Anaconda, 37, 77
Andean Mountains (Andean Plateau), 4, 7, 11, 23, 78, 81, 87, 176
Angarova, Galina, 198–99
Angola, 164
Antarctica, 18
anti-mining activism (anti-mining networks), 22–23, 173–204
Antofagasta, Chile, 113
Appalacia, 197
Apple, 68
aquifers, 9–10, 13, 92
Arcadium Lithium, 55
archaea, single-cell, 12–13
Argentina, 3, 18, 37, 54, 103, 107, 108, 141, 192–97

Argonne National Laboratory, 133, 135
Arkansas, 55, 206
artemia (brine shrimp), 10–11
Asahi Kasei, 48–50
astronomy, 12
Atacama Desert, 3, 5–7, 9–12, 22, 23, 55, 68, 75, 77–81, 81, 87, 89, 92–94, 98, 102, 107, 111, 113, 118, 155, 158–61, 168, 177, 193, 194, 198, 208, 209; *See also* Atacama Salt Flat (Salar de Atacama)
Atacama Salt Flat (Salar de Atacama), *1,* 3–5, 8–13, 11, 21, 23, *31,* 77–80, 86, 87, 90–95, 98, 100, 106, 107, 110, 115, 119–21, 155, 157, 165–68, 187, 193–95, 206
Atacameño people, 3, 4, 7, 10, 95–99, 119, 160, 196, 212; *See also* Council of Atacameño Peoples
Atomic Energy Commission, 53–54, 128
austerity, 103, 153
Australia, 9, 18, 28, 54–55, 68, 178, 187
Austria, 128
authoritarianism, 35
automakers (auto industry), 82, 127, 153–54, 156, 156–61
automobiles, *See* cars
Automotive and Mobility Industries Unit (European Commission), 140
avocados, 111, 112
Azorella atacamensis, 11

Bachelet, Michelle, 83, 85, 86, 88, 109
bacteria, 10, 12–13
Balcázar, Ramón, 193, 195
Bannock people, 182
Barroso mine (Portugal), 175, 177, 196
Bartell, Ed, 202–3
BASF, 161
batteries
  cell phone, 52, 162, 197
  critical minerals in, 69
  energy used to charge, 70–71
  and "green dominance," 135–37
  hybrid, 153
  import tariffs on, 137
  lead-acid, 34, 51
  lithium in, 5, 15–16, 25, 27, 30, 46, 46–52, 54–58, 65–68, 88, 102, 108, 126–27, 129, 130, 133, 135, 138–39, 141, 144, 148–49, 153–55, 157–58, 208, 213
  price of, 56–58
  production of, 59, 129–30, 140, 141, 145, 160
  rechargeable, 5, 15–16, 48–50
  size range of, 210
  sodium, 20, 153
  sustainable, 156–59, 210–11
Battery Engineering, Inc., 49–50
bauxite, 16, 191
beef, 62, 131, 148
Benchmark Mineral Intelligence, 16, 18, 134, 154–55
Benchmark Minerals Summit, 134
beryllium, 53
BHP, 113
bicycles, 26, 50–51, 67, 209, 211
Biden, Joe, and administration, 24, 134–37, 142, 144, 169
Big Greens, 164
biodiversity, 10, 12, 23, 60, 91, 168, 184, 188–90
biomass, 34
Bitran, Eduardo, 86–88
Bitran, Sergio, 114
BLM, *See* Bureau of Land Management
"blood diamonds," 164
BMW, 140, 157, 165
Bolivia, 3, 4, 7, 37, 81, 104, 107–8, 139, 149, 193, 196
boom-and-bust cycles, 17, 29, 35, 58, 62–63, 152
Boric, Gabriel, 105–7, 109, 110, 115, 116, 118–20, 194, 195
boron, 28, 187
Boston, Mass., 49–50
Bosworth, Kai, 202
Boticas, Portugal, 175
Boulanger, Aimee, 163–65, 167–69
brake pollution, 70
Brazil, 18, 26, 27, 39, 108, 176, 180–81
brine (brine deposits), 8–13, 15, 29, 68, 77, 78, 84, 87–94, 98, 115, 133, 148–49, 159–60, 168, 187, 188, 206, 216
brine shrimp *(artemia),* 10–11
British Empire, 26
brownfields, 206

INDEX 267

Brumadinho, Brazil, 180–81
Brussels, Belgium, 125
Buenos Aires, Argentina, 196
Buffalo Ranch (Nevada), 202
buffer zones, 64–65
Bukele, Nayib, 246
Bund, Der (newspaper), 159
Bureau of Energy Resources (US State Department), 134
Bureau of Land Management (BLM), 141, 145, 179–81, 183–84, 190, 200, 202
bureaucrats and bureaucracy, 22, 38, 80, 82, 83, 93–94, 115, 125–28, 137, 143, 145, 169, 190, 212
Burns Paiute Tribe, 198
Buryat people, 198
buses, 67–68, 117, 209, 210, 213
buybacks, stock, 63
BYD, 52, 54, 102, 153, 210

Cáceres, Spain, 174–75, 196
Calama, Chile, 23, 75
calcium hydroxide, 90, 241
Caldor Fire, 29
California, 29, 132, 189
camcorders, 50, 56
Camp David, 44
Canada, 18, 62, 68–69, 141
"Cancer Alley," 197–98
"cancer villages," 132
"capital discipline," 63
capital flight, 28–29, 115
capital mobility, 21–22
capitalism
    carbon-free, 205
    disaster, 81
    extractive, 9, 30, 55, 65, 87, 94, 106, 164, 180
    "fossil," 51, 55, 205, 206
    global, 21–22, 25, 36, 40–41, 46, 61, 170, 198
    "green," 9, 17, 24, 25, 30, 58, 66, 89, 137–39, 143, 155–57, 169, 176, 194, 205, 213
    industrial, 26, 130
    lithium, 55, 155
    origins of, 33
    state's role in, 52–54, 56–57, 127–30
car ownership, 50, 51, 66

"Caravan of Death," 75
carbon dioxide, 29
carbon emissions, 5, 15, 56, 144
carbon energy, *See* fossil fuels (fossil fuel industry)
carbon footprint, 9, 15, 20, 139, 144
carbon-free capitalism, 205
Cardoso, Fernando Henrique, 39
Caribbean, 40
carob trees, 92
cars, 15, 20, 50–52, 57, 58, 69, 71–72, 130, 156, 210–11
Carson City, Nev., 35
Carter, Jimmy, and administration, 43–44
Castle, The (Kafka), 80
cathodes (cathode materials), 20, 48, 49, 57, 58, 102, 108, 127, 138
CATL, 54, 140, 153
Cayo, Juan Carlos, 99
CBD, *See* Center for Biological Diversity
CCP (Chinese Communist Party), 51
cell phones (cell phone batteries), 52, 161, 162, 197
Center for Biological Diversity (CBD), 187–91
Central Asia, 53
CEPAL, *See* Economic Commission for Latin America and the Caribbean
CERA (Certification of Raw Materials), 170
certification, 162, 166, 168–70
Chaves, Portugal, 204
chemosynthesis, 13
Chery, 153
Chevron, 207
Chevy Bolt, 68
Chicago Mercantile Exchange (CME), 150
child labor, 167
Chile, 3–7, 18, 22, 23, 25, 41–42, 54–55, 60, 68, 72–95, 97, 100, 100–121, 126–27, 139, 152, 158, 160, 161, 176, 187, 189, 190, 192–98, 212; *See also specific headings, e.g.:* Atacama Salt Flat (Salar de Atacama); Santiago
China, 18, 23, 24, 27, 34, 50–55, 53, 57, 62, 67, 102, 108–9, 126, 127, 129–32, 134, 134–38, 135, 140–41, 149, 153, 196, 197

INDEX

Chinese Communist Party (CCP), 51
CHIPS and Science Act (2022), 136
Christophers, Brett, 60
chromium, 17
Chuquicamata mine (Chile), 75
circular economy (circularity), 70, 139, 144, 157, 208–9
Clean Technologies Institute, 88, 102
climate action (climate activism), 9, 23, 112, 137, 152, 156, 185–86, 208, 210, 211, 213
Climate and Community Institute, 212
climate change (climate crisis), 5, 11, 13, 17, 19, 23, 27, 29, 45, 55–58, 70, 91, 104, 126, 135, 161, 186, 188, 204, 205
climate denial, 51, 186
climate mitigation, 19, 58, 71
Clinton, N.J., 47
cloud forests, 60
Club of Rome, 45
CME (Chicago Mercantile Exchange), 150
coal (coal power), 16, 26, 27, 55, 64, 71, 154, 163, 198, 205, 206
cobalt, 16, 68, 72, 153, 158, 162, 165
Codelco, 76, 82, 118–19, 195
coffee, 26, 58
Cold War, 41, 44, 77, 80, 128
Colla people, 194
colonization and colonialism, 5–6, 13, 17, 24, 26, 33–40, 42, 43, 74, 99–101, 103, 121, 176, 178, 193, 205
Columbus, Christopher, 33
Committee on Environment, Rights of Nature, Natural Commons, and the Economic Model, 112
commodities (commodity markets), 40, 42, 55, 57, 59, 62–63, 66, 79, 104, 131, 140, 142, 148–52, 154, 155, 161
commodities super cycle, 62
"commodity frontiers," 26
computerized inventories, 45
Confederation of Copper Workers (Chile), 75
"conflict resources," 164
Congo, Democratic Republic of, *See* Democratic Republic of Congo
consent, prior, *See* prior consent
consultation, prior, *See* prior consultation

consumption, reducing, 20, 66
container shipping, 27, 45, 67, 82
copper (copper mining), 6, 10, 16–19, 21, 23, 24, 34, 40, 41, 53, 60, 62–64, 68, 72–77, 79, 81, 82, 91, 92, 94, 97, 101, 103, 107, 111, 113, 119, 131, 148, 149, 176, 185, 191, 192, 195, 198
CORFO, 78, 84–86, 238
corporations, *See* multinational corporations
Córrego do Feijão iron ore mine (Brazil), 180–81
corruption, 35, 79, 85–86, 103, 134, 165, 208
cost per kilowatt-hour (kWh), 56, 58
Costa Rica, 107
cotton, 24, 148, 158
Council of Atacameño Peoples, 86, 94–100, 110, 118–20
Covas do Barroso, Portugal, 173–77, 203–4; *See also* Barroso mine
Covas River, 21, 203–4
COVID-19 pandemic, 24, 57, 65, 103, 110, 126, 178, 181
critical habitats, 189–90
critical minerals (critical raw materials), 16, 18–19, 24, 24–25, 44, 61–62, 67, 69–70, 104, 126, 131–39, 141, 143, 147, 152, 179, 180, 186, 189, 203, 209
Critical Minerals Strategy (report), 133
Critical Raw Materials Act (2024), 138–39
Crowell, Bradley, 143–45
crustaceans, 11
Cubillos, Sergio, 97–100
Cultural Survival, 198, 199
Czech Republic, 138

Dann sisters, 179
Day of National Dignity (Chile), 73–74, 107
Death Valley, 29
Debrecen, Hungary, 140
decarbonization, 17, 29, 70–72
Decree No. 2886 (Chile), 77
Deep River Resistance, 183
Defense Production Act, 135
degrowth, 20, 25
deindustrialization, 140

demand destruction, 153
Demeter, 138
democracy, 41, 79, 103–5, 112, 168, 170, 182, 185–86, 192
Democratic Republic of Congo (DRC), 144, 162, 165, 257
democratic socialism, 74
Deng Xiaoping, 52
dependency theory, 38–43, 218
"deposits" (geological category), 59
deregulation, 130, 131; *See also* fast tracking
desalination plants, 113
desert tortoise, 188
deserts, 189; *See also specific deserts, e.g.*: Atacama Desert
DGA (General Water Directorate), 92
Díaz, Carlina, 93
direct lithium extraction (DLE), 160, 188, 206
Directorate-General for Internal Market, Industry, and Small and Medium Enterprises (European Union), 125
disaster capitalism, 81
disinvestment, 115, 206
"disturbance footprint," 183
dividends, stock, 63
Division of Minerals (Nevada), 144, 145
DLE, *See* direct lithium extraction
DOE, *See* US Department of Energy
Domeyko Mountains, 4, 5
Donnelly, Patrick, 187–90, 190
Dorador, Cristina, 111–13, 194
Dow Chemical, 74–75
downstreaming, 152
DRC (Democratic Republic of Congo), 144, 162, 165, 257
drought, 11, 58, 97, 177, 204
Duck Valley Indian Reservation, 184
Dutch Indies, 39

Earth Day, 45
Earthworks, 163–65, 164, 191
ecomodernists, 20
Economic Commission for Latin America and the Caribbean (CEPAL), 38–39, 41
economies of scale, 20, 56–57, 116
ecosocialism, 117

ecosystems, 4, 6, 9, 13, 20, 45, 64, 90, 92, 107, 111, 114, 179, 185, 189, 195
Ecuador, 23, 60, 103, 106–7, 192
Egypt, 103
EIS, *See* environmental impact statement
EJAtlas, 177
El Salvador, 107, 246
electric buses, 67–68, 117
electric mobility, 48, 50–52, 67, 70, 72, 155, 164, 210
electric vehicles (EVs), 16, 18, 19, 25, 48, 50–54, 56–58, 65, 67–72, 83, 102, 116, 127, 129, 130, 132, 134–37, 140, 145, 147, 152–57, 162, 163, 165, 166, 186, 194, 209–11
electricity (electrification), 15–16, 38, 71, 186
electronics industry, 82, 131–32, 162, 164
emerging powers, 17–18
Emerman, Steve, 180–81, 260
emissions, 5, 15, 56, 58, 70, 71, 90, 156, 205, 210, 211
emissions targets, 20, 139, 156
enclave economies, 39, 52
endorheic basins, 8
"energy communities," 206
energy crisis (1970s), 43–44
Energy Policy and Conservation Act, 43
energy transition, 6, 9, 15–17, 19, 20, 27–29, 34, 58–59, 61–65, 68, 72, 91, 103–4, 107, 126, 130, 134, 135, 137, 143–45, 152, 154, 176, 178, 185–86, 189, 204–8, 211, 212, 214
England, Industrial Revolution in, 33
"entrepreneurial state," 56–57
environmental, social, and governance (ESG), 60–62, 147, 155, 162
Environmental Assessment Service (SEA), 242–43
environmental impact statement (EIS), 179, 180, 183
environmentalism (environmental activism), 23, 45, 60, 103, 106, 111–14, 116–18, 121, 132, 139, 143–44, 160, 164, 168, 170, 175–79, 183, 186–88, 190, 191, 193, 195, 199, 202
ERM, 168
Escondida mine (Chile), 113

ESG, *See* environmental, social, and governance
ethical branding, 162
EU, *See* European Union
EU Battery Alliance, 138
Europe, 23, 57, 127, 128, 131, 140, 169–70
European Commission, 125–27, 133, 138–40, 252
European Investment Bank, 138
European Union (EU), 23–25, 27, 46, 50, 54, 62, 125–27, 129–30, 133, 137–40, 160, 163, 174, 196, 199; *See also* European Commission
Evans, Jon, 141, 142
evaporation (evaporation ponds), 8–9, 11, 13, 87, 98, 155, 160, 187, 188, 207
EVs, *See* electric vehicles
executive orders, 24, 133–35, 141, 250
export bans, 62
expropriation, 74–75, 86–88, 114
externalizing, of socio-environmental costs, 34, 42
extractive capitalism, 9, 30, 55, 65, 87, 94, 106, 164, 180
extractive economies, 62, 79–81, 101, 104
extractive frontiers (resource frontiers), 6, 9, 17, 21, 23–27, 29, 33–35, 43, 46, 53–55, 61, 78–81, 91, 100, 118, 121, 170, 174, 176, 189, 191, 194, 195, 198–200, 203, 205, 212, 214
extractivism, 97, 105, 116, 176, 192, 193
Extramadura region (Spain), 174
extreme temperatures, 30
extremophiles, 12–13
Exxon, 47, 48, 55, 56, 207
Exxon Valdez, 199

Facebook, 117
Fairphone, 161
Falk, Will, 260
Fallon Naval Air Station, 179
Fannon, Francis, 134
fast tracking, 130, 141, 203
feasibility studies, 135
Fernandes, Aida, 173–75, 177, 203
Fernandes, Nelson, 173–74
finance (financial markets), 27, 62, 66, 115, 127, 131
financial crisis (2008), 131

Firestone, 74–75
Fisher, Irving, 69
Flamencos, Los, National Reserve (Chile), *1, 4, 31*
flamingos, 4, 10–11, 121, 198
flexible contracts, 150
flooding, 6–8, 11, 23, 29
flows, stocks vs., 69
Flying Pigeon, 51
Foote Mineral Co., 77–78
forced labor, 53, 156
Ford, Gerald, and administration, 43, 44
Ford, Henry, 26–27, 154
Ford Motor Company, 26–27, 165
Fordism, 26–27
foreclosures, 131
forest fires, 29, 204
forestry, 82, 113; *See also* logging and timber
Fort McDermitt Paiute-Shoshone Reservation and Tribe, 182, 198
fossil capital (fossil capitalism), 51, 55, 205, 206
fossil fuels (fossil fuel industry), 15, 29–30, 34, 43, 45, 47, 64, 67, 70, 87, 156, 160, 175, 178, 185, 186, 202, 205–8, 210
FPIC (free, prior, and informed consent), 185
fracking, 21, 205–7
France, 128, 129, 138
fraud, 82–83, 85, 165; *See also* corruption
free, prior, and informed consent (FPIC), 185
free markets, 76, 128
free trade (free trade agreements), 24, 27, 87, 127, 136, 154
freshwater, 9–10, 13, 22, 77, 89–94, 113, 168; *See also* aquifers
friend-shoring, 27, 62, 134
frontline communities, 61, 106, 164, 180, 192, 201
Fujian Province, China, 140
futures contracts, 150

Galicia region (Spain), 174, 175
Ganfeng, 54, 55
Garces, Ingrid, 91
GBRW, *See* Great Basin Resource Watch

INDEX 271

General Mining Law (1872), 142, 169, 200
General Motors (GM), 153–54, 165
General Water Directorate (DGA), 92
geoeconomics, 19, 62, 63, 126, 127, 132, 133, 137, 138, 141, 160
geology, 35, 59, 62, 68, 77–78, 135
geopolitics, 17–19, 22, 27, 41, 45–46, 66–67, 103–4, 125, 134, 147, 151, 159, 160, 214
geothermal energy, 8, 160, 188
Germany, 51, 138, 140, 158–61, 196
Ghana, 109
ghost towns, 28, 35, 178
Gigafactory (Tesla), 189
GIZ, 161
glaciers, 114
Glatz Brahm, Pedro, 116–17
Glencore, 55
global capitalism, 21–22, 25, 36, 40–41, 46, 61, 121, 170, 198
global inequality, *See* inequality
global interdependency, 43
Global North, 43, 45–46, 72, 121, 127, 129, 131, 133, 159, 196–99, 214
Global South, 24, 33, 43, 45–46, 62, 72, 86, 87, 95, 100–102, 104, 105, 115, 121, 131, 152, 196, 198, 199, 214
global warming, *See* climate change (climate crisis)
Global Witness, 162
globalization (global trade), 24, 45, 127, 151, 154
GM, *See* General Motors
goats, 97
gold, 6, 21, 23, 24, 28–29, 33, 53, 176, 178, 179, 192, 198
Goldfield, Nev., 28–29, 178
Goodenough, John, 49
Gotion, 54
graphite, 16, 19, 49, 68
grazing, 97
Great Acceleration, 45
Great Basin, 178
Great Basin Resource Watch (GBRW), 178–81, 191
Great Powers, 17–18, 24, 45–46, 147, 197, 203
green bonds, 155
green branding, 162

"green capital accumulation," 157
green capitalism, 9, 17, 24, 25, 30, 58, 66, 89, 137–39, 143, 155–57, 166, 169, 176, 178, 194, 205, 213
green consumers, 156–57
green dominance, 67, 121, 126–31, 135–37
green economy, 24, 121, 144, 199
green extractivism, 176
"green mining," 23, 55, 160
"green nationalism," 132
"green premium," 154–55
green technologies, 17, 20, 24, 132, 193, 213; *See also specific technologies, e.g.:* solar energy (solar power)
Greenbrushes mine (Australia), 54
greenhouse gases, 70
Greenland, 62
greenwashing, 99, 147, 155, 166, 170, 176, 207
Group of 77 (G77), 40
Grubert, Emily, 29
Guatemala, 107
Gulf of Mexico, 43
Gutierrez, Gonzalo, 109–10

Hadder, John, 179–82, 188, 197, 200
Handley, Peter, 125, 139–40
hazardous waste, 207
herding, 97
high-income nations, 19, 25, 34, 42
Hinkey, Daranda, 182–84, 200–201
Hispaniola, 33
home energy storage, 136
Honduras, 107
Hong Kong, 103
Horizon Europe, 138
housing density, 71, 211
How Europe Underdeveloped Africa (Rodney), 39
Hubbert, M. King, 21
human rights (human rights abuses), 53, 72, 95, 114, 134, 151, 155, 158, 162–63, 170, 184–85, 197, 208
Hummer, 71
Hungary, 102, 140
hunger strikes, 97–98, 185
hybrid batteries, 153
Hyde Park (Boston neighborhood), 50

INDEX

Iberian Peninsula, 204
ICEs (internal combustion engines), 69–71, 156; *See also* cars
IEA, *See* International Energy Agency
illegal trading, 85
IMF (International Monetary Fund), 61
imperialism, 26, 33, 100
India, 53
Indigenous peoples and communities, 3–5, 13, 23, 25, 26, 33, 83–84, 88, 90–92, 94–100, 103, 106, 110–11, 118–20, 141–44, 157, 163, 167, 168, 170, 174, 176, 178–82, 184, 185, 191, 193–202, 207, 208, 212, 213; *See also specific groups, e.g.:* Atacameño people
Indonesia, 104
industrial capitalism, 26, 130
industrial ecology, 210
industrial policy, 50, 127–30, 136, 137
Industrial Revolution, 33
industrialization, 34, 35, 62, 107–8
industry certification agencies, 162; *See also* certification
inelasticity (inelastic demand), 151
inequality (incl. global inequality), 19, 24, 25, 34–35, 39, 42, 103–5, 131
inflation, 58, 103, 110, 118
Inflation Reduction Act (IRA) (2022), 136, 139, 142, 206
Infrastructure Investment and Jobs Act (2021), 135
Initiative for Responsible Mining Assurance (IRMA), 163–69
innovation, 17, 27, 49, 55–57, 84, 101, 116, 137
innovation funds, 138
Inorganic Chemistry Laboratory (Oxford University), 47, 49
Intag Valley (Ecuador), 60, 61
intercalation, 48
interdependency, global, 43
internal combustion engines (ICEs), 69–71, 156; *See also* cars
International Council on Mining and Metals, 95, 170
International Energy Agency (IEA), 16, 18, 69, 152, 210
International Labor Organization, 184–85

international law, 184–85
International Monetary Fund (IMF), 61
inventories, computerized, 45
invierno boliviano, 6–7
Ioneer, 178, 187–90
Iraq, 40, 103
IRMA (Initiative for Responsible Mining Assurance), 163–69
iron (iron ore), 16, 17, 20, 26, 34, 49, 176, 181, 191
irrigation, 4, 7
Italy, 24, 126

Japan, 51, 52, 132
Jiangxi Province, China, 54
joint ventures, 36, 51, 60, 78, 106, 115, 116, 129, 154
Jujuy, Argentina, 141, 195–96
"just in time" production techniques, 127

Kafka, Franz, 80
Kanagawa, Japan, 48
Kentucky, 54, 205
Killiches, Franziska, 157–61
Kings River, 201
Klein, Naomi, 81
Klubock, Thomas Miller, 75
Koktokay mine, 53, 231
Korean War, 53, 128, 135
Kracht, Willy, 115–16
Kunza language, 99
kWh, *See* cost per kilowatt-hour

La Paz, Bolivia, 196
labor (labor movement), 23, 28, 33–34, 38, 42, 52, 53, 60, 75–76, 85, 86, 156, 166–68, 184–85
laissez-faire, 76
Lake Baikal, 198
lanthanum, 131–32
Las Condes neighborhood (Santiago, Chile), 80, 115
Las Vegas, Nev., 28, 178
Latin America, 24, 34, 37–40, 38, 65, 73, 100, 104, 106, 108, 111, 131, 139, 163, 175–76, 191–93; *See also specific countries*
Latin American Observatory of Environmental Conflicts (OLCA), 192

INDEX

lead (lead-acid batteries), 34, 51
Lebanon, 103
left-wing parties (the left), 23, 38, 86, 105, 106, 114, 117–18, 144, 195
Lehman Brothers, 131
Lenny-Pessagno, Ellen, 89–90
Licancabur Volcano, 3
Lickanantay people, *See* Atacameño people
Limits to Growth, The (report), 45
Lisbon, Portugal, 196
lithium
   in batteries, 5, 15–16, 25, 27, 30, 46, 46–52, 54–58, 65–68, 88, 102, 108, 126–27, 129, 130, 133, 135, 138–39, 141, 144, 148–49, 153–55, 157–58, 208, 213
   in Bolivia, 107–8, 149, 196
   brine deposits of, 8–9, 12–13, 15, 68, 77, 78, 84, 89–94, 148–49, 159–60, 187, 188, 206
   in Chile's Atacama Salt Flat, 3, 5–10, 12–13, 55, 77–79, 91–94, 98, 106, 119, 165, 193–95, 206
   in China, 18, 27, 53–55, 57, 102, 130–31
   demand for, 16, 18, 54, 57–58, 65, 68, 71, 130, 147, 206, 211
   and energy transition, 6, 15–16, 19, 58, 72, 83, 178
   and extractive frontier, 6, 23, 25, 27, 78, 91, 121, 174, 189, 191, 194, 195, 198, 203
   as "fixed" resource, 21–22
   "green," 23, 55, 147–55, 158–63, 165, 166
   nationalization efforts, 22, 79, 86, 88, 104, 106, 108–10, 194, 195
   in nuclear weapons, 44, 53, 128
   and plant life, 28
   price of, 57–58, 65, 102, 130, 142, 149–55
   properties of, 15, 48
   supply of, 18, 19, 54, 59, 65–66, 77, 108–9, 125, 129–31, 139–41, 147–49, 149, 154, 186
   sustainable, 154–55, 165
Lithium Americas Corporation, 141–43, 153–54, 165, 181, 183, 184, 201
lithium capitalism, 55, 155

lithium carbonate, 89, 102, 149
lithium cobalt oxide, 49
Lithium for Chile, 84, 86
lithium hydroxide, 55, 150
lithium iron phosphate, 20, 49, 102, 153
"lithium majors," 55
lithium manganese oxide, 49
Lithium Nevada, 181, 260
"lithium rush," 28, 142, 143
Lithium Supply & Markets Conference, 147, 162, 178
"lithium triangle," 193
LitioMx, 108
Livent, 55, 155, 165
llama, 97
LME (London Metal Exchange), 150
logging and timber, 24, 148, 175
logistics (logistics revolution), 27, 45, 83
London Metal Exchange (LME), 150
long-nose harlequin frog, 60
López Obrador, Andrés Manuel, 108
Los Angeles, Calif., 198
Louisiana, 197
low-carbon technologies, 61
low-income countries, 19, 25, 34, 43
lumber, 148; *See also* timber and logging

magma, 8
magnesium, 149
"Making Clean Energy Clean, Just & Equitable" campaign, 191
"malaise speech" (Carter), 43–44
Malaysia, 26
Mali, 54
manganese, 16, 17, 49, 53, 68, 72
manufacturing, 16, 24–26, 34, 51, 56, 57, 84, 108, 109, 121, 128, 129, 136
Mao Zedong, 51
maps, 120
Marcellus Shale, 205–6
Maricunga Salt Flat (Chile), 120, 194
Marshall Plan, 128
Martín Bravo, Juan José, 112
Martínez de Olcoz Cerdan, Javier, 148–49
mass transit (urban transit), 20, 71, 208, 211, 213
Mazzucato, Mariana, 56
McDermitt caldera, 201
McKinney, Gary, 184

McNeill, John, 45
Mehdi, Ahmed, 153
Mehech, Ignacio, 115
Mercedes-Benz, 157, 161, 165
metals, 19, 24, 34, 58, 64, 67–70, 131–32, 156, 164, 179; *See also specific metals, e.g.:* lithium
Mexico, 37, 51, 54, 102, 108, 109, 176, 178
Microsoft, 165
middle class, 19, 42
Middle East, 37, 39, 40
middle-income countries, 19
"mid-transition," 29
Mina do Barroso lithium project, 175, 177, 196
mine waste, 64–65, 69, 205–7
mineral stockpiling, 44, 77
Mining Code of 1874 (Chile), 6
mining companies (mining industry), 8, 9, 13, 28, 33, 36, 37, 54, 60, 63, 64, 72, 75, 83, 84, 92–96, 114, 142, 149–52, 154–57, 159, 161, 162, 164, 166–67, 170, 176, 186, 196, 206; *See also specific companies, e.g.:* SQM
Mining Law (1872), *See* General Mining Law
MiningWatch Canada, 68–69
Ministry of Mining (Chile), 110
Mitchell, Harrison, 162–63
Model S (Tesla), 68–69
Montalegre, Portugal, 175
Montana, 201
Moore, Jason W., 21
Morales, Evo, 107–8
Morgan Stanley, 149
Mountain Pass mine (California), 132
mountaintop removal, 9
Movement for the Defense of Water, Land, and the Environment, 112–13
Mujica, Felipe, 81–82
multinational corporations, 19, 23, 36–37, 40–42, 45, 63, 74–77, 86, 95, 104, 108, 110, 115, 116, 152, 154, 157, 161, 163, 164, 175, 192–93, 212; *See also specific corporations, e.g.:* Albemarle
Mundaca, Francisco, 96, 98–99
Muñoz, Lesley, 194
Murkowski, Lisa, 133

Musalem Jara, Mónica, 94
Musk, Elon, 199

NAM (Non-Aligned Movement), 41
Namibia, 109
National Lithium Commission (Chile), 83–84, 109
national security, 18, 19, 43, 61, 67, 76, 126, 133, 136, 186
nationalism, resource, *See* resource nationalism
nationalization of resources, *See* resource nationalization
natural gas, 21, 37, 38, 205–6
Natural Resources Defense Council, 143
neocolonialism, 33, 39
neodymium, 131–32
neoliberalism, 74, 76, 105, 127
nepotism, 85, 239
net-zero emissions, 210
Nevada, 21, 25, 28, 91, 143–45, 176–91, 196, 201, 254; *See also* Thacker Pass mine site (Nevada)
Nevada Division of Environmental Protection, 181, 184
New International Economic Order, 40–42
New York State, 205
NGOs, 68–69, 158, 162–70, 167, 170, 175, 187, 191, 194, 197–99; *See also specific organizations, e.g.:* Amnesty International
nickel, 16, 34, 53, 68, 72, 109, 148, 153, 185, 199
NIMBY, 145, 186
nitrates, 6, 81
Nixon, Richard, and administration, 43, 44, 74
Nobel Prize, 49
Non-Aligned Movement (NAM), 41
nonmetallic minerals, 34
Norilsk, Russia, 199
Nornickel, 199
Norris, Eric, 152, 153
North Africa, 40
North Carolina, 53
North Sea, 43
Northern Paiute people, 178, 182
nuclear power, 77, 80–85

nuclear weapons, 25, 44, 53, 128, 179
Numu (Northern Paiute) people, 178, 182

Obama, Barack, and administration, 132
obsidian, 201
"obsolescing bargain," 87, 119
Occupy Wall Street, 131
OECD (Organisation for Economic Co-
    operation and Development), 61
offtake agreements, 149, 154
Ohio, 54
oil (oil companies), 21, 24, 33, 35–45, 47,
    55, 62, 70, 76, 101, 107, 108, 131, 148,
    149, 192, 205–7
"oil revolution," 42
oil shock (1970s), 42, 47, 56, 131
oil spills, 199
Okinawa, 132
OLCA (Latin American Observatory of
    Environmental Conflicts), 192
onshoring, 25, 27, 46, 62, 125, 127,
    132–35, 139–41, 144, 145, 160, 174,
    196–97
OPEC, *See* Organization of Petroleum
    Exporting Countries
"open markets," 27
open-pit mines, 28, 183
opium, 24
OPSAL (Plurinational Observatory of
    Andean Salt Flats), 193–95
Oregon, 202
Organisation for Economic Co-operation
    and Development (OECD), 61
Organization of Petroleum Exporting
    Countries (OPEC), 39–46, 46, 108,
    131
Ormat Technologies, 188
Oxford University, 47, 49
oysters, 11

Padilla, Cesar, 192–93
Paiute people, 90, 178, 182, 182–83, 198,
    200–202
Pakistan, 53
Paley Commission, 44
Panama, 107
Panasonic, 49
path dependency, 101, 130
patrimonio, 38

Peehee Mu'huh massacre, 182
Peehee Mu'huh protest camp, *171*,
    200–201
Peine, Chile (Peine Indigenous Commu-
    nity), 92, 94, 97, 168
Pennsylvania, 77, 205–6
Pentagon, *See* US Department of
    Defense
People of Red Mountain, 182, 184, 200,
    201, 260
"Periodic Table of Commodities Returns,"
    152
permits (permitting), 18, 28, 36, 60, 66,
    93, 133, 135, 141–42, 145, 180, 181,
    184, 190, 196, 202–3
Peru, 81
Petorca Province, Chile, 112–13
petroleum coke, 49
photosynthesis, 13
phytoplankton, 10
Piedmont Lithium, 165
Piñera, Sebastián, 195
"pink tide," 38
Pinochet, Augusto, 22, 41, 74–77, 79, 81,
    82, 85, 91, 103, 105, 192, 239
"pipeline populism," 202
pipelines, 6, 206
Pitt River Indians, 182
place-based investments, 22, 61, 174, 177
plant life, 11–12, 28, 189–90
plantations (plantation-style agricul-
    ture), 26–27, 36, 37, 39, 111, 112
playas, 178, 189
Plurinational Observatory of Andean
    Salt Flats (OPSAL), 193–95
pollution, 29, 51, 197–98
polyextreme environments, 10
Ponce Lerou, Julio, 239
Ponte, Stefano, 157
Porto, Portugal, 196
Portugal, 21, 25, 90, 129, 138, 173–76,
    196, 198
potassium, 88
potatoes, 58
Potosí region (Bolivia), 108, 196
poverty, 19, 35, 39, 42, 174–75; *See also*
    low-wealth countries
precipitation, 7, 10, 35; *See also* rain
    (rainfall)

prior consent, 118, 142, 168, 184–85
  free, prior, and informed consent (FPIC), 185
prior consultation, 60, 98, 107, 111, 142, 167, 177–78, 182, 184–85, 196, 201
produced water, 205–7
profits and profitability, 17, 22, 36, 45, 58–61, 63, 65–67, 72, 74, 79, 87, 130, 152, 157, 195, 209, 213
Project Independence, 43
ProtectThackerPass (website), 183
Public Citizen, 170
public lands, 28, 142, 183, 187, 202
Pueblo communities, 198
Pulgar, Antonio, 121

Qinghai Province, China, 54
Quinn River, 201

railroads, 6, 38
rain (rainfall), 4–8, 11, 23, 187; *See also* flooding
rainbows, 7
rare earth elements, 16, 17, 131–32
Raw Materials Union (European Commission), 125–26, 139–40
RCS Global, 162, 163
R&D, *See* research and development
Reagan, Ronald, and administration, 128
rechargeable batteries, 5, 15–16, 48–50
recycling, 16, 25, 68, 70, 129, 132, 135, 139, 141, 144, 161, 209–13
referenda, 107, 117, 195
regulatory capture, 36, 79
Renault, 160
renewables (renewable energy), 15–17, 19, 23, 29, 59, 65, 121, 144, 160, 178, 185, 188, 205, 208; *See also* energy transition
Reno, Nev., 178, 179, 182, 184
Reno-Sparks Indian Colony, 183, 198
Republican Party, 134
research and development (R&D), 56, 82, 101, 108, 130, 135, 138
"reserves" (geological category), 59
Resolution 1173 (UN Security Council), 164
Resource Conservation and Recovery Act, 207

"resource curse," 35
resource frontiers, *See* extractive frontiers
resource nationalism, 37, 38, 42, 46, 86, 104, 107, 111, 112, 121
resource nationalization, 22, 37, 37–38, 40–42, 73–76, 79, 81, 86, 88, 104, 106, 108–10, 114–15, 194, 195
resource scarcity, 45
resource security, 42, 46, 125, 137
resource sovereignty, 88, 104
"resources" (geological category), 59
Responsible Lithium Partnership, 160–61
"responsible" mining, 138, 162–65
Responsible Mining Map, 165–66
"Responsible Raw Materials Report," 158–59
"revolving door," 158, 180
Rhine River Valley, 159–60
Rhyolite Ridge, 27–28, *123*, 178, 187–90
rich nations, *See* high-wealth nations
"right to say no, the," 185
Rio Tinto, 55, 196
River Rouge plant (Ford), 26
road blockades, 86, 97, 119, 196
rock-to-metal ratio, 68
Rockwood, 94–95, 97
Rodney, Walter, 39
Roosevelt, Theodore, 28
royalties, 75, 76, 84–85, 87, 88, 94–95, 97, 101, 142, 180
rubber, 24, 26, 26–27
Rudolph, William E., 77
Russia (Russian Federation), 53, 126, 147, 160, 196, 198, 199; *See also* Soviet Union

St. Marys, Pa., 206
Salar de Atacama, *See* Atacama Salt Flat
salmon, 82
Sam, Inelda, 201
Sam, Ox, 182
San Pedro, Chile, 3, 7, 23, 78, 96–98, 193, 194
Sand Mountain, 179
sandstorms, 4
Santa Rosa Peak, 182
Santiago, Chile, 22, 35, 80, 89, 105–6, 116, 147, 155, 192, 193, 198, 208

satellite imagery, 64
Savannah Resources, 174, 196
Save the Mountain, 175
Scott, James, 82
SEA (Environmental Assessment Service), 242–43
Securities and Exchange Commission (SEC), 85
semiconductors, 19, 136, 137, 153
Serbia, 196, 198
"Seven Sisters," 39
sheep, 97
Shenzhen, China, 52
Shock Doctrine, The (Klein), 81
"shoring," 62
Shoshone people, *See* Western Shoshone people
Siberia, 198, 199
Sichuan Province, China, 54, 57–58
Sierra Club, 163–64
Sierra Nevada mountains, 29
silicon, 16
silver, 6, 24, 179, 191, 196
Silver Legacy Casino (Reno, Nev.), 179
Silver Peak (Silver Peak Range), 21, 28, 78, 178, 187; *See also* Rhyolite Ridge
single-cell archaea, 12–13
Sino-Soviet split, 53
SIRGE Coalition, 198–99
"situation of dependency," 39–41
slavery, 33
Slobodian, Quinn, 52
SMA (Superintendency of the Environment) (Chile), 92
Smackover Formation, 206
Smart, Myron, 200, 201
smelting, 53
Snake War, 182
Socaire community, 119–20
social engineering, 169
socialism, 41, 73, 74, 117
Socialist Party (Chile), 85, 114
socio-environmental costs, externalizing of, 34, 42
sodium, 153
sodium batteries, 20, 153
sodium carbonate, 90, 241
sodium nitrate, 238
Solanum chilense (wild desert tomato), 11

solar energy (solar power), 16, 16–17, 19, 89, 90, 101, 132, 139, 188, 208
solar (UV) radiation, 4, 10, 11
Sony, 49, 50, 56
South Carolina, 54
South Dakota, 53
South Korea, 51
Southeast Asia, 40
Southern Oregon University, 183
sovereignty, national, 37, 38, 40, 41, 45, 88
Soviet Union, 37, 41, 53, 231
soybeans, 148
Spain, 138, 174–75, 196
Spanish Empire, 5, 196
special economic zones (China), 52
spodumene, 9, 55
spot markets, 149
SQM, 9, 22, 55, 77–79, 82–98, 101, 102, 106, 119–20, 150, 155, 165–68, 196, 238, 239, 242–43
Sri Lanka, 26
Standard Oil, 37
state, role of, in a capitalist economy, 52–54, 56–57, 127–30
state-owned companies and enterprises, 36, 104, 109, 114, 117, 120, 128
state-sponsored violence, 28–29
steel, 26, 38, 69, 154
Stellantis, 160
stock buybacks, 63
stock dividends, 63
stocks, flows vs., 69
Strategic Petroleum Reserve, 43
subsidies, 36, 52, 57, 82, 129, 130, 136, 137; *See also* tax breaks (incl. tax credits)
sugar, 24, 40
sunk costs, 22, 61, 79, 87
Superintendency of the Environment (SMA) (Chile), 92
supply and demand, 19, 50, 58, 66–67, 150
supply chains, 22–27, 30, 35, 53, 54, 57–58, 65–68, 88, 90, 91, 102, 108, 109, 117, 126–30, 132–36, 138–41, 143–45, 152–54, 156–60, 163–65, 176, 186, 194, 197, 199, 208, 209, 212, 213
Supreme Court (Chile), 102

sustainability (sustainable development), 23, 91, 93, 95, 115, 129–30, 138–40, 143, 154–57, 159, 162
Sustainable Battery Regulation, 139, 140, 163, 199
sustainable lithium, 154–55, 165
Sustainable Lithium (website), 89
"sustainable sourcing," 156, 162, 163
SUVs, 67, 71
Switzerland, 159
synthetic graphite, 16, 49
synthetic nitrates, 81
Szychowska, Joanna, 140

tailpipe emissions, 70
Taíno people, 33
Taiwan, 132
Taltal, Chile, 6
Tanzania, 109
tar sands, 64
tariffs, 129, 136–37
tax breaks (incl. tax credits), 66, 75, 129, 130, 133, 136–38, 206, 207
Tea Party, 131
technology transfers, 51
telecommunications, 38, 128
temperatures, extreme, 30
"Ten Cities, Ten Thousand Vehicles" contest, 52
terraforming, 9
Tesla, 54, 68–69, 117, 155–56, 165, 166, 189, 199, 210
Thacker Pass Concerned Citizens, 202
Thacker Pass mine site (Nevada), 141, 142, 153–54, *171,* 177–86, 181, 196, 198, 200–203
Thailand, 102
Thatcher, Margaret, 128
think tanks, 210
Third World, 38–42, 45, 74, 144; *See also* Global South
Thuringia, Germany, 140
Tianqi, 54–55, 57, 150
Tibet, 54
Tiehm's buckwheat *(Eriogonum tiehmii),* 28, *123,* 187, 189, 191
Tiffany's, 164, 166
Tilopozo plains (Chile), 92
timber and logging, 24, 148, 175

tin, 24, 37, 198
tire pollution, 70
tobacco, 24
Toconao, Chile (Toconao community), 7, 23, 96, 119–20
tourism, 3, 7, 94, 96, 97, 143, 177, 193
toxic mud, 180–81
toxic waste, 207
trade barriers, 61
trade deficits, 51
trade protectionism, 19; *See also* tariffs
trade union confederations, 86
transportation sector, 15, 56, 209
trickle-down economics, 129
tritium, 128
Truman, Harry S., and administration, 44
Trump, Donald, and administration, 24, 62, 133–35, 137, 141, 180, 190, 250
Tsingshan Holding Group, 102
tungsten, 53, 198
Tunisia, 103
Turner, James Morton, 47

Uighurs, 53
Ukraine, Russian invasion of, 126, 147, 160, 252
UN, *See* United Nations
UN Commission on Trade and Development (UNCTAD), 38–39, 74
UN Declaration on the Rights of Indigenous Peoples, 185
UN Security Council, 164
underdevelopment, 39, 42
unequal exchange, 39, 197
UNITA, 164
United Fruit Company, 37
United in Defense of Covas do Barroso, 177
United Kingdom, 54, 81, 128–29
United Nations (UN), 38–39, 74, 174
United States; *See also specific headings*
"American national identity" in, 71
carbon emissions from, 15, 56, 144
and Chile, 73–75, 87
as colonizer, 34, 178
and critical minerals/resources, 43, 189
and energy transition, 212

INDEX 279

EV production/market in, 50, 57, 68
forest fires in, 29
government loans in, 28, 190
and Indigenous peoples, 90, 142, 178, 183, 185, 191, 200
industrial policy in, 129, 136
lithium mining and processing in, 27, 46, 53–54, 141–43, 187, 196–97, 199, 206
military aid to Ukraine, 252
mineral stockpiling in, 44
mining in, 44, 66, 133, 189–90
multinational corporations based in, 37, 55, 74–75, 78
onshoring efforts in, 46, 62, 127, 132–35
and OPEC, 42, 43, 45
"peak oil" prediction for, 21
political upheavals in, 126, 138
rare earth minerals in, 132
tariffs in, 137
tax breaks/credits in, 133, 136–38, 206, 207
and Third World, 41, 45
2008 financial crisis in, 131
during World War II, 128
United States Geological Survey (USGS), 59, 68
University of Antofagasta, 91
University of New Mexico, 198
upstream mineral supplies, 61–62
urban transit, *See* mass transit
US Congress, 44, 132–34, 136, 139, 143, 169
US Department of Defense, 129, 137
US Department of Energy (DOE), 133, 135, 142, 143, 190, 206
US Department of Justice, 85
US Department of the Interior, 133, 190
US Fish and Wildlife Service (USFWS), 189–90
US Global Investors, 152
US State Department, 134
USGS, (United States Geological Survey), 59, 68
Uyuni Salt Flat (Bolivia), 108

Valdebenito, Marcelo, 115
Valdivia, Pedro de, 5

Valle de la Luna (Valley of the Moon), 7
value-added production, 126–27
value proposition, 125
vanadium, 179
variable pricing, 150
Venezuela, 39, 40
Verisk Maplecroft, 109
Vernon, Raymond, 87
vertical integration, 26, 153–54
videoconferencing, 181–82
Vilches, Carolina, 112–13
violence, state-sponsored, 28–29
Visher, Mike, 144–45
Vivar, Jerónimo de, 5
Volkswagen, 157–61, 165
Vulcan Energy Resources, 159–60

Wallerstein, Immanuel, 227
Wang Chuanfo, 52
War of the Pacific, 81
War Production Board, 44, 128
Wassuk Range, 178
wastewater, 69, 205–7
Water Code (Chile), 91
water management, 160, 161, 168
water rights, 85, 91
wells, 6, 8, 92, 94
West Africa, 164
Western Australia, 9
Western Shoshone Defense Project, 191
Western Shoshone people, 178, 179, 182, 183, 191, 198, 200–202
wetlands, 11, 98, 113–14, 120, 121, 193, 202
whales, 11
WhatsApp, 117
Whitehouse, Sheldon, 143
Whittingham, Stanley, 48, 49
Wilbert, Max, 260
wild desert tomato *(Solanum chilense)*, 11
wind energy (wind power), 15–17, 23, 58, 101, 132, 203, 208
Winnemucca, Nev., 182
Wolfsburg, Germany, 158
Wood Mackenzie, 18
working class, 38, 42, 74
World Bank, 16–17
World War II, 44, 53, 128
Wuhu, China, 153

xenophobia, 24, 197
Xinjiang Province, China, 53

Yacimientos de Litios Boliviano (YPL), 108
Yacimientos Petrolíferos Fiscales (YPF), 37
Yes to Life, No to Mining, 177, 191
Yoshino, Akira, 49–50
yttrium, 131–32

Zawadski, Alexi, 141
zero-carbon economy, 13, 17, 155–56
Zero Carbon Lithium, 138, 160
zero-carbon lithium mines, 138
zero emissions, 58, 71, 90, 156, 205, 210, 211
zero-sum formulations, 178, 208, 211
Zimbabwe, 18, 54, 108
Zimmermann, Erich, 35
zinc, 17, 34, 72
Zoom, 181–82, 184